Contributions to Management Science

The series *Contributions to Management Science* contains research publications in all fields of business and management science. These publications are primarily monographs and multiple author works containing new research results, and also feature selected conference-based publications are also considered. The focus of the series lies in presenting the development of latest theoretical and empirical research across different viewpoints.

This book series is indexed in Scopus.

More information about this series at http://www.springer.com/series/1505

Antonio Leotta
Editor

Management Controlling and Governance of Family Businesses

Theoretical Insights and Empirical Evidence from Italy

Springer

Editor
Antonio Leotta
Department of Economics and Business
University of Catania
Catania, Italy

ISSN 1431-1941 ISSN 2197-716X (electronic)
Contributions to Management Science
ISBN 978-3-030-47740-0 ISBN 978-3-030-47741-7 (eBook)
https://doi.org/10.1007/978-3-030-47741-7

This Springer imprint is published by the registered company Springer Nature Switzerland AG
The registered company address is: Gewerbestrasse 11, 6330 Cham, Switzerland

Dedicated to our families

Contents

Contributors

Gaia Bassani Department of Management, Economics and Quantitative Methods, University of Bergamo, Bergamo, Italy

Cristiana Cattaneo Department of Management, Economics and Quantitative Methods, University of Bergamo, Bergamo, Italy

Francesca M. Cesaroni Department of Economics, Society, Politics, University of Urbino Carlo Bo, Urbino, Italy

Elena Cristiano Department of Business Economics and Law, University of Calabria, Rende, Italy

Claudia Frisenna Department of Economics and Business, University of Catania, Catania, Italy

Antonio Leotta Department of Economics and Business, University of Catania, Catania, Italy

Carmela Rizza Department of Economics and Business, University of Catania, Catania, Italy

Davide Rizzotti Department of Economics and Business, University of Catania, Catania, Italy

Daniela Ruggeri Department of Economics and Business, University of Catania, Catania, Italy

Annalisa Sentuti Department of Economics, Society, Politics, University of Urbino Carlo Bo, Urbino, Italy

List of Figures

Beyond the Founder. Which Conditions Can Favor or Hinder the Professionalization of Family Firms?

Internationalisation in Family Businesses. The Case of Mamagra

Discussing and Concluding Remarks

List of Tables

Introduction

Antonio Leotta

Families are the elementary communities that constitute society. Their dynamics involve emotions and interests which are shaped in family members' relations. Families often believe in core values, which influence, and are influenced by, the social context around them. When a family is involved in a business enterprise, the latter expresses the view of the family, and its aptitude to survive and develop over time is mostly the consequence of the family dynamics and of the ability of the family to absorb the culture and values of the social context where the business is born and develops. Therefore, the family and the business form a unitary system of forces where economical and emotional concerns are merged. The aptitude of a family business to survive and develop depends on the ability of the family to acquire managerial and financial culture and to speak and listen to financial language. The willingness of the entrepreneur to take the investment risk and seize new opportunities must be balanced with his/her aptitude to verify the feasibility of the new project, especially in financial terms. The entrepreneur should also recognize in his/her children the abilities to manage the business: this is a critical requisite for the survival of the firm. Furthermore, when a professional manager is hired to guide the family business in a development path, introducing administrative innovations in line with the managerial principles of doing business, the professional manager needs to learn and respect the family values and cultures where the business comes from. Those of family and business are two worlds that need to be merged for they can constitute a sound family business reality. Such a merging is the fundamental challenge of a family business. It requires the founder of the business and his/her family members to overcome the view of the family, focused on familiar habits and emotional constraints, in order to adopt the family business perspective as a *melting-pot* of familiar and managerial principles. A family business develops and grows by entering international markets,

A. Leotta (✉)
Department of Economics and Business, University of Catania, Catania, Italy
e-mail: antonio.leotta@unict.it

A. Leotta (ed.), *Management Controlling and Governance of Family Businesses*,
Contributions to Management Science,
https://doi.org/10.1007/978-3-030-47741-7_1

to spread its products and services; accessing financial markets, to sustain strategic investments; and transferring knowledge and experience from senior to junior generations, to survive over time, behind the founder's vision of the business. For the family business to deal with all these challenges, a unitary system of principles and values needs to be developed. The main thesis of this book argues that the core of such a system lies in the integration of familiar and managerial principles and values.

The extant literature on family business has been developed around the distinctive features of a family firm, such as the presence of a family whose values and dynamics influence the business in its aptitude to grow, to enter international markets, to survive over the current generations and to access financial markets. Such topics are strongly interrelated, and their linkages need further investigations. Administrative innovations are required for the family business to solve conflicts and promote cooperation, improving its search for efficiency and effectiveness. Management control and governance systems can be the administrative innovations a family business needs to introduce if it wants to deal with all its challenges by a unitary way. Little has been studied on the role of management control and governance systems in family firms. Recently, management control scholars have been invited to invest more in the field of family business, investigating on the role of management accounting and control systems in this setting. What are the specific features and roles of management control and governance systems in family firms? How do such systems can help family business actors in dealing with the main business challenges?

In order to address the above questions, this volume conceptualizes a system view of the main challenges that characterize family businesses, namely managerialization and professionalization, succession, internationalization and relations with financial markets. The need to develop a unitary view of these challenges, based on a holistic approach, is derived from the opportunity to investigate their interrelations. This view embraces the use of management control and governance systems, since the introduction and use of such systems, as argued by recent studies, play a relevant role being the main subject of managerialization and professionalization, and facilitating firm succession, internationalization and relations with financial markets. This is the core argument of the book and is developed theoretically, in a first part of the volume, and applied, in the second part, in interpreting and discussing field and empirical evidence on Italian cases of family business.

The book contributes in different ways. First, it offers an updated review of the studies that have dealt with the main family business topics. Second, it suggests various insights to help family businesses to survive and grow up. Third, it attempts to deal with a relevant point, not developed enough in the scientific literature, namely the role of governance and control systems in family firms. Finally, it highlights the main linkages between the principle family business challenges, discussing on how the business can take advantage from the governance and control systems in handling those challenges. The theoretical propositions, drawn on the extant literature, are developed into a conceptual framework which guides the interpretation of the fields and empirical results discussed in the second part of the volume.

The development of a system view of the main business challenges, included the introduction of management control and governance systems, makes the book distinctive as a means to develop a deeper understanding of the role of management control and governance systems in family firms. In so doing, the reader is invited to contextualize the role of such systems within the challenges that make a family firm distinctive. In these terms, the introduction of management control and governance systems may be the consequence of a succession process which facilitates the firm managerialization/professionalization and international growth. At the same time, management control and governance systems may contribute to reinforce the process of succession if their introduction has been successfully led by a representative of the junior generation. Such an innovation may have contributed to the acceptance of his/her leadership amongst family and non-family business members.

As mentioned above, the book is organized in two main parts: the first develops the theoretical propositions of the book and its main thesis. After defining family businesses, in a first chapter, the principle family business challenges, namely managerialization and professionalization, family business succession, internationalization and relations with financial markets, are discussed in each of the following chapters, reviewing the literature on the topics. This discussion is inspired from the perspective of the development and growth of a family business. The last chapter of the first part presents a conceptual framework where all the main challenges discussed previously are linked together and are proposed to be managed through a systems package composed of management control and governance systems. This package constitutes the unitary system of principles and values that lies in the integration of familiar and managerial views.

In the second part of the volume, the main thesis of the book, just mentioned, is used as the interpretive framework which guides the discussion of the evidence drawn from case studies and statistical analyses accomplished on Italian family firms. The focus on Italy, as the national context of the empirical analyses, is due to the high diffusion and relevance of family businesses in the Italian economy. The research approach privileges interpretive case studies. Field evidence is offered on Italian family businesses located in different areas of the country and operating in various industries, such as the market for nutraceuticals and cosmeceuticals, in the case of Greenlife; the market for yellow flours, breakfast cereals and other products (flour for breading, cous cous) destined for human consumption, in the case of Molino Nicoli S.p.A.; the food packaging sector, in the case of Teseo S.p.A.; the machinery industry for construction markets, in the case of Volta S.p.A.; and the market for olive oils, in the case of Mamagra.

The case studies report episodes around managerialization and professionalization, succession and internationalization, considered as important family business challenges. The main objective of the field research is to show how these challenges are interrelated, as argued in the theoretical part of the volume, and how their management has involved a unitary view which integrates familiar and managerial principles and values. Field evidences drawn from case studies are integrated with a quantitative investigation on the relations between family business and financial markets. A regression analysis was run on data gathered from a sample of family-owned businesses listed in the Italian stock market. The aim was to verify hypotheses based on the theoretical propositions formulated in the first part of the volume, which were related to the role of governance mechanisms in protecting financial investors, therefore facilitating financial support for family business development and growth.

The volume ends with a discussing and concluding section, aimed to offer an interpretation of the field and empirical evidences from the theoretical lens developed in the conceptual framework proposed earlier.

Some terminological clarification is needed. In all the volumes, the terms *family business* and *family firm* will be used with the same meaning, while the term *governance* will refer to both the traditional content given in the specific literature and the new meaning which will be proposed in the theoretical framework developed in Chapter "Governing Family Businesses. A Research Map". This new meaning of the term governance will be often associated with the term *governing* and with the expressions of *governance systems package, governance package, governing systems package.*

Governing Family Business Challenges. Theoretical Insights

An Overview of Family Business. Profiles, Definitions and the Main Challenges of the Business Life Cycle

Antonio Leotta, Carmela Rizza, and Daniela Ruggeri

Abstract This chapter defines the unit of analysis of the volume, which is the family firm. The characteristics describing the specific aspects of such firms are outlined and considered along the main phases of the family firm life cycle. The chapter sets out the static and dynamic coordinates required for examining the main challenges that a family firm needs to deal with along its development path. Since the present chapter is something of an overture for the entire volume, the main family business challenges will be outlined, and each is the subject of the following chapters.

Keywords Family business definitions · Family business challenges · Family business life cycle

1 Introduction

Family business is a very important phenomenon around the world and deserves research attention for many reasons. Firstly, family firms seem to have specific profiles and features that make them distinctive from non-family firms. One of the most acknowledged features is the influence of one or more families over the business. This suggests investigating family member relationships and their dynamics, as well as those with non-family members. Secondly, the distinctive profiles and features of family firms entail that the development and growth of family firms may follow patterns of behaviour that can differ from the development patterns followed by non-family firms. Thirdly, if family firms follow patterns of development and growth that are different from the patterns followed by non-family firms, then the

A. Leotta · C. Rizza (✉) · D. Ruggeri
Department of Economics and Business, University of Catania, Catania, Italy
e-mail: c.rizza@unict.it

A. Leotta
e-mail: antonio.leotta@unict.it

D. Ruggeri
e-mail: d.ruggeri@unict.it

A. Leotta (ed.), *Management Controlling and Governance of Family Businesses*, Contributions to Management Science,
https://doi.org/10.1007/978-3-030-47741-7_2

role played by governance and control systems may be different. Such roles need to be explored.

The present chapter is thought of as an overview of the first, theoretical, part of the volume. It thus needs to define the distinctive profiles and features of a family business; as such business is the unit of analysis for the research. As will be discussed in the second section, the very essence of a family business is the intention of a family, or a number of families, to shape the vision of the business (Chua et al. 1999). How the family or families shape the vision of the business, however, influencing its path of development and growth, depends on how young or mature the family business is, which forms the organisational and environmental context of the family business. Following the contribution by Quinn et al. (2018), the second section will discuss four important dimensions which differ between family and non-family firms: architecture, governance, entrepreneurship and stewardship (Craig and Moores 2015, 2017). These dimensions are examined so as to discuss the role played by dimensions that are distinct to family businesses, dealing with the challenges of family business growth and development: in the relations between family and non-family members (managerialisation-professionalisation); in the relations between generations (succession); and in the relations between family business and its markets (such as international and financial markets). The choice of discussing architecture, governance, entrepreneurship and stewardship as specific dimensions of a family business is also due to the focus of the present volume on the role played by governance and control systems in managing the main family business challenges.

Accordingly, the third section outlines the context of the family business, which involves the relationships between the family business and its environment. As will be discussed, such relations differ according to the stage of the business development path. The literature suggests that the development path of a family business is appropriately represented through a life-cycle model whose phases describe the organisational and environmental characteristics of a family business along its maturity stages.

Sections two and three together set the static and dynamic coordinates required for examining the main challenges a family business needs to deal with as it develops. As the present chapter is something of an overture for the entire volume, the main family business challenges will be outlined and will be the subject of each of the following chapters. The challenges in question have been selected according to the most relevant family business studies. They involve managerialisation-professionalisation, family business succession, internationalisation and access to financial markets. The fourth section in the present chapter outlines and offers an introductory discussion of these challenges, which will be the subject of the following chapters.

Some methodological choices in the writing of the chapter need to be clarified. Firstly, the content of each section is not intended to offer an exhaustive recognition of the various perspectives in the family business literature. The focus of the volume is restricted to the perspective of governance and control systems in family business. It is from this perspective that the present volume aims to describe how family businesses can manage their main challenges. Secondly, the approach followed in the volume, which is mostly qualitative and process-oriented, has influenced the selection of the specific profiles and features of family business, and, thereby, its definition. The privilege given to the essence approach, which underlines the distinctiveness of the influence of the family or families in a family business, is functional to the study of the role of governance and control systems as constructed in the relationships between family and non-family members through the various stages of the family business life cycle.

The present chapter contributes to the volume by defining the unit of analysis and the main logical assumptions of the research. The latter can be outlined in the following propositions:

1. The distinctive profiles and features of family firms make them different from non-family firms in dealing with the main business challenges that come from the various stages of the development path.
2. This distinctiveness can be investigated by studying the specific role played by governance and control systems in managing family business challenges.

2 Family Businesses Profiles and Features

Defining a family firm is one of the classic problems of family business research and is also called the "definition problem" (Astrachan et al. 2002). It is a never-ending story, as no resolution has been achieved yet, as the viewpoints of the scholars who have dealt with such a problem, and their research purposes, are different. A common starting point is the definition proposed by Chua et al. (1999), according to which: "The family business is a business governed and/or managed with the intention to shape and pursue the vision of the business held by a dominant coalition controlled by members of the same family or a small number of families in a manner that is potentially sustainable across generations of the family or families" (cf. p. 25). Thus, the very essence of a family business is the intention of a family, or a number of families, to shape the vision of the business. This behavioural approach, which has been called the "essence approach", was further developed in 2003 by Chrisman et al. (2003, p. 9), who stated that the essence of a family firm consists of the: "(1) intention to maintain family control of the dominant coalition; (2) unique, inseparable, and synergistic resources and capabilities arising from family involvement and interactions; (3) a vision set by the family controlled dominant coalition and intended for transgenerational pursuance; and (4) pursuance of such a vision". We consider the essence approach seminal, as it encompasses most of the family business features.

The essence approach assumes that a family business is a business influenced by one or more families. This assumption has focused on a number of dimensions through which the influence can be exerted. According to Astrachan et al. (2002), there are three important dimensions of family influence that should be considered: power, experience and culture. Analysing the power dimension, the authors sustain that a family can influence a business through the extent of its ownership, governance and management involvement. The authors also add: "This level of influence via ownership, management, and governance is, therefore, viewed as interchangeable as well as additive" (Astrachan et al. 2002, p. 48). Obviously, the measurement of influence via each of these three ways needs to consider the legal requirements of the country to which the business is subject. The experience dimension of family influence refers to succession and the number of family members who contribute to the business. Various authors suggest that a business should be seen as a family business when a transfer to the next generation is intended (Barach and Ganitsky 1995; Birley 1986; Heck and Trent 1999; Ward 1987, 1988). It is commonly accepted that each succession adds experience to the family and the company. The number of family members involved in ownership, governance and management is also a relevant source of experience for the family and the business. Finally, the culture dimension refers to the sharing of assumptions and values between the family and the business, and to the family's commitment to the business (Gallo 2000). Other authors consider the culture dimension in terms of whether the CEO, the managers or the owners perceive it as a family business or not. The overlap of company and family values is the most considered element of culture dimensions, but its evaluation can be problematic. For example, as Astrachan et al. (2002) pointed out: "the values of an organization might well be rooted in family values of a former generation, but not necessarily manifest in the current family" (cf. p. 50). Such a criticality, which seems to be an operational concern, is related to the complex nature of the family business concept and will be considered later in this section.

According to the arguments outlined above, Astrachan et al. (2002) developed a F-PEC index of family influence which enables comparisons across businesses concerning the level of family involvement. Such an index has the ability to avoid a cut-off distinction of family versus non-family firms, allowing a continuum of family business typology, based on the degree of the three subscales derived from the three components of family influence. Accordingly, Mustakallio et al. (2002) summarised the various definitions of family business into six categories: ownership, management, generational transfer, the family's intention to continue as a family business, family goals and the interaction between the family and the business.

Another feature of the essence approach to family business is that the influence of the family or families refers to a family's or multiple families' visions of the business. It is a cultural dimension that overcomes the economic interest in the business. Instead, the business is seen by family members as a way to pursue their values.

Another feature, which the essence approach highlights as a distinctive element of family businesses, is the transgenerational pursuance of the family vision of the business. Since the family vision needs to be sustained across family generations, the dynamics of family successions are important for the business to survive. The relationships between older and junior generations, the leadership constructed by the latter, and the preparation of the succession process are issues involved in the feature of succession, which represents another distinctive concern of family businesses and of their research. The transgenerational horizon of a family business gives the family business system a dynamic dimension. This, on the one hand, has been perceived by Astrachan et al. (2002) as a source of experience and considered as one of the three components of family involvement. On the other hand, this transgenerational horizon is a source of instability, since it may hinder the survival of the family firm. As reported by Songini et al. (2013), indeed: "The Family Firm Institute estimated that only 30% of all US family businesses survive into the second generation, only 12% make it to the third generation, and as few as 3% make it to the fourth generation or beyond" (cf. p. 78). This decreasing rate of survival can be explained by the growing complexity of the family business governance and management from the first to the following generations due to the increasing number of families involved, as the descending founder's family. Relationships change from siblings in the first family generations, to cousins within the descending family's generations, making the governance and management of the business more complex and difficult.

A recent contribution by Quinn et al. (2018) provided a framework called AGES, articulated in four dimensions (architecture, governance, entrepreneurship and stewardship) in order to explain the main differences between family and non-family firms. This framework seems useful in identifying some characteristics of the family firms. In the first dimension, a family firm's architecture is characterised by less complex and less formal structures than those of non-family firms. This is due to the great power and discretion in decision-making given to managers in family firms, which allows them more flexibility (Craig and Moores 2015, 2017). These differences between family and non-family firms are more pronounced among small firms and less among large firms (Hiebl 2013; Speckbacher and Wentges 2012). It thus seems that when getting larger and older, family firms increasingly rely on more formal management accounting and control systems (Amat et al. 1994; Giovannoni et al. 2011; Moores and Mula 2000; Moores and Yuen 2001). When growing in size, family firms become more similar to non-family firms in terms of formal management accounting and control instruments. Management accounting tools are characterised by information systems and technology architecture, two main aspects with potential for studies that consider the peculiarities of family business. Quinn et al. (2018) suggested paying closer attention to the specifics of family firms when adopting accounting information systems (or not) and to the barriers to be overcome for successful implementation in a family business context.

In the second dimension, a family firm's governance is a particularly challenging task given a family firm's longstanding stakeholder structure, which involves family members, top management and a board of directors. The ownership stakes are often passed from one generation to the next within the family. The owner family's members usually take on multiple roles in managing and governing the firm (Tagiuri and Davis 1996), thereby blurring the governance relationships. Also, family members, as managers, often make the most important business decisions (Gallo and Sveen 1991). The emotional attachment to family firm ownership may detract from the firm's focus on economic goals. A typical family firm thus violates almost all of the underlying assumptions of traditional governance theories. Mustakallio et al. (2002) developed and tested a model of family firm governance that incorporated both formal and social control aspects of governance. In particular, they emphasised that family firms require a governance structure characterised by formal control that fits the complexity of their stakeholder structure, minimising opportunism and governance mechanisms based on social control that promote cohesion and shared vision within the family. Drawing on agency theory and social theories, they examined the effect of different governance mechanisms on the quality of strategic decision-making.

Other contributions have applied alternative perspectives to agency theory to study the owner-manager relationship, recognizing a social role to the family business, such as the stewardship theory (Davis et al. 1997; Donaldson and Davis 1991), which sees managers as pro organisational and trustworthy team players whose goals naturally align with those of the principals. Stewardship-oriented managers derive higher utility from pro-organisational, collectivist behaviour than from individualistic, self-serving behaviour (Davis et al. 1997). Stewardship theory has advanced as an alternative framework to explain governance issues in family firms (Corbetta and Salvato 2004; Jaskiewicz and Klein 2007; Pieper et al. 2008). For example, Pieper et al. (2008) found that relatively high levels of family commitment to the business and an overlap of values between the owning family and management result in fewer formal governance structures, such as boards of directors. One possible explanation for this finding is that family firms may rely on more informal governance structures.

In the third dimension of Quinn et al.'s framework, contributions have showed that family firms may be reluctant to introduce more formal management control systems, such as strategic planning, due to the fear of losing their entrepreneurial spirit (Mintzberg and Waters 1982; Nordqvist and Melin 2008, 2010). The relationship between family business entrepreneurship and the design of management accounting and control systems may not necessarily be complementary. The design of such systems may very much depend on the form of entrepreneurship in family firms (Kallmuenzer et al. 2017).

Finally, family members are often serving the family business rather than their own interests, which is why researchers have applied the stewardship theory in family business research (Madison et al. 2016; Neubaum et al. 2017; Siebels and zuKnyphausen-Aufseß 2012). In a family firm characterised by stewardship, there is less need for formal monitoring and control (Hiebl 2013). As suggested by Quinn et al. (2018), it could be interesting to explore the roles that multi-generational families have had in the operations and development of the accounting function in these contexts. It would be of interest to review accounting records over an extended historical timeframe to gain insights into the family business sub-system interplay, as suggested by Gersick et al.'s (1997) three-circle model. As indicated above, such research could not only be of historical interest, but could also inform current family business practice (Quinn et al. 2018, p. 541).

The relevance of family values and the emotional attachment to them have been examined through the socio-emotional wealth approach which, according to Songini et al. (2013), originated "from the strong emotional overtone characterizing various dynamics of family business, from strong family values permeating the organization, and from altruistic behaviour typically found among family owners" (cf. p. 76). From this perspective: "factors like emotional attachment, sibling involvement, sense of legacy, family control, and concern for reputation, among many others, give family firms their distinctiveness" (Gomez-Mejia et al. 2011, p. 692). The socio-emotional wealth perspective therefore points out that the management decisions of many family owners are driven more by socio-emotional factors than by economical ones. Related to this approach is the concept of "familiness", which is considered a central concept in the family business research (Frank et al. 2010), and has been defined by Habbershon and Williams (1999) "as the unique bundle of resources a particular firm has because of the systems interactions between the family, its individual members, and the business" (cf. p. 11). The concept of familiness therefore derives from a commonly accepted view of a family business as "the consequence of two overlapping and interacting systems (…): the emotion-oriented family system that focuses on noneconomic goals on one hand and the results-oriented business system that focuses on economic goals on the other" (Stockmans et al. 2010 in Songini et al. 2013, p. 75).

According to the literature reviewed above, a family business profile and it related features can be outlined and summarised in the following way. Generally speaking, a family business is a complex social system derived from two overlapping and interacting social sub-systems: the family sub-system, which is socio-emotionally oriented, and a business sub-system, which is economically oriented. Interactions between the two sub-systems occur via three main dimensions, power, experience and culture, and are intended to pursue the family's vision of the business in a transgenerational horizon. The social system of a family business is thus of a dynamic nature.

A further reflection is noteworthy with respect to the cultural view of the family business system, as a set of different values which tend to become more different moving forward across generations. Stockmans et al.'s (2010) view of a family business is the junction of family and business sub-systems based on two different sets of values, socio-emotional and economical, which motivate the family and the business sub-systems, respectively. Furthermore, within the familiar sub-system, further differences in values can be observed from both a static and a dynamic perspective. From a static perspective, different values may emerge from the different families involved in the business, especially when the family business is behind the first family generation. From a dynamic perspective, old and junior generations may be motivated by different values. We believe that both the static and the dynamic perspectives on the difference between the socio-emotional values within the familiar sub-system can potentially explain the rate of family business failures, which is higher than non-family failures. In our view, these differences in values deserve to be investigated in order to better understand how any kind of innovation, product, process or administration can be introduced into a family business.

3 Family Businesses Life-Cycle Model

The organisational life-cycle theory has many appealing aspects to explain the sequential stages of firm growth and development. These stages present unique sets of effectiveness and difficulties that firms face throughout their life cycles. Although the description of these stages varies across studies, a common assumption is that they refer to transitions, sometimes marked by trauma and crisis (Phelps et al. 2007).

In general, scholars agree that the current life-cycle stage of an organisation is crucial for both management and future plans, allowing the recognition of competencies, as well as constraints, for overcoming the growing pains in the future. The life-cycle theory describes the expected obstacles for each stage, which can help the firms to diagnose their problems and reframe their strategies accordingly (Adizes 1979; Greiner 1998; Quinn and Cameron 1983).

Greiner (1998) pointed out that each stage in a firm's development is the result of a former state, implying that the development comes in sequential order. Although rapid environment changes require firms to be more adaptive and flexible, rather than following a certain passage of development, the organisational life-cycle theory is still a useful tool with which to evaluate a firm's current status and to interpret a firm's dynamics.

The three-circle conceptual model by Gersick et al. (1997) has generally been used when focusing on family business contributions and considers family business as a complex system comprised of three overlapping sub-systems, ownership, business, and family, which move through a sequence of stages over time. In particular, transitions involve an organisation in fundamental choices that will profoundly shape its future; they require particular attention and are fundamental for business continuity. The movement between stages does not happen instantly, rather many systems can exist as a hybrid of two stages for an extended period of time. However, periods of transition between stages occur at predictable times and follow a typical course, and then the understanding of the underlying structure of transition periods could better help to manage these periods more effectively, increasing the chances of family business continuity (Gersick et al. 1997).

According to the model by Gersik et al. transitions are characterised by six components: the continuous accumulation of developmental pressures, the trigger, disengaging, exploring alternatives, choosing and commitment to the new structure. First of all, the developmental pressures that accompany families and their businesses are constantly at work, creating the need and a readiness for change. Once the accumulated pressure is activated, the system has an opportunity to make fundamental changes that bring it more in alignment with its resources, environment and goals. This alignment lasts for a moment immediately after the transition, and then new developmental pressures begin again. The trigger that sets the transition in motion may be either a temporal alarm or an event, and it comes from the accumulated developmental pressures in the system. Disengaging is the time when the old structure is coming to an end, and a new configuration must be found. Exploring alternatives involves considering different forms for the new ownership structure and then measuring their viability against the dreams, talents and capabilities of the participants. This is a process of testing, learning and revising. Managing this exploration phase is the most important leadership challenge of transitions. Choosing, at the end, is related to select an alternative.

In Gersick et al.'s (1997) view, the stages of family business ownership are: a controlling owner, where the source of the family business centrality is launched (culture, strategy and values); sibling partnership, where formalisation emerges, managers need new qualifications and knowledge, structures and processes must be aligned with the whole industry, and information systems become truly important to an adequate coordination; and a cousin consortium, which suggests the development of policies to protect the company's interests. Between these three stages, three types of ownership transitions can occur: recycles (changing individuals, but retaining the same basic structure of ownership); devolutionary transitions (moving to a less complex structure); and evolutionary transitions (moving to a more complex structure).

Other contributions in this field have presented different models for the organisational life cycle, with a different number of stages (Heck et al. 2006; Phelps et al. 2007; Songini and Vola 2015). All of these studies drew on Quinn and Cameron's (1983) model, which highlighted four main developmental stages: the entrepreneurial stage, collectivity stage, formalisation and control stage, and structure elaboration and adoption stage.

The entrepreneurial stage is generally characterised by the biggest driving force behind growth, which is the founder's motivation and commitment. In this stage, creativity is encouraged and tasks are not coordinated in systemised ways but rather "frantic" (Adizes 1979). As Adizes (1979) specified, "dreaming" and entrepreneurship are the activities necessary to get an organisation off the ground during this first stage. Business success tends to be defined in this stage, characterised by easy and quick communication between members and also towards the market response. The business is structurally and financially unstable, whereas the decision-making process is simple and quick as a leader takes all responsibilities (Greiner 1998). This stage is continued until the entrepreneur realises that the firm needs to introduce a formal structure in order to increase efficiency in production. An increase in the firm's size could mean that it becomes harder for the entrepreneur to be involved on their own. On this point, Lippitt and Schmidt (1967) argued that the ownership role is limited to the founder, however this ownership role cannot reach further, since the founder is unable to handle all matters as the firm grows.

The second stage, called collectivity, is related to cooperation, where firms generally keep their informal structures with one-person ownership while realising the importance of production efficiency. No action for change takes place, however. When these obstacles emerge, it is necessary to focus more on human resource management, and interpersonal skills become more important. Quin and Cameron (1983) emphasised the sense of family and cooperativeness among members, high member commitment, and personalised leadership, as the main characteristics of this stage. Even if production efficiency is recognised as relevant, the reason behind the slow transition is the founder's resistance against the delegation of responsibilities to other managerial roles, which entails a depersonalisation of procedures (Adizes 1979; Amat et al. 1994; Moores and Mula 2000; Moores and Yuen 2001; Quinn et al. 2018).

The third stage, formalisation and control, is the most radical and occurs when firms put more emphasis on control and administrative work. Organisational stability, efficiency of production, rules and procedures, and conservative trends are the main characteristics of this developmental stage (Quin and Cameron 1983). There is still the essence of entrepreneurship, however the institution is more depersonalised and the sense of specialisation is strengthened (Adizes 1979). Communication becomes hierarchical (Greiner 1998), and jobs between executives and lower-level managers are separated so that the functional level of production is divided from the decision-making unit. Adizes (1979) refers to this stage as that of an adolescent organisation.

Finally, the fourth stage, called structure elaboration and adoption, is the "one in which the organization monitors the external environment in order to renew itself or expand its domain, or both" (Quin and Cameron 1983, p. 44). Maturity represents the stability of the organisation, but this is not the most desirable stage. This stage is typical of older and bigger firms where both production and managerial structures are balanced. Phelps et al. (2007) claim that at the level of maturity, firms tend to have a lower failure level but that "younger and smaller firms exhibit the highest growth rates" (Phelps et al. 2007, p. 3). Thus, maturity might provide firms with market security but this is no longer accompanied by high growth. They define the maturation as "a realization of the potential inherent in organizations", emphasising the importance of internal structure and the lack of external influences such as innovation. The main challenge of this stage is that firms must learn to regain their creativity in order to sustain further growth. In this stage, leadership style changes from hierarchical to more collaborative and participative. Greiner (1998) refers to dual organisational structure as when firms divide tasks into a habit structure, which deals with daily work, and a reflective structure, which promotes creativity.

4 Main Challenges of Family Businesses

Recent decades have seen an increase in research into the field of family business, to identify the kind of firm that could be identified as a family firm, and making great efforts to trace a life-cycle model for family firm (Anglin et al. 2017; Basco 2017; Carney et al. 2015). In doing so, the literature has focused on differences between family and non-family firms in terms of: strategic decisions (Boellis et al. 2016; Gomez-Mejia et al. 2011; Muñoz-Bullón and Sanchez-Bueno 2011; Strike et al. 2015); general management accounting and control tools (Salvato and Moores 2010; Quinn et al. 2018); governance mechanisms (Mustakallio et al. 2002); and so on. Highlighting these differences has helped academics to identify the peculiarities of family firms, tracing new possible paths of research that are still unexplored.

Astrachan (2010) identified ten areas of research relevant to strategic thinking in family business. Family influence means that family businesses have characteristics that differentiate them from non-family businesses, for example they are value-driven (Denison et al. 2004; Olson et al. 2003), pursuing other than merely financial goals (Astrachan and Jaskiewicz 2008; Gomez-Mejia et al. 2007), relying on networks and long-term relationships which foster trust and altruism (Anderson et al. 2005), and they are frequently characterised by a long-term perspective (Le Breton-Miller and Miller 2006). The latter is determined by the presence of long-tenured CEOs (Miller et al. 2008) who are careful when investing capital, preferring longer investment horizons (Sirmon and Hitt 2003). This long-term orientation can generate a risk aversion in innovation that means the firm does not survive on the market. This problem is evident in family firms that have moved beyond the founder generation (Hiebl 2013, 2014). Given the strong presence of family firms in national contexts, various contributions have investigated the long-term survival and sustainability of family firms, even if their sources of longevity are not well understood. On one hand, family commitment and cohesion are important drivers of longevity and sustainability, whereas consistent family values and a coherence between family and business values are crucial for maintaining family ownership in the long term (Pieper 2008); on the other hand, some evidence suggests that family influence can also have detrimental effects for the business and the family group (Miller and Le Breton-Miller 2003; Miller et al. 2008), for example ownership disperses and control over the business could decrease (Schulze et al. 2003).

Focusing on what could represent the competitive advantage of family firms, some evidence suggested that family relationships can be a source of competition in addition to other firm specific resources (Eddleston et al. 2008). These relationships can add and shed resources to the business in various ways, facilitating the decision-making and governance processes (Sirmon and Hitt 2003), but "the sources from where these resources emerge, the ways in which they change over time, and the means through which they can be nurtured and preserved are not well explored" (Astrachan 2010, p.8).

Another important aspect that characterises family firms is their conservative planning and organic expansion which could limit their growth compared to that of non-family firms. Some contributions have highlighted that when a family firm achieves growth through internationalisation, the results are mixed. Some evidence suggests that family businesses are relatively slow to internationalise (Fernandez and Nieto 2006; Graves and Thomas 2006), emphasising that long-term orientation and non-family management are positively related to international growth (Claver et al. 2009). Astrachan (2010) noted that there is very little research that addresses the intentionality of internationalisation in family firms, with success in starting or expanding international activities, calling for more research in this area.

From a long-term perspective, longevity and competitive advantage are among the challenges for family firms. A recent contribution offered by Quinn et al. (2018) suggested further exploring the use of management accounting and control in family firms in order to advance future research. Research into management accounting and control in family firms has increased considerably in recent years (Giovannoni et al. 2011; Leotta et al. 2017; Songini and Gnan 2015; Speckbacher and Wentges 2012), motivated by the fact that family firms display considerable differences in the way they implement and use management accounting and control systems compared to non-family firms. For instance, several contributions adopting agency theory (Dekker et al. 2013, 2015; García Pérez de Lema and Duréndez 2007; Songini and Gnan 2015; Speckbacher and Wentges 2012) argued that family firms have less need for formal management accounting and control tools, due to the separation of ownership and control, which occurs less often than in non-family firms.

Quinn et al. (2018) discussed future research on management accounting and control in family firms around four dimensions, architecture, governance, entrepreneurship and stewardship, the AGES framework, which are used to explain the main differences between family and non-family firms (Craig and Moores 2015, 2017), as discussed in the second section of the present chapter. Architecture refers to the structures and systems in place to deliver a firm's strategy. While structures comprise the organisational roles and responsibilities formally assigned to people, systems are related to rules and procedures which support and control people as they carry out the roles and responsibilities assigned to them. Governance refers to the "processes that are needed to provide oversight of the direction, control and accountability functions of the firm" (Craig and Moores 2015, p. 137). Entrepreneurship relates to a family firm's strategy, and to their need to act entrepreneurially in order to survive in the market. Finally, the stewardship dimension considers the disposition of family members to behave in the interest of the family business, showing a willingness to collaborate with each other.

Combining the life-cycle model arguments and the family firm features and profiles, we next introduce the main challenges that family firms have to deal with, namely professionalisation and managerialisation, succession, internationalisation and access to financial markets, outlining the role that governance and control systems may play when supporting the firm in facing such challenges.

Professionalisation is one of the most frequent challenges that a family firm has to face. A family firm needs to move from a life-cycle stage characterised by the dominant figure of the founder, where decision-making processes are simple, quick and centralised to the founder themselves (Greiner 1998), to a stage of development where the founder needs to change their entrepreneurial approach, and take a more professional one (Howorth et al. 2016; Stewart and Hitt 2012). At this stage, the owner recognises that the firm needs a more formal structure in order to increase efficiency or to undertake growth. That requires more delegation and formalised practices that could help them and their staff when doing business.

It is not only business considerations that play a role in such firms, but also family interests and those of other owners. This is why family firms are often described as systems comprising three sub-systems: the family system, the business system and the ownership system (Gersick et al. 1997). However, not all family firms are fully family-owned and family-managed.

Contributions to the family firm literature have highlighted that the professionalisation process starts with the involvement of external non-family managers (Dekker et al. 2013). They are usually characterised by a wide experience, and managerial skills enabling them to increase the level of technical knowledge and to support the firm in its growth, affording other challenges such as internationalisation, succession or the decision to enter financial markets. Professionalisation can also be promoted by the owner, who executes their authority by adopting professional processes in firm decision-making (Kelly et al. 2000; McConaughy 2000), or professionally educated family business successors, who make positive contributions to professionalisation (Cabrera-Suárez et al. 2001; Lee et al. 2003; Gedajlovic et al. 2004; Zahra et al. 2008), abandoning traditions that are inconsistent with professional norms.

Some contributions have noted that family managers are often seen as nonprofessional managers due to their relationship to the firm and their background (Hall and

Nordqvist 2008, Lee et al. 2003; Sacristán Navarro and Gómez Ansón 2009). They are characterised by an affective relationship with the family and are more oriented to instinctive decision-making (Schein 1995; Kets de Vries 1985).

The very challenge of family firm professionalisation is thus how the new professional manager integrates their managerial and professional view of doing business with the historically embedded view of the family who developed the business.

Indeed, research shows that non-family managers and directors can bring important external knowledge and experience to family firms (Klein and Bell 2007; Bammens et al. 2011; Bettinelli 2011; Siebels and zuKnyphausen-Aufseß 2012; Hiebl 2014; Tabor et al. 2018).

In particular, when boards and management teams are composed of both family and non-family members, the governance structure can have important implications for the design of management accounting and control systems in family firms. The composition of boards and management teams in family firms seems to have an impact on the use and design of management accounting and control systems (Songini et al. 2013; Songini and Gnan 2015). At the same time, management accounting and control systems can support the family in monitoring non-family managers (Hiebl et al. 2012).

Studies which have investigated professionalisation and governance often include references to professional non-family actors such as Chief Financial Officers (CFOs), controllers or accountants as drivers of this process (Amat et al. 1994; Giovannoni et al. 2011; Stergiou et al. 2013; Hiebl 2014, 2017; Huerta et al. 2017). These external experts often activate the professionalisation of a family firm's governance by designing and implementing management accounting and control systems. Studies that aim to understand the professionalisation process of both the business and the family would be interesting for both research and practice. Accordingly, the professional manager requires "an in-depth enough understanding of the owner family's dominant goals and meanings of being in business (…)" during the professionalisation process (Hall and Nordqvist 2008, p. 63). In doing so, the professional manager has the role of transferring technical knowledge to the family and the non-family organisational actors, who need to become accustomed to the managerial, impersonal principles of being in business. Increasing the levels of delegation and responsibility requires more information and more formalised mechanisms in an organisation (Moores and Yuen 2001; Songini and Vola 2015). The challenge of professionalisation intertwines with another important challenge, "the managerialisation", which involves the introduction of formal management control systems (Songini and Vola 2015).

The management accounting literature focused on family firms has highlighted the low diffusion of managerial control systems related to a widespread entrepreneurship, and strong connections between the family and the firm at governance and management levels, which cause lower agency costs (Schulze et al. 2001; Songini 2006). The rare presence of these tools characterises family firms which are in the earlier stage of their life cycle, where the owner generally uses informal managerial control systems to make decisions (Songini and Gnan 2015). When a family firm grows up, however, it has to cope with the increased complexity of the environment and the firm. In this context, the owner needs to adopt a more professional approach as seen in the professionalisation process (Moores and Yuen 2001; Songini and Vola 2015). The new managerial principles followed by the external non-family manager lead them to introduce more formalised management accounting tools which help in mitigating problems related to delegation and responsibilities, mechanisms of merit and the objectification of the business's goals. Managerialisation can be seen as an important challenge for all organisational actors involved in the family firm, who have to acquire new technical knowledge in order to manage the new accounting tools. In this context, the founder plays a special role in coordinating and monitoring the progress made in the various organisational areas in designing the performance indicators, setting targets for each measure and assessing performance (Giovannoni and Maraghini 2013).

Accordingly, professionalisation and managerialisation can be seen as two interdependent challenges, where the role played by the management accounting systems is crucial. The professionalisation process could be started by professionals and managerial tools that help the family firm to realise a more formal, structured and institutionalised organisation. At the same time, the introduction of new management accounting tools configures the managerialisation process, which helps a family firm to better manage delegation and authority among family and non-family members.

Another important challenge for a family firm is succession, a particular process that involves the family firm when leadership at the top of the firm, and often ownership, are transferred (Le Breton-Miller et al. 2004). This process could occur in case of the incumbent's death or unexpected retirement, or when the founder wants to prepare the successor for the business, ensuring the firm's existence through the next generation (Trow 1961; Dyer 1986; Ward 1987; Lansberg 1988, 1999; Sonnenfeld and Spence 1989; Malone 1989; Handler 1990; Sharma et al. 2001; Dyck et al. 2002; Cabrera-Suárez et al. 2001; Le Breton- Miller et al. 2004; Giovannoni et al. 2011).

When the leadership is transferred from one family member to another, the successor is selected and trained in order to develop appropriate skills and experience to lead the organisation in its next phase (Dyck et al. 2002).

According to Le Breton-Miller et al. (2004), one of the most critical challenges for a family firm lies in ensuring competent family leadership across generations. Poor preparation during the succession processes determines the failure of many family firms that do not survive into the third generation (Birley 1986; Miller et al. 2003). During the succession preparation process, all organisational actors, family and non-family members, are involved in social interaction that could become complex if the successor is not recognised as the leader after the leadership transfer. Studies in management accounting have highlighted how management accounting tools can facilitate internal communication and interaction, helping a founder to transfer their knowledge across generations (Kelly et al. 2000; Giovannoni et al. 2011). These tools help to rebuild conditions of trust and legitimacy among the successors and between the successors and the rest of the organisation establishment (Busco et al. 2006; Bracci and Maran 2012). Some studies focused on the family firm field have highlighted that an external professional manager can make an important contribution in favouring the succession process (Morris 1996; Salvato and Corbetta 2013).

The presence of a professional manager who guides the family firm towards growth has been identified as a lever in the process of internationalisation. The latter represents another important challenge that family firms have to manage in the stages of their life cycle.

Generally, the processes of internationalisation require new assets and investments that expose the family business to new forms of debt. The choice to expand business boundaries implies that the family members are not averse to risk, but they have to be prompt when opening their business to new markets and new forms of risks. This growth step could be facilitated by the presence of non-family professional managers on the board of directors, able to offer alternative orientations to the management's choices and to generate new knowledge and information (George et al. 2005; Cerrato 2012; Calabrò 2013) even if it means a loss of control with regard to strategic management. Finally, another important challenge for the family firm is the strategic decisions that the family owners must take when the firm is listed on the financial market. When a family firm increases in size and the organisation becomes more complex, the owners consider the possibility of entering the financial markets. When a family firm becomes a listed firm, its strategic decisions can be approved by the family and non-family members who work inside the firm, but the impact on the small investors, who are passive and external to strategic decisions, could be negative. The small investors could perceive a risk of expropriation if the family owners make decisions that lead to the maximisation of the family interests rather than the firm's interests (Morck and Yeung 2003). In this situation, family owners often prefer to maintain their corporate control for a long time and the stability of the firm, reducing the growth and investment possibilities, and demonstrating risk averse behaviour (Schulze et al. 2001; Graves and Thomas 2006).

In summary, a family firm has to face many challenges, and these differ among the life-cycle phases. In the following chapters, the present volume will deal with the main topics of family businesses discussed in the extant literature, namely managerialisation-professionalisation, succession, internationalisation and access to financial markets, with the aim of understanding how governance and control systems can help family firms to face the main challenges that come from the business.

5 Conclusions

Recognising the relevance of family businesses, this chapter focused on the profiles and features that distinguish family from non-family firms. The literature on family business has highlighted that the presence of family values and dynamics affects the ability of a business to grow, to enter international markets, to survive over the future generations and to access financial markets. Recently, management control scholars have been invited to invest more in the fields of family business, investigating the role of management accounting and control systems in such settings. This has prompted further investigations into the dynamics between family and non-family members, and how these could affect the development and growth of family firms. Little has been done on the role of governance and control systems in family firms, however, exploring how control systems work in these firms.

Starting from this gap, the present chapter aimed to trace an overview of the main theoretical points that could be defined as the characteristics and profiles of family businesses, trying to systematise them, in order to offer an interpretation that could sustain further theoretical development in this field.

Organisational life-cycle theory was used to pursue this aim, as it offers appealing theories to explain the sequential stages of firm growth and development, allowing the recognition of competencies as well as constrains for each stage. Following this view, several models have been proposed to highlight the differences between the various stages and the criticalities of transition periods. Following Quinn and Cameron (1983), we recognised four main stages: entrepreneurial, cooperation, adolescent, and maturity. Starting from entrepreneurial stage, family firms were characterised by the founder's motivation and commitment, with low coordination mechanisms. When an entrepreneur recognises the need to increase efficiency with delegation of responsibilities, the cooperation stage occurs. The business becomes more depersonalised and the sense of specialisation is strengthened; this allows more formalised communication, and this stage is referred to as that of an adolescent organisation. Finally, maturity represents the stability of the organisation, but it requires the regaining of creativity in order to sustain further growth.

The use of the life-cycle model to discuss how such profiles and features are linked to a particular stage of the business development path allowed us to examine the main challenges of a family business along its development path, namely managerialisation/professionalisation, internationalisation, firm succession and access to financial markets. Such topics are strongly interrelated and their connections need further investigation.

The need to develop a unitary view of these challenges, based on a holistic approach, derives from the opportunity to investigate the main interrelationships among them. This view embraces the use of management control and governance systems, since the introduction and use of such systems, as argued by some recent studies, play a role in facilitating managerialisation/professionalisation, internationalisation, firm succession and access to financial markets.

This chapter contributes to an updated review of studies that have dealt with the main family business topics, suggesting various insights to help family businesses to survive and to grow up. In doing so, it questioned the role of governance and control systems in family firms, in managing the main family business challenges. In these terms, the introduction of a management accounting system may be the consequence of a succession process and, in the meantime, may facilitate a firm's managerialisation/professionalisation and growth. At the same time, a management accounting system may contribute to reinforcing the process of succession if its introduction has been successfully led by a representative of the junior generation. This offers some reasons for a better investigation of interrelationships between managerialisation and successions, as well as for other family business challenges.

References

Adizes I (1979) Organizational passages: diagnosing and treating lifecycle problems of organizations. Organizational Dyn 8(1):3–25. https://doi.org/10.1016/0090-2616(79)90001-9

Amat J, Carmona S, Roberts H (1994) Context and change in management accounting systems: a Spanish case study. Manage Acc Res 5(2):107–122. https://doi.org/10.1006/mare.1994.1008

Anderson AR, Jack SL, Dodd SD (2005) The role of family members in entrepreneurial networks: beyond the boundaries of the family firm. Family Bus Rev 18:135–154. https://doi.org/10.4337/9781785364884

Anglin AH, Reid SW, Short JC, Zachary MA, Rutherford MW (2017) An archival approach to measuring family influence: an organizational identity perspective. Family Bus Rev 30:19–36. https://doi.org/10.1177/0894486516669254

Astrachan JH (2010) Strategy in family business: toward a multidimensional research agenda. J Family Bus Strat 1:6–14. https://doi.org/10.1016/j.jfbs.2010.02.001

Astrachan JH, Jaskiewicz P (2008) Emotional returns and emotional costs in privately held family businesses: advancing traditional business valuation. Family Bus Rev 21:139–149. https://doi.org/10.1111/j.1741-6248.2008.00115.x

Astrachan JH, Klein SB, Smyrnios KX (2002) The F-PEC scale of family influence: a proposal for solving the family business definition problem. Family Bus Rev XV(1): 45–58. https://doi.org/10.1111/j.1741-6248.2002.00045.x

Bammens Y, Voordeckers W, Gils AV (2011) Boards of directors in family businesses: a literature review and research agenda. Int J Manag Rev 13(2):134–152. https://doi.org/10.1111/j.1468-2370.2010.00289.x

Barach JA, Ganitsky JB (1995) Successful succession in family business. Family Bus Rev 8(2):131–155. https://doi.org/10.1111/j.1741-6248.1995.00131.x

Basco R (2017) Where do you want to take your family firm? A theoretical and empirical exploratory study of family business goals. Bus Res Q 4. https://doi.org/10.1016/j.brq.2016.07.001

Bettinelli C (2011) Boards of directors in family firms: an exploratory study of structure and group process. Family Bus Rev 24(2):151–169. https://doi.org/10.1177/0894486511402196

Birley S (1986) Succession in the family firm: the inheritor's view. J Small Bus Manage 24(3):36–43. https://doi.org/10.1111/j.1741-6248.1994.00133.x

Boellis A, Mariotti S, Minichilli A, Piscitello L (2016) Family involvement and firms' establishment mode choice in foreign markets. J Int Bus Stud 47:929–950. https://doi.org/10.1057/jibs.2016.23

Bracci M, Maran L (2012) The role and use of management accouting systems (MAS) in family firms: a case study Piccola Impresa/Small Business 3: 129–153. https://doi.org/10.14596/pisb.35

Busco C, Riccaboni A, Scapens RW (2006) Trust for accounting and accounting for trust. Manag Acc Res 17:11–41. https://doi.org/10.1016/j.mar.2005.08.001

Cabrera-Suàrez K, De Saa-Pèrez P, Garcìa-Almeida D (2001) The succession process from a resource-and knowledge-based view of the family firm. Family Bus Rev 14:37–46. https://doi.org/10.1111/j.1741-6248.2001.00037.x

Calabrò A, Torchia M, Pukall T, Mussolino D (2013) The Influence of ownership structure and board strategic involvement on international sales: the moderating effect of family involvement. Int Bus Rev 22:509–523. https://doi.org/10.1016/j.ibusrev.2012.07.002

Carney M, van Essen M, Gedajlovic ER, Heugens PPMAR (2015) What do we know about private family firms? A meta-analytical review. Entrep Theory Pract 39: 513–544. DOI: 10.1111/etap.12054

Cerrato D, Piva M (2012) The internationalization of small and medium-sized enterprises: the effect of family management, human capital and foreign ownership. J Manag Governance 16:617–644. https://doi.org/10.1007/s10997-010-9166-x

Chrisman JJ, Chua JH, Sharma P (2003) Current trends and future directions in family business management studies: toward a theory of the family firm. Coleman Found White Pap Ser. https://doi.org/10.1111/j.1540-6520.2005.00098.x

Chua JH, Chrisman J, Sharma P (1999) Defining the family business by behaviour. Entrep Theory Pract 19–39. https://doi.org/10.1177/104225879902300402

Claver E, Rienda L, Quer D (2009) Family firms' international commitment: The influence of family-related factors. Family Bus Rev 22:125–135. https://doi.org/10.1177/0894486508330054

Corbetta G, Salvato CA (2004) The board of directors in family firms: one size fits all? Family Bus Rev 17(2):119–134. https://doi.org/10.1111/j.1741-6248.2004.00008.x

Craig JB, Moores K (2015) The A-GES framework: Understanding the family business difference. In: Newbert SL (ed) Small business in a global economy: creating and managing successful organizations. Praeger, Santa Barbara, pp 123–154

Craig JB, Moores K (2017) Leading a family business: best practices for long term stewardship. Praegar Publishing, Santa Barbara

Davis JH, Schoorman FD, Donaldson L (1997) Toward a stewardship theory of management. Acad Manag Rev 22(1):20–47. https://doi.org/10.2307/259223

Dekker J, Lybaert N, Steijvers T, Depaire B (2015) The effect of family business professionalization as a multidimensional construct on firm performance. J Small Bus Manage 53(2):516–538. https://doi.org/10.1111/jsbm.12082

Dekker JC, Lybaert N, Steijvers T, Depaire B, Mercken R (2013) Family firm types based on the professionalization construct: exploratory research. Family Bus Rev 26(1):81–99. https://doi.org/10.1177/0894486512445614

Denison D, Lief C, Ward JL (2004) Culture in family-owned enterprises: Recognizing and leveraging unique strengths. Family Bus Rev 17:61–70. https://doi.org/10.1111/j.1741-6248.2004.00004.x

Donaldson L, Davis JH (1991) Stewardship theory or agency theory: CEO governance and shareholder returns. Aust J Manage 16(1):49–64. https://doi.org/10.1177/031289629101600103

Dyck B, Mauws F, Starke A, Mischke GA (2002) Passing the baton. The importance of sequence, timing, technique and communication in executive succession. J Bus Ventur 17:143–162. https://doi.org/10.1016/S0883-9026(00)00056-2

Dyer WG Jr (1986) Cultural change in family firms: anticipating and managing business and family transitions. Jossey-Bass, San Francisco

Eddleston KA, Kellermanns FW, Sarathy R (2008) Resource configuration in family firms: linking resources, strategic planning and technological opportunities to performance. J Manage Stud 45:26–50. https://doi.org/10.1111/j.1467-6486.2007.00717.x

Fernandez Z, Nieto MJ (2006) Impact of ownership on the international involvement of SMEs. J Int Bus Stud 37:340–351. https://doi.org/10.1057/palgrave.jibs.8400196

Frank H, Lueger M, Nosè L, Suchy D (2010) The concept of '"Familiness"' literature review and systems theory-based reflections. J Fam Bus Strat 1:119–130. https://doi.org/10.1016/j.jfbs.2010.08.001

Gallo M.A. (2000) Conversation with S Klein at the IFERA meeting held at Amsterdam University

Gallo MA, Sveen J (1991) Internationalizing the family business: facilitating and restraining factors. Family Bus Rev 4(2):181–190. https://doi.org/10.1111/j.1741-6248.1991.00181.x

Gedajlovic E, Lubatkin MH, Schulze WS (2004) Crossing the threshold from founder management to professional management: a governance perspective. J Manage Stud 41(5):899–912. https://doi.org/10.1111/j.1467-6486.2004.00459.x

George G, Wiklund J, Zahra A (2005) Ownership and the internationalization of small firms. J Manage 31:31(2): 210–233. https://doi.org/10.1177/0149206304271760

Gersick KE, Davis JA, McCollom HM, Lansberg I (1997) Generation to generation: life cycles of the family business. Harvard Business Press, Boston

Giovannoni E, Maraghini MP (2013) The challenger of integrated performance measurement systems. Integrating mechanisms for integrated measures. Accounting, Auditing & Accountability 26(6):978–1008. https://doi.org/10.1108/AAAJ-04-2013-1312

Giovannoni E, Maraghini MP, Riccaboni A (2011) Transmitting knowledge across generations: the role of management accounting practices. Family Bus Rev 24(2):126–150. https://doi.org/10.1177/0894486511406722

Gomez-Mejia LR, Haynes KT, Nunez-Nickel M, Jacobson KJL, Moyano-Fuentes J (2007) Socioemotional wealth and business risks in family-controlled firms: evidence from Spanish olive oil mills. Adm Sci Q 52:106–137. https://doi.org/10.2189/asqu.52.1.106

Gomez-Mejia LR, Cruz C, Berrone P, De Castro J (2011) Thebind that ties: socioemotional wealth preservation in familyfirms. Acad Manage Ann 5:653–707. https://doi.org/10.1080/19416520.2011.593320

Graves C, Thomas J (2006) Internationalization of Australian family businesses: a managerial capabilities perspective. Family Bus Rev 19:207–223. https://doi.org/10.1111/j.1741-6248.2006.00066.x

Greiner L (1998) Evolution and revolution as organizations grow. Harv Bus Rev 76(3):55–68. https://doi.org/10.1007/978-1-349-20317-8_25

Habbershon TG, Williams ML (1999) A resource-based framework for assessing the strategic advantages of family firms. Family Bus Rev 12:1–25. https://doi.org/10.1111/j.1741-6248.1999.00001.x

Hall A, Nordqvist M (2008) Professional management in family businesses: Toward an extended understanding. Family Bus Rev 21:51–69. https://doi.org/10.1111/j.1741-6248.2007.00109.x

Handler WC (1990) Succession in family firms: a mutual role adjustment between entrepreneur and next generation family members. Entrep Theory Pract 15(1):37–51. https://doi.org/10.1177/104225879001500105

Heck RKZ, Scannell TE (1999) The prevalence of family business from a household sample. Family Bus Rev 12(3):209–224. https://doi.org/10.1111/j.1741-6248.1999.00209.x

Heck RKZ, Danes SM, Fitzgerald MA (2006) The family's dynamic role within family business entrepreneurship. In: Poutziouris PZ, Smyrnios KX, Klein SB (eds) Handbook of research on family business, Edward Elgar Cheltenham, UK Northampton, MA, USA, pp 80–105

Hiebl MRW (2013) Risk aversion in family firms: What do we really know? J Risk Financ 14(1):49–70. https://doi.org/10.1108/15265941311288103

Hiebl MRW (2014) A finance professional who understands the family: family firms' specific requirements for non-family chief financial officers. RMS 8(4):465–494. https://doi.org/10.1007/s11846-013-0112-6

Hiebl MRW (2017) Finance managers in family firms: an upper-echelons view. J Fam Bus Manag 7(2):207–220. https://doi.org/10.1108/JFBM-07-2016-0014

Hiebl MRW, Feldbauer-Durstmüller B, Duller C, Neubauer H (2012) Institutionalisation of management accounting in family businesses–Empirical evidence from austria and Germany. J Enterprising Cult 20(4):405–436. https://doi.org/10.1142/S0218495812500173

Howorth C, Wright M, Westhead P, Allcock D (2016) Company metamorphosis: professionalization waves, family firms and management buyouts. Small Bus Econ 47:803–817. https://doi.org/10.1007/s11187-016-9761-6

Huerta E, Petrides Y, O'Shaughnessy D (2017) Introduction of accounting practices in small family businesses. Qual Res Account Manag 14(2):111–136. https://doi.org/10.1108/QRAM-01-2015-0008

Jaskiewicz P, Klein SB (2007) The impact of goal alignment on board size and board composition in family-owned businesses. J Bus Res 60(10):1080–1089. https://doi.org/10.1016/j.jbusres.2006.12.015

Kallmuenzer A, Strobl A, Peters M (2017) Tweaking the entrepreneurial orientation—performance relationship in family firms: the effect of control mechanisms and family-related goals. RMS. https://doi.org/10.1007/s11846-017-0231-6
Kelly LM, Athanassiou N, Crittenden WF (2000) Founder centrality and strategic behavior in family-owned firm. Entrep Theory Pract 25(2):27–42. https://doi.org/10.1177/104225870002500202
Kets de Vreis MF (1985) The dark side of entrepreneurship. Harv Bus Rev 8(6):160–167
Klein S, Bell FA (2007) Non-family executives in family businesses: a literature review. Electron J Fam Bus Stud 1(1):19–37. https://doi.org/10.1177/0894486517734683
Lansberg I (1988) The succession conspiracy. Family Bus Rev 1(2):119–143. https://doi.org/10.1111/j.1741-6248.1988.00119.x
Lansberg I (1999) Succeeding generations: realizing the dream of families in business. Harvard Business School Press, Boston
Le Breton-Miller I, Miller D (2006) Why do some family businesses out-compete? Governance, long-term orientations, and sustainable capability. Entrep: Theory Pract 30: 731–746. https://doi.org/10.1111/j.1540-6520.2006.00147.x
Le Breton-Miller I, Miller D, Steier LP (2004) Toward and integrative model of effective FOB succession. Entrep Theory Pract 28:305–328. https://doi.org/10.1111/j.1540-6520.2004.00047.x
Lee KS, Lim GH, Lim WS (2003) Family business succession: appropriation risk and choice of successor. Acad Manag Rev 28(4):657–666. https://doi.org/10.5465/amr.2003.10899446
Leotta A, Rizza C, Ruggeri D (2017) Management accounting and leadership construction in family firms. Qual Res Account Manag 14(2):189–207. https://doi.org/10.1108/QRAM-09-2015-0079
Lippitt G, Schmidt W (1967) Crises in a developing organization. Harv Bus Rev 45(6):102–112. https://doi.org/10.12776/qip.v22i3.1177
Madison K, Holt DT, Kellermanns FW, Ranft AL (2016) Viewing family firm behavior and governance through the lens of agency and stewardship theories. Family Bus Rev 29(1):65–93. https://doi.org/10.1177/0894486515594292
Malone SC (1989) Selected correlates of business continuity planning in the family business. Family Bus Rev 2(4):341–353. https://doi.org/10.1111/j.1741-6248.1989.tb00003.x
McConaughy DL (2000) Family CEOs vs. nonfamily CEOs in the family-controlled firm: an examination of the level and sensitivity of pay to performance. Family Bus Rev 13(2):121–131. https://doi.org/10.1111/j.1741-6248.2000.00121.x
Miller D, Le Breton-Miller I (2003) Challenge versus advantage in family business. Strategic Organization 1:127–134. https://doi.org/10.1177/1476127003001001222
Miller D, Le Breton-Miller I, Scholnick B (2008) Stewardship vs. stagnation: an empirical comparison of small family and non-family businesses. J Manage Stud 45:51–78. https://doi.org/10.1111/j.1467-6486.2007.00718.x
Miller D, Steier L, Le Breton-Miller I (2003) Lost in time: intergenerational succession, change and failure in family. J Bus Ventur 18:513–553. https://doi.org/10.1016/S0883-9026(03)00058-2
Mintzberg H, Waters JA (1982) Tracking strategy in an entrepreneurial firm. Acad Manag J 25(3):465–499. https://doi.org/10.1111/j.1741-6248.1990.00285.x
Moores K, Mula J (2000) The salience of market, bureaucratic, and clan controls in the management of family firm transitions: some tentative Australian evidence. Family Bus Rev 13(2):91–106. https://doi.org/10.1111/j.1741-6248.2000.00091.x
Moores K, Yuen S (2001) Management accounting systems and organizational configuration: a life-cycle perspective. Acc Organ Soc 26(4–5):351–389. https://doi.org/10.1016/S0361-3682(00)00040-4
Morck R, Yeung B (2003) Agency problems in large family business groups. Entrep Theory Pract 27(4):367–382. https://doi.org/10.1111/1540-8520.t01-1-00015
Morris MH (1996) Factors influencing family business succession. Int J Entrep Behav Res 2(3):68–81. https://doi.org/10.1108/13552559610153261

Muñoz-Bullón F, Sanchez-Bueno MJ (2011) The impact of family involvement on the R&D intensity of publicly traded firms. Family Bus Rev 24(1):62–70. https://doi.org/10.1016/j.techfore.2018.02.021

Mustakallio M, Autio E, Zahra SA (2002) Relational and contractual governance in family firms: effects on strategic decision making. Family Bus Rev 15:205–222. https://doi.org/10.1111/j.1741-6248.2002.00205.x

Neubaum DO, Thomas CH, Dibrell C, Craig JB (2017) Stewardship climate scale: an assessment of reliability and validity. Family Bus Rev 30(1):37–60. https://doi.org/10.1177/0894486516673701

Nordqvist M, Melin L (2008) Strategic planning champions: social crafts persons, artful interpreters and known strangers. Long Range Plan 41(3):326–344. https://doi.org/10.1016/j.lrp.2008.02.007

Nordqvist M, Melin L (2010) The promise of the strategy as practice perspective for family business strategy research. J Fam Bus Strat 1(1):15–25. https://doi.org/10.1016/j.jfbs.2009.12.001

Olson PD, Zuiker VS, Danes SM, Stafford K, Heck RKZ, Duncan KA (2003) The impact of the family and the business on family business sustainability. J Bus Ventur 18:639–666. https://doi.org/10.1016/S0883-9026(03)00014-4

Pérez G, de Lema D, Duréndez A (2007) Managerial behaviour of small and medium-sized family businesses: an empirical study. Int J Entrep Behav Res 13(3):151–172. https://doi.org/10.1108/13552550710751030

Phelps R, Adams R, Bessant J (2007) Life cycles of growing organizations: a review with implications for knowledge and learning. Int J Manag Rev 9(1):1–30. https://doi.org/10.1111/j.1468-2370.2007.00200.x

Pieper TM, Klein SB, Jaskiewicz P (2008) The impact of goal alignment on board existence and top management team composition evidence from family-influenced businesses. J Small Bus Manage 46(3):372–394. https://doi.org/10.1111/j.1540-627X.2008.00249.x

Quinn M, Hiebl MRW, Moores K, Craig JB (2018) Future research on management accounting and control in family firms: suggestions linked to architecture, governance, entrepreneurship and stewardship. J Manag Control 28:529–546. https://doi.org/10.1007/s00187-018-0257-1

Quinn R, Cameron K (1983) Organizational life-cycles and shifting criteria of effectiveness: some preliminary evidence. Manage Sci 29:33–51. https://doi.org/10.1287/mnsc.29.1.33

Sacristán NM, GómezAnsón S (2009) Do families shape corporate governance structures? J Manag Organ 15(3):327–345. https://doi.org/10.1017/S1833367200002650

Salvato C, Moores K (2010) Research on accounting in family firms: past accomplishments and future challenges. Family Bus Rev 23(3):193–215. https://doi.org/10.1177/0894486510375069

Salvato C, Corbetta G (2013) Transitional leadership of advisors as a facilitator of successors' leadership construction. Family Bus Rev 26(3):235–255. https://doi.org/10.1177/0894486513490796

Schein EH (1995) The role of the founder in creating organizational culture. Family Bus Rev 8(3):221–238. https://doi.org/10.1111/j.1741-6248.1995.00221.x

Schulze WS, Lubatkin MH, Dino RN (2003) Exploring the agency consequences of ownership dispersion among the directors of private family firms. Acad Manag J 46:179–194. https://doi.org/10.5465/30040613

Schulze WS, Lubatkin MH, Dino RN, Buchholtz AK (2001) Agency relationships in family firms: theory and evidence. Organ Sci 12:99–116. https://doi.org/10.1287/orsc.12.2.99.10114

Sharma P, Chrisman JJ, Pablo AL, Chua JH (2001) Determinants of initial satisfaction with the succession process in family firms: a conceptual model. Entrep Theory Pract 25(3):17–35. https://doi.org/10.1177/104225870102500302

Siebels JF, zuKnyphausen-Aufseß D (2012) A review of theory in family business research: the implications for corporate governance. Int J Manag Rev 14(3):280–304. https://doi.org/10.1111/j.1468-2370.2011.00317.x

Sirmon DG, Hitt MA (2003) Managing resources: linking unique resources, management, and wealth creation in family firms. Entrep: Theory Pract 27:339–358. https://doi.org/10.1111/1540-8520.t01-1-00013

Songini L, Vola P (2015) The role of professionalization and managerialization in family business succession. Manage Control 1:9–43. https://doi.org/10.3280/MACO2015-001002
Songini L (2006) The professionalization of family firms: theory and practice. In Poutziouris PZ, Smyrnios KX, Klein SB (eds) Handbook of family business research. UK, Edward Elgar Publishing.
Songini L, Gnan L (2015) Family involvement and agency cost control mechanisms in family small and medium-sized enterprises. J Small Bus Manage 53(3):748–779. https://doi.org/10.1111/jsbm.12085
Songini L, Gnan L, Malmi T (2013) The role and impact of accounting in family business. J Fam Bus Strat 4(2):71–83. https://doi.org/10.1016/j.jfbs.2013.04.002
Sonnenfeld JA, Spence PL (1989) The parting patriarch of a family firm. Family Bus Rev 2(4):355–375. https://doi.org/10.1111/j.1741-6248.1989.tb00004.x
Speckbacher G, Wentges P (2012) The impact of family control on the use of performance measures in strategic target setting and incentive compensation: a research note. Manag Account Res 23(1):34–46. https://doi.org/10.1016/j.mar.2011.06.002
Stergiou K, Ashraf J, Uddin S (2013) The role of structure and agency in management accounting control change of a family owned firm: a Greek case study. Crit Perspect Acc 24(1):62–73. https://doi.org/10.1016/j.cpa.2012.09.007
Stewart A, Hitt MA (2012) Why can't a family business be more like a nonfamily business? Modes of professionalization in family firms. Family Bus Rev 25(1):58–86. https://doi.org/10.1177/0894486511421665
Stockmans A, Lybaert N, Voordeckers W (2010) Socioemotional wealth and earnings management in private family firms. Family Bus Rev 23(3):280–294. https://doi.org/10.1177/0894486510374457
Strike VM, Berrone P, Sapp SG, Congiu L (2015) A socioemotional wealth approach to CEO career horizons in family firms. J Manage Stud 52:555–583. https://doi.org/10.1111/joms.12123
Tabor W, Chrisman JJ, Madison K, Vardaman JM (2018) Nonfamily members in family firms: a review and future research agenda. Family Bus Rev 31(1):54–79. https://doi.org/10.1177/0894486517734683
Tagiuri R, Davis J (1996) Bivalent attributes of the family firms. Family Bus Rev 9(2):199–208. https://doi.org/10.1111/j.1741-6248.1996.00199.x
Trow DB (1961) Executive succession in small companies. Adm Sci Q 6(2):228–239. https://doi.org/10.2307/2390756
Ward JL (1987) Keeping the family business healthy: how to plan for continuing growth profitability and family leadership. Jossey-Bass, San Francisco
Ward JL (1988) The special role of strategic planning for family businesses. Family Bus Rev 1(2):105–117. https://doi.org/10.1111/j.1741-6248.1988.00105.x
Zahra SA, Hayton JC, Neubaum DO, Dibrell C, Craig J (2008) Culture of family commitment and strategic flexibility: the moderating effect of stewardship. Entrep Theory Pract 32–6:1035–1054. https://doi.org/10.1111/j.1540-6520.2008.00271.x

Professionalization and Managerialization in Family Firms: A Still Open Issue

Cristiana Cattaneo and Gaia Bassani

Abstract This chapter reviews the extant literature on managerialization and professionalization, highlighting the main and overlapping differences between the two concepts. Professionalization and managerialization are viewed as business challenges as they need to be dealt with for the family business to survive. These challenges are discussed, and their determinants and effects in terms of organizational performance are examined. Published case studies on professionalization and managerialization are investigated using the theoretical perspectives most often considered in the literature. The chapter uses a systemic view approach to emphasize the need to tackle the above challenges.

Keywords Professionalization · Managerialization · Management control system · Professional · Family business

1 Introduction

For many years, researchers have studied family firms as a mysterious object and very different from non-family firms. The authors consider company structure and the central role of the family in every area in the organization, as well as other often intangible characteristics, such as relationships, flexibility and speed in decision processes, knowledge, and so on. Additionally, the family dimension throws up many challenges, specifically, but not only, during growth, succession, and professionalization.

Professionalization is a key issue in the life of family businesses because it leads to a shift from an "entrepreneurial" dimension to a "managerial" one (Howorth et al. 2016; Stewart and Hitt 2012). The question is crucial, due to its impact on governance,

C. Cattaneo (✉) · G. Bassani
Department of Management, Economics and Quantitative Methods, University of Bergamo, Bergamo, Italy
e-mail: cristiana.cattaneo@unibg.it

G. Bassani
e-mail: gaia.bassani@unibg.it

A. Leotta (ed.), *Management Controlling and Governance of Family Businesses*, Contributions to Management Science,
https://doi.org/10.1007/978-3-030-47741-7_3

on the firm's management, and on performance. Moreover, professionalization intertwines with the evolution of management accounting systems and managerialization. In fact, some authors (e.g., Songini and Vola 2015) describe managerialization as the introduction of formal management control systems. In general, the question of managerialization arises when the growth of the company challenges information systems. The decision-making process asks for more information and more formalized mechanisms in the organization. In family business, the issue is also crucial in the phase of succession and poses many questions. Thus, the prevalent literature has argued that family firms have very scarce formal control systems, while informal relations and control systems prevail (Cattaneo and Bassani 2015).

Much of the empirical and theoretical literature on family business examines professionalization and managerialization. Many authors have defined the two concepts in different ways and others have debated the same arguments without labeling their results with the terms professionalization and managerialization. Recently, the concept of professionalization has become pervasive (e.g., Camfield and Franco 2019; Dekker et al. 2015; Stewart and Hitt 2012). Culasso et al. (2018, p. 49), for example, defined professionalization "as the phenomenon during which professional managers become part of the management in a family business, and/or the implementation of formal management control systems to support the managerial decision-making process" (Giovannoni et al. 2011).

With regard to professionalization and managerialization, the main areas of attention concern how the business is run and who manages it. Mechanisms and managers are the key elements in the survival and growth of the business. To accomplish these, the manager controls ambition and mechanisms are often referred to as practices influencing behavior and supporting organizations in their accomplishment of objectives (El Masri et al. 2017). It is not a case if many studies on professionalization and management control systems describe the link with these concepts and firm performance (e.g. Dekker et al. 2015; Durendez et al. 2016; Stewart and Hitt 2012). This applies also to small- and medium-sized enterprises (SMEs) (Fang et al. 2017). Moreover, as a family business progresses with efforts toward professionalization, a formal and rational control and compensation system based on overall organizational goals is introduced. A tight relationship between the two concepts exists and is more evident if we observe longitudinally managers, the introduction and use of institutionalized practices, and formal management control systems. Hatum et al. (2010) suggested observation of the life-cycle role of the founder, control systems, the professionalization of the management team, and ownership issues.

The two processes are described separately in more detail herein. They are worth the attention of those who wish to analyze the main characteristics of the two processes. Thus, we begin by describing the process of professionalization, and this is followed by the review of studies about managerialization. We then synthesize our findings into a discussion where the relationship between the two concepts emerges. Finally, we conclude and propose avenues for future research.

2 Professionalization

2.1 *The Evolutionary Meaning of Professionalization*

Entrepreneurship and governance literature has focused on professionalization as a process that contributes to a more formalized, structured, and institutionalized corporation (e.g., Daily and Dalton 1992; Dekker et al. 2015; Gedajlovic et al. 2004).

For long time, professionalization in family firms was considered equivalent to the involvement of external non-family managers in supporting the firm to meet several challenges: growth, internationalization, and succession. In these crucial phases in the firm's life, the literature argues that only external professionals have the characteristics properly to manage the firm (Dekker et al. 2013). This assumption is underpinned by the belief that non-family managers are more able than family members to achieve the strategic goals of the firm due to their skills and abilities (Pérez de Lema and Duréndez 2007) and adequate management training (Chittoor and Das 2007). In general, the meaning of "professional" is not unequivocal but is mainly related to people with a strong educational background and a wide experience that give them legitimacy (Hwang and Powell 2009). Stewart and Hitt (2012) developed this description by adding certain less obvious features, such as the adoption of a moral code and the need for continued improvement of skills and status. The aforementioned literature argued that only external non-family managers possess these characteristics.

By contrast, family managers are often seen as non-professional, regardless of their background and relationship to the company (Hall and Nordqvist 2008). For this reason, Corbetta (1995) and others referred to the presence of non-family managers as an opportunity to increase technical knowledge that is lacking within the family. A number of studies have suggested that to increase the family business's profitability and longevity family managers should be replaced by non-family ones (Barth et al. 2005; Bloom and Van Reenen 2007; Corbetta 1995; Daily and Dollinger 1992; Dyer 1988; Gulbrandsen 2005).

Moreover, some authors have observed different personality types in family and non-family members, and these can explain why external managers are more able to lead the company through its life cycle. Previous contributions indicated three areas that define a CEO's personality: (i) relationships with people, (ii) thinking styles, and (iii) feelings and emotions (Kelleci et al. 2019).

With regard to the first point, the literature has suggested that family CEOs have a greater preference for control and have strong opinions on what is necessary to balance family and business (Dyer 1989; Schein 1995). Consequently, they are independent in making decisions (Kets de Vreis 1985; Miller 2015).

Many authors have argued that thinking styles among family members have specific elements. Family CEOs are influenced by affective relations with the family and by the desire to perpetuate family dynasties, and this makes them less methodical, organized, systematic and aware of details (detail conscious). Furthermore, they are more oriented to instinctive decision making rather than numbers, data or statistical information (data rational) (Kets de Vries 1985; Schein 1995). Finally, the need to guarantee a future for the family forces the family CEO into forward thinking, setting goals from a strategic perspective. Otherwise, family CEOs are not very interested in understanding the motives and behavior of people. This trait is partly related to independence in decision making.

Considering the third (feelings and emotions), the family CEO is very deeply emotionally involved in the destiny of the firm, as he or she identifies itself with the firm and the family's future intertwines with it. For this reason, family CEOs tend to be worried, are not relaxed, and are somewhat distrusting of people around them (Cannella and Shen 2001).

Recently, Kelleci et al. (2019) investigated the personalities of 25 non-family CEOs and 19 family CEOs in Belgian private firms. They examined the traits outlined in the literature above and found, as was partly expected, that non-family CEOs are more democratic and less independently minded that family CEOs, although both tend to emphasize control. Furthermore, non-family CEOs are more relaxed, less worried, and more trusting than family CEOs. In addition, non-family CEOs are characterized as being more detail conscious, more data rational, and more behavioral.

This evidence seems to indicate that non-family CEOs have a more balanced personality and are more flexible in their behavior. These traits should be conditions for a more "professional" management of the firm.

Despite the abundance of literature that suggested that professionalization could be pursued only by hiring external managers, a more balanced view has been presented. The seminal work of Dyer (1989) underlined that the process of professionalization could be realized through the hiring of new professional managers but could also involve other actors: family members of the organization and non-family members already working in the firm. A business could have all three types of professionals or none. In fact, the process of professionalization does not necessarily imply the presence of family members in managerial roles. Alternatively, the professionalization of family members (Camfield and Franco 2019) or employees may lead to professionalization of the firm, in the sense described above. In any case, as has already been mentioned, when we talk about professionals, we depict a person who gains legitimacy and authority through his or her brilliant scholastic and experiential background (Hwang and Powell 2009). Moreover, professionals develop a specific knowledge that is not generally applicable to all contexts.

Other authors (Bennedsen et al. 2007; Berenbeim 1990; Chittoor and Das 2007; Levinson 1971; Lin and Hu 2007; Zhang and Ma 2009) underline the usefulness of going beyond a family/non-family dichotomy. This is underpinned by the belief that professionalization may or may not originate from family members. These authors argue that the matter is more related to professionalization process than to who drives it (family or non-family).

Whatever problems do arise, professionalization leads to a profound change in identity and organization, and it challenges both family and non-family members. In fact, both have problems relating to professionalization. Family managers have difficulties being accepted as professionals and they have to share social skills to earn a role among other members. Non-family managers have to show the capacity to face idiosyncratic family values and behaviors (Hall and Nordqvist 2008; Lee et al. 2003; Sacristán Navarro and Gómez Ansón 2009) and to accord their values and behaviors with the identity of the firm. In particular, the harmonization of non-family member managers and family members is a key issue in professionalization. Finally, when professionalization requires a profound change in the organizational culture, the presence of a high level of parental altruism (Lubatkin et al. 2005) is a barrier to change.

The complexity of professionalization means that it is a multidimensional concept. Dekker et al. (2013, 2015) listed certain variables: (i) non-family involvement in governance systems, (ii) financial control systems, (iii) human resources control systems, (iv) decentralization of authority, and (iv) top-level activity. Other studies on professionalization have included as a condition the presence of formal financial control mechanisms, such as human resource control mechanisms and financial strategic systems (El Masri et al. 2017; Giovannoni et al. 2011; Hiebl and Mayrleitner 2017; Hatum et al. 2010). Songini (2006) outlined some elements of professionalization: formal mechanisms of governance, strategic planning systems, management control systems, and the involvement of non-family members on the board and in management (Flamholtz and Randle 2007; Howorth et al. 2016; Mustakallio et al. 2002; Yildirim-Öktem and Üsdiken 2010; Zhang and Ma 2009). Recently, Camfield and Franco (2019) studied the topic of personal values and proposed a framework that connects these to professionalization and succession. In particular, the authors mentioned eight factors of professionalization: management systems, management policies, non-family involvement in management, family involvement in management, organizational development, decentralization of authority, top-level action, and social and cultural aspects.

Figure 1 gives an overview of aspects of professionalization that have been discussed in the literature and are reinterpreted by authors. We emphasize the fact that, if one takes a very broad view, professionalization involves people, mechanisms, culture, and the whole firm.

2.2 *Relevant Factors in Processes of Professionalization*

As indicated, professionalization is a complex phenomenon, especially in the case of family firms, and it often leads to a profound change in the organization. Stewart and Hitt (2012) underlined that professionalization is fundamentally firm specific. In fact, the result of this process depends on many forces and interactions inside and outside the firm itself.

Professionalization appears to be a response to **context** and **external factors**. For example, Hatum et al. (2010) compared two Argentinian firms and their adaptability under competitive turmoil. The authors provided evidence of the positive effect of professionalization on the top managers when dealing with competition. Moreover, in some national cultures, family owners face undesirable pressures from

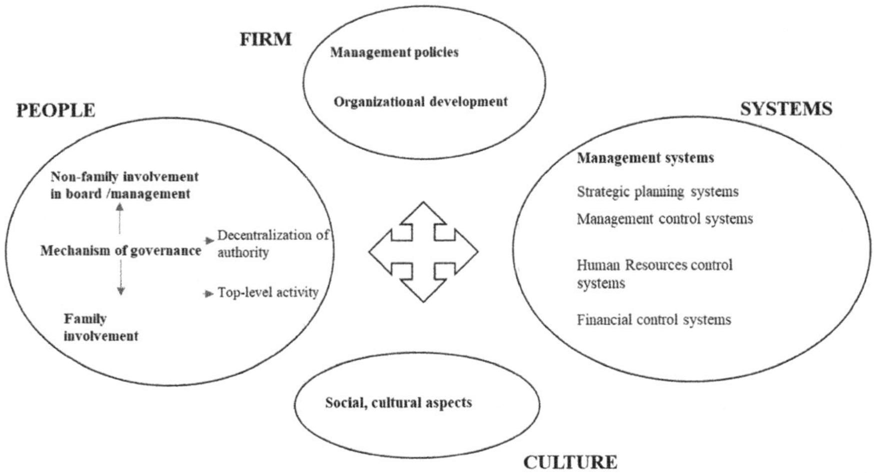

Fig. 1 Aspects of professionalization: a synthesis

webs of kinship when deciding whether or not to professionalize by hiring non-family professionals (Fletcher et al. 2009). In other contexts, the choice to professionalize by using family professionals can be an objective consequence of being unable to pay market wages (Carrasco-Hernandez and Sánchez-Marin 2007; Cater and Schwab 2008; McConaughy 2000). Sinha et al. (2017) investigated how the religion of the family living environment and in particular the religious belief of the owner could affect the process of professionalization, for instance in the area of human resources. Fang et al. (2017) underlined how industrial sectors can affect the decision of hiring non-family managers. The authors investigated 965 SMEs in the retail and manufacturing industries. They concluded that family firms are not favorable toward hiring externally when operating in sectors where information asymmetries make it difficult to monitor managers.

Hiebl (2017) studied financial managers in family firms through the lens of upper echelon theory. He examined the influence of objective situations on upper echelon characteristics and considered such conditions as the external environment (e.g., stakeholders, the labor market, and environmental characteristics) and the organizational situation (e.g., firm and board characteristics).

Some studies have found no correlation between professionalization of management and levels of education (Tsui-Auch 2004), while others have indicated that professionalization is not explicitly related to formal qualifications or objective goals based on the principle of merit (Stewart and Hitt 2012).

Other authors have studied how professionalization could be a lever in the process of **internationalization**. For example, Moya (2010) investigated the history of a multinational publishing group and discovered professionalization to be a key element in the international growth of the group. Ray et al. (2017) studied 303 leading firms in India to test the influence of family involvement on internationalization.

The authors observed that firms with a strong presence of family in their management are more averse to internationalization. In addition, the authors noticed that higher foreign institutional ownership moderates this effect. Finally, firms managed by non-family professionals are more open to internationalization.

Many authors have argued that the decision to professionalize in a family firm is a matter of **ability** and **willingness**. Stewart and Hitt (2012) stated that a family firm was not able to professionalize if it did not want to do so. De Massis et al. (2014, p. 346) defined "ability" as the "family owner's discretion of the family to direct, allocate, add to or dispose of a firm's resources" i.e. discretion to act (Chrisman et al. 2015). Moreover, the meaning of ability includes skills, competencies, and the experience to do something. Willingness is the disposition to act (Chrisman et al. 2015) and to regard every process as one that could shape the future of the firm: internationalization, succession (Richards et al. 2019), innovation (Chrisman et al. 2015), professionalization, and so on.

As Hiebl and Mayrleitner (2017) suggested, "for family firms to professionalize, these firms must be both be able and willing to do so." The authors analyzed a case study of the professionalization of management accounting in a family firm. They argued that professionalization can have two possible paths: one driven by family members or one driven by non-family members. In the studied case, family members drive the process and this naturally mitigates influence of non-family members. They argued that, when non-family members drive professionalization, they can gain higher influence in the firm.

Another important issue, partly relating to the question of ability and willingness, concerns the **values**, **beliefs**, and **personalities** of the family members and ultimately non-family members involved in the process of professionalization. In the previous paragraph (Kelleci et al. 2019), we described the traits of non-family members and family members, highlighting how non-family CEOs are independent minded, democratic and data rational, behavioral, detail conscious, conscientious, relaxed, non-worrying, and trusting. Moreover, Hiebl (2017) considered upper echelon theory, i.e., the theory that investigates the link between the personal characteristics of the top management and their strategic choices and organizational outcomes. The author attributed to non-family finance managers eight characteristics: age, functional track, other carrier experiences, education, socioeconomic roots, financial position, group characteristics, and leadership style. His literature review provided evidence to show that in family firms, non-family financial managers occupy a more traditional role (e.g., accounting and taxes) than they do in non-family firms. Their support for strategic decisions is limited; these lie mainly in family hands. Non-family financial managers contribute to the introduction of advanced tools and techniques only if they are able to avoid conflicts and maintain continuous and open dialogue with the family members.

Camfield and Franco (2019, p. 2) indicated that "personal values are guides for the selection and assessment of action, situations and people, which create pattern of behavior throughout people lives, delimiting their behavior." The authors emphasized that, in family firms, there are three components of personal values: family values, shared values, and individual values. The first one are the values connected to belonging to the family and other external related contexts. Shared values mean having a set of values that persist in the family and in the environment where the firm lives. Finally, individual values are the guide for behavior of single members of the family. The authors proposed a framework in which the factors of professionalization, described in the previous paragraph, and values and factors of succession interact with each other and shape the management in family firms. It is important to reiterate that values are extremely influential in professionalization decisions and processes, and professionalization can affect the dynamic evolution of values in family firms.

Johannisson and Huse (2000, p. 356) argued that a family business has "to accommodate different **world-views**, even contrasting ideologies." Specifically, the authors argued that the family firm lies at the intersection of three different ideologies: entrepreneurialism, paternalism, and managerialism. In a study of 12 family firms, the authors observed that professionalization of the board enforces managerialism and challenges paternalism and entrepreneurialism. They concluded by suggesting that the process must be properly managed and conflicts must be ironed out, and this will make for an improved firm.

The relationships between family and non-family members are affected by, for example, **mechanisms of governance**. Astrachan (2010) studied this matter through the lenses of agency theory and stewardship theory. Agency theory focuses the attention on the opportunistic behavior of managers and the moderating role of control mechanisms (Davis et al. 1997; Fama and Jensen 1983; Jensen and Meckling 1976; Ross 1973). This contrasts with stewardship theory (Davis et al. 1997; Donaldson and Davis 1991), which argues that managers are pro-organization and reliable people, and no formal control mechanism is necessary (see Sect. 3.1).

Furthermore, in processes of professionalization, some caution is necessary. For example, taking into consideration familiness (Tagiuri and Davis 1996) is fundamental, by distinguishing the stakeholders' interests from the family, its individual members, and the business. Family businesses see contrasts daily between these different interests, and the solution goes beyond the replacement of family managers with non-family ones. Tagiuri and Davis (1996) described clearly the nature of these relationships and the confusion they cause. Socioemotional factors are at the core of this confusion (Craig and Lindsay 2002; Lansberg 1983; Sorensen 1999), and non-family and family members are involved. Concerning the problems that a family business faces during the process of professionalization, the majority of authors have referred to leaders' mental model of the business (Chua et al. 1999; Stewart and Hitt 2012) and their competences and skills in managing the paths of development. Some studies have revealed only a slight inclination of CEOs to accept non-family professional as managers (Gilding 2005; Selekler-Goksen and Öktem 2009). As part of the professionalization process, the authority to decentralize and delegate decision making powers (Chittoor and Das 2007; Dekker et al. 2015; Gedajlovic et al. 2004) could be seen as important issues.

Finally, when professionalization requires a profound change in the organizational culture, the presence of a high level of parental altruism (Lubatkin et al. 2005) is a barrier of change.

2.3 Professionalization and Performance

Many authors have investigated the question of whether family businesses perform better than non-family ones. They have arrived at two opposing conclusions. Some authors have suggested that family businesses perform better thanks to flexibility, to long-term orientation, and to the strong relationship between family members. In contrast, some authors have argued that family businesses are weaker and less performative due to the absence of professionals. They have seen family relationships as a limit to managing family firms. Similarly, these authors have suggested that professionalization contributes to improved performance in family businesses, and most of them have referred to the presence of external managers. These have the skills and competencies to improve performance due to their experience and their less emotive approach. However, we have shown how there is a complex and delicate equilibrium in family businesses that leads to: (i) different ways of professionalizing and (ii) relationships between family and non-family members that are influenced by personality and many other psychological factors.

Lin and Hu (2007) argued that the choice between a family and a professional CEO is a critical issue for a family entrepreneur. The authors found a significant relationship between a firm's operating characteristics and the CEO's skills and professional background. Thus, both family CEOs and professional CEOs can support family business performance as long as CEOs are hired by suitable firms and appropriate governance mechanisms exist. If a family firm has a high requirement for managerial skills in its operations, using a professional manager as a CEO can improve the firm's performance. When there is an opportunity for expropriation in a family firm, the firm's performance will be better if the CEO is a family member. Bennedsen et al. (2007) echoed Lin and Hu's (2007) results, showing that family CEO underperformance is particularly significant in fast-growing industries, industries with highly skilled labor forces, and relatively large firms.

For example, Binacci et al. (2016), in their analysis of 500 Italian family-controlled firms, investigated how the composition of non-family top management can affect performance. They considered the size and length of tenure in the non-family team and the diversity of functional backgrounds. The authors found that all such characteristics increase performance, but beyond a certain level size and tenure diversity have a negative effect.

Therefore, we can argue that the relationship between professionalization and performance is not unequivocal and depends on the combination of several objective and subjective factors.

Usually, the professionalization process benefits from the implementation of management control systems supporting professionals' decisions. In this sense, management control systems could play an important role in improving performance, as we describe in a later part of this chapter.

3 Managerialization

The role of management control systems, even in small family businesses, has attracted increasing attention within the management literature. In general, quantitative and qualitative studies have revealed that family businesses make less use of formalized management control systems than non-family firms (Hiebl and Mayrleitner 2017). The evidence is greater in the case of SMEs (García Pérez de Lema and Duréndez 2007). In a similar manner (Fang et al. 2017; Johannisson and Huse 2000), the scenario is changing with regard to the introduction of formalized control systems in small family enterprises.

3.1 Definitions and Theoretical Approaches

It is worth briefly restating the definition of managerialization provided by Songini and Vola (2015) who described the managerialization process as the introduction of formal management control systems. Formal management control systems mitigate problems relating to mechanisms of merit, authority delegation, and objectifications of the business's goals. In previous research, Songini (2006) identified under the umbrella of governance mechanisms the board of directors (Mustakallio et al. 2002; Yildirim-Öktem and Üsdiken 2010; Zhang and Ma 2009), formal strategic planning (Dekker et al. 2013), and performance evaluation systems (Chua et al. 2009; Dekker et al. 2013; Gedajlovic et al. 2004). These address all the issues mentioned above. Thus, in terms of governance, a first relevant question concerns the relationships between family and non-family members. Astrachan (2010) explained this relationship through the lens of agency theory or the stewardship theory.

In the first case, we can see the importance of control mechanisms in moderating opportunistic and individualistic managers' behavior (Davis et al. 1997; Fama and Jensen 1983; Jensen and Meckling 1976; Ross 1973). Jensen and Meckling (1976) and Tosi et al. (2003) proposed in this regard the introduction of mechanisms such as the extension of bargaining, compensation policies, and the board of directors. Prencipe et al. (2014) argued that agency behavior is more common than stewardship behavior when there is a greater number of family directors, officers, generations, and votes, and finally when more executives fall under the family influence.

In the second case, scholars who have carried out research on family businesses in accordance with the stewardship theory (Davis et al. 1997; Donaldson and Davis 1991) argued that a "collectivistic model of man" (Astrachan 2010, p. 11) can avoid the possible opportunistic behaviors of managers who are seen as reliable and pro-organization persons. This conceptualization puts more emphasis on the design of accountability and control systems that manage governance relations, especially mechanisms that address social controls. Recently, a multitude of studies have given an account of how this theoretical approach has a positive impact not only on behavior, but also on firm performance (Davis et al. 2010; Eddleston and Kellermanns 2007; Zahra et al. 2008).

The agency and stewardship theories therefore emphasize, respectively, formal and informal/social controls that mitigate the relationships between family and non-family managers and owners. Thus, under different circumstances, both views can be usefully applied to family businesses (Breton-Miller and Miller 2011).

3.2 How the Design of Formal Management Control Systems Mitigates Critical Issues

Beyond theoretical approaches, several management control studies on family businesses have referred to problems and issues detected in the contexts under analysis. When family and non-family managers coexist in a family business, the **principle of merit** should be a critical lever of peaceful coexistence. Payment systems based on incentives (Chua et al. 2009; Dekker et al. 2013) and evaluation systems based on personal performance (Dekker et al. 2013; de Kok et al. 2006; Reid and Adams 2001) safeguard the rights and merits of non-family managers.

Sinha et al. (2017) depicted a process of professionalization in which, as a result of much effort, a formal and rational compensation mechanism based on overall organizational goals is introduced. Though employee performance could be based on objective criteria, often the personal views of the family owners' overshadows decisions. An objective mechanism for performance evaluation is thus needed which takes into account both the hard and soft dimensions of performance. New appraisal system is introduced, with rewards linked to performance. However, in the Sinha et al. (2017) specific case study, owners continued to disburse discretionary rewards outside the formal system, but they were urged to consult the non-family human resources manager beforehand.

The principle of merit and the performance orientation of managers find support not only in the introduction of reward and compensation systems (Ward 2004), but in general in the design and use of performance evaluation systems (Chua et al. 2009; Dekker et al. 2013; Gedajlovic et al. 2004).

A second critical issue that should be addressed is the "**sense of family**." Family and non-family members can follow a different path in experiencing this. Craig and Moores (2005, 2010) conducted an action research project during which they designed a balanced scorecard on which metrics of business coexist in a delicate balance with kinship/family system indicators. The kinship/family indicators have roots in the sense of family, a system largely based on the concept of need. The authors described the sense of family as cooperation, unity, emotional bonding, a rare sense of responsibility, and loyalty to the group as a system.

The kinship/family indicators describe the perspectives of the family as: (i) property, (ii) employee, (iii) family itself, and (iv) community. In terms of family as a property, the authors suggested that business needs to take an intragenerational orientation in the sense of distinguishing itself from its competitors by immediately pursuing a focus on long-term growth with a minimal environmental impact. With the family as employee's perspective, they wanted to understand how all family members could be encouraged to work for the company, even though it is not an automatically acquired right. This process of involvement can be pursued through the generations by kinship education. Thus, family businesses distinguish themselves from non-family businesses according to their spontaneous perpetuation of intragenerational values. The whole family is involved in the promotion of an intensive communication between relatives, spreading a sense of mutual support for the attainment of common dreams. Finally, the family members interviewed for the study address their sense of family to the community in which the business is engaged, promoting a sense of awareness of and responsibility toward this natural context.

The design of performance evaluation systems encountered realistic measurement difficulties due to the presence of non-economic goals, long-term and intragenerational orientation, and, as already mentioned, compensation policies when family and non-family managers coexist (Chua et al. 2009).

Clear evidence of the tight relationship between family and business goals can be seen with the introduction of formal strategic planning (Rue and Ibrahim 1996; Sharma et al. 1997). Rue and Ibrahim analyzed 128 American family SMEs with the aim of understanding the role and degree of implementation of strategic planning. From the analysis, it emerged how planning practices are much more sophisticated than acknowledged in small-sized companies. In addition, more than 80% of the strategic planning analyzed contain a significant sophistication in corporate performance objectives. In 40% of cases, the authors noticed that IT systems support the monitoring of strategic objectives with periodic signs of deviation.

When the owners and managers introduce formal strategic planning, usually the **delegation process** is a real and precise element of the organizational structure (Chua et al. 2009; Songini and Gnan 2009). The delegation process is the third critical issue that is addressed in this paragraph. The design of formal strategic planning can be challenging. More than 30 years ago, Ward (1988) conducted an analysis of over 2000 firms. He found six interdependent assessment steps that are important for designing strategic planning. These were: (i) the family's commitment to business, (ii) the business's health, (iii) the business alternatives, (iv) family and personal goals, (v) the selection of business strategy, and (vi) the family's interests and capabilities. The assessment of all these aspects paves the way for a delegation process also in terms of (intragenerational) succession. Educating and training the new generation in business can be facilitated by a planning system. During the design of strategic planning, including documentation and process, more tacit values, strategies, and actions emerge. The new generation, and also family and non-family managers, can benefit from the process (Giovannoni et al. 2011; Mazzola et al. 2008). **Intragenerational succession** is the fourth critical issue addressed by management control systems.

This succession process should be understood in a larger frame in which a family firm's management desires to preserve the business in the long term. Thus, strategies and decision making in a family business are more addressed to the firm's survival than on mere wealth maximization (Prencipe et al. 2014).

3.3 How the Use of Formal Management Control Systems Affects Firm Performance

If the design of systems is not without struggle, their use is much more difficult to detect in the family context. In Upton et al.'s (2001) survey, the majority of fast-growth family firms stated that they prepare written formal plans, tie planning to actual performance, and adjust management compensation accordingly with the intent to pass the firm to next generation. Other research has found the use of management control systems in family contexts where firms focus on antecedents rather than consequences, and in particular performance. In a study on management control choices, for example, Speckbacher and Wentges (2012) argued that founding family involvement in top management teams is associated with less frequent use of performance measures in strategic target setting and incentive practices. Moreover, Filbeck and Lee (2000) unearthed the use of more sophisticated financial management techniques in more established and larger family businesses with an outside board of directors or a non-family member in financial decision-making roles.

El Masri (2017) focused his analysis on the use of management control systems and came to some interesting conclusions. Inspired by the dual role of control systems (Simons 1995; Tessier and Otley 2012), he introduced the concept of calibration that involves three activities: determining a graduation, adjusting the calibration for a particular purpose, and comparing it to a standard of reference for calibration. Empirical evidence showed how the family firms calibrate management control systems by graduating them for particular purposes. The author theorized a link between particular purposes and the family business identity of the firm.

With regard to the calibration of management control systems and firms' life moments, Moores and Mula (2000) obtained evidence of the presence of both formal and informal controls and showed that the salience of these varies according to the life cycle of the family firm. Specifically, they found that family firms use various combinations of clan, bureaucratic, and market-based control that become more reliant on management accounting-type controls as firms mature. It was only when family firms move beyond the collectivity stage to formalization and control and the elaboration of structure and adaption stages that they begin to utilize accounting-based controls such as budgets, costing, quality and inventory standards, and profit and investment centers.

All the studies above referred to the use of management control systems, but without any evidence of the effects on company performance. Moving in a more general direction, the extant literature has included numerous analyses addressing the dilemma of the effect of family involvement in performance (for details, see Stewart and Hitt 2012), and how theoretical approaches such as stewardship theory

(Davis et al. 2010; Eddleston and Kellermanns 2007; Zahra et al. 2008) or agency theory (Songini and Gnan 2015) affect firm performance. Durendez et al. (2016) provided an exception, suggesting that an intensive use of management control systems positively influence companies' level of performance. The authors collected personal interviews with 900 managers in Spain who belonged to belonging to family and non-family firms in industry, construction, and services, all competitive arenas. The management control systems analyzed were enterprise resource planning, balanced scorecards, cost accounting systems, budgets, financial and economic analysis, strategic planning, and so on.

According to Salvato and Moores (2010) and Prencipe et al. (2014), investigations into management control systems in family firms are still scarce. In particular, knowledge of the use of management control systems and their effects is not available. Studies focused on elements of professionalization, including the presence of management control systems, present a confused picture on how these single elements affect performance.

Though the presence of formal management control systems in family businesses is usually related to the presence of non-family professionals, Dekker et al. (2013) showed a correlation that had hitherto been missed. Their results stated that two clusters (about 84% of the family businesses from their data set) in which there are formal financial control systems and human resource control systems have low non-family professionals' involvement in governance systems. The next section addresses this issue.

4 A Tight Relationship

The separate analysis of the meaning and contents of professionalization and managerialization highlights a multiplicity of visions, with some overlapping between the two concepts. However, we cannot consider them as two sides of the same coin.

In a broad sense, professionalization of a firm indicates the shift from an entrepreneurial firm to a managerial one. This complex and very challenging process could be realized in two complementary ways: (i) professionals (people with specific characteristics, skills and backgrounds) and (ii) mechanisms and tools befitting a more formal, structured, and institutionalized firm. Managerialization also concerns the introduction of management control systems, including governance mechanisms, reward systems, performance systems, and so on.

Our study makes some relevant points. First of all, the meaning of professional cannot be limited to external people but also to family members and internal non-family members, who can become professionals through different paths.

Secondly, professionalization involves primarily people but concerns mechanisms and tools as well, especially of governance, which can balance relationships between family and non-family members and manage delegation of authority. In other words, professionalization of a firm implies processes of managerialization.

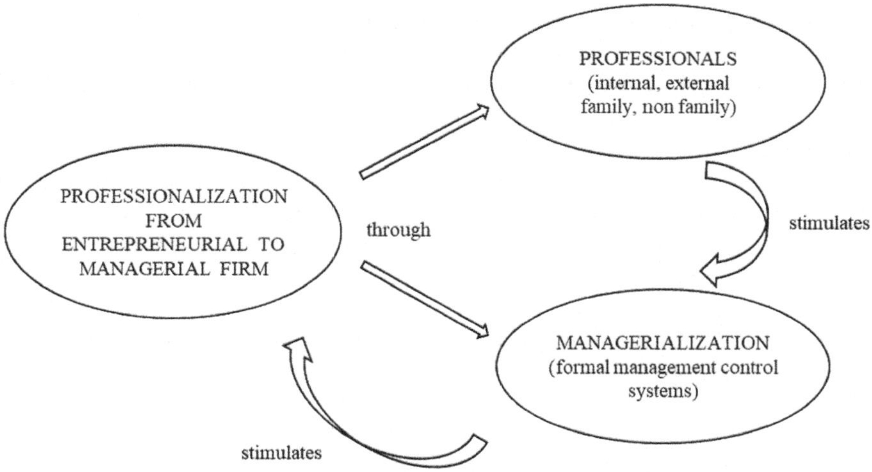

Fig. 2 Relationship between professionalization and managerialization

Thirdly, in light of the above, managerialization is a part of professionalization. However, managerialization is not necessarily realized through professionals, either internal or external, but can arise from a need in the firm that is promoted by the entrepreneur or other change agents. It is worth underlining that managerialization can stimulate processes of professionalization of people (both family and non-family, internal and external) as the introduction of new tools and mechanisms ask for more and more qualified skills and competencies.

We summarize our findings and interpretations in Fig. 2.

5 Conclusion and Research Agenda

The contributions to the topics of professionalization and managerialization provide us with some important and interesting insights into family businesses. Some questions are answered, and new problems are presented that need to be explored. The following are the issues that we think are most important; they should be addressed in future research on professionalization and management control systems in family businesses.

Our first issue is the current state of academic research into professionalization and managerialization. We need to understand the boundaries of the two topics and the contributions that professional and family managers make during the implementation and use of management control systems. Conversely, it would be useful to analyze how some control systems, such as compensation mechanisms and performance management systems, evaluate family and non-family CEOs and managers during their operational activities. Identifying the direction of the interplay between professionalization and managerialization is challenging. Moreover, is information from management control systems useful for promoting a more formalized and external capabilities culture in the family business? Should family professionals be part of the web of high skilled persons who counterbalance the professional power of non-family professionals? And how do formal management control systems affect company performance?

Another important issue is the impact of professionalization on innovation processes. To understand this, family businesses need to be studied not only in a close context, but as an open space containing internal and external actors who interact with each other.

Identifying the interplay between management control systems and innovation is another issue. Management accounting and control literature has recently addressed this noteworthy topic. Do formal management control systems stimulate innovative products and processes? Or do formal management control systems reduce the innovative culture of a family business?

Existing literature has focused on professionalization in the presence of family or non-family professionals. However, the coexistence of family and non-family professionals needs to be investigated. The existence of balancing systems that facilitate coexistence between the two types of professionals is a further avenue for research.

Finally, it is important to analyze how (family and non-family) middle managers and employees participate in professionalization processes. Are they active participants or not? Do family and non-family members form such a cohesive group?

The need to understand the peculiarities of challenging processes inside family businesses is urgent. Increased competition and worldwide economic pressures challenge unprepared businesses to offer prompt and complex solutions. As family businesses dominate the international setting, academics, owners, and managers should be prepared for future scenarios. This chapter provides additional insights into the ways family businesses can be made to work effectively.

References

Astrachan JH (2010) Strategy in family business: Toward a multidimensional research agenda. J Fam Bus Strategy 1:6–14. https://doi.org/10.1016/j.jfbs.2010.02.001

Barth E, Gulbrandsen T, Schønea P (2005) Family ownership and productivity: The role of owner-management. J Corp Finan 11:107–127. https://doi.org/10.1016/j.jcorpfin.2004.02.001

Bennedsen M, Nielsen KM, Pérez-González F, Wolfenzon D (2007) Inside the family firm: the role of families in succession decisions and performance. Q J Econ 122(2):647–691. 10.1162/qjec.122.2.647

Berenbeim RE (1990) How business families manage the transition from owner to professional management. Fam Bus Rev 3(1):69–110. https://doi.org/10.1111/j.1741-6248.1990.00069.x

Binacci M, Peruffo E, Oriani R, Minichilli A (2016) Are all Non family members (NFMs) equal? The impact of NFM characteristics and diversity on family firm performance. Corp Governance An Int Rev 24(6):569–583. https://doi.org/10.1111/corg.12130

Bloom N, Van Reenen J (2007) Measuring and explaining management practices across firms and countries. Q J Econ 122:1351–1408. https://www.jstor.org/stable/25098879

Camfield C, Franco M (2019) Theoretical framework for family firm management: relationship between personal values and professionalization and succession. J Fam Bus Manage 9(2):201–227. https://doi.org/10.1108/JFBM-06-2018-0020
Cannella AA, Shen W (2001) So close and yet so far: promotion versus exit for CEO heirs apparent. Acad Manag J 44:252–270. https://doi.org/10.2307/3069454
Carrasco-Hernandez A, Sánchez-Marin G (2007) The determinants of employee compensation in family firms: empirical evidence. Fam Bus Rev 20(3):215–228. https://doi.org/10.1111/j.1741-6248.2007.00096.x
Cater J, Schwab A (2008) Turnaround strategies in established family firms. Fam Bus Rev 21:31–50. https://doi.org/10.1111/j.1741-6248.2007.00113.x
Cattaneo C, Bassani G (2015) Sistemi di controllo formali nelle PMI familiari: una presenza possibile? Small Bus 1:31–52. https://doi.org/10.14596/pisb.176
Chittor R, Das R (2007) Professionalization of management and succession performance—a vital linkage. Fam Bus Rev 20(1):65–76. https://doi.org/10.1111/j.1741-6248.2007.00084.x
Chrisman JJ, Chua JH, De Massis A, Frattini F, Wright M (2015) The ability and willingness paradox in family firm innovation. J Prod Innov Manag 32(3):310–318. https://doi.org/10.1111/jpim.12207
Chua JH, Chrisman JJ, Sharma P (1999) Defining the family business by behavior. Entrepreneurship Theor Pract 23(4):19–39. https://doi.org/10.1177/104225879902300402
Chua JH, Chrisman JJ, Bergiel EB (2009) An agency theoretic analysis of the professionalized family firm. Entrepreneurship Theor Pract 33:355–372. https://doi.org/10.1111/j.1540-6520.2009.00294.x
Corbetta G (1995) Patterns of development of family businesses in Italy. Fam Bus Rev 8(4):255–265. https://doi.org/10.1111/j.1741-6248.1995.00255x
Craig JB Lindsay NJ (2002) Incorporating the family dynamic into the entrepreneurship process. J Small Bus Enterp Dev 9 (4):416–430. 10.1108/14626000210450586
Craig J, Moores K (2005) Balanced scorecard to drive the strategic planning of family firms. Fam Bus Rev 18(2):105–122. https://doi.org/10.1111/j.1741-6248.2005.00035.x
Craig J, Moores K (2010) Strategically aligning family and business systems using the Balanced Scorecard. J Fam Bus Strategy 1:78–87. 10.1016/j.jfbs.2010.04.003ss
Culasso F, Giacosa E, Manzi LM, Dana L (2018) Professionalization in family businesses. How to strenghten strategy implementation and control, favouring succession. Manage Control 1:45–71. https://doi.org/10.3280/MACO2018-001003
Daily CM, Dollinger MJ (1992) An empirical examination of ownership structure in family and professionally managed firms. Fam Bus Rev 5:117–136. https://doi.org/10.1111/j.1741-6248.1992.00117.x
Daily CM, Dollinger MJ (1993) Alternative methodologies for identifying family- versus nonfamily-managed businesses. J Small Bus Manage 31(2):79–90
Davis JH, Schoorman FD, Donaldson L (1997) Toward a stewardship theory of management. Acad Manage Rev 22(1):20–47. https://www.jstor.org/stable/259223.
Davis JH, Allen MR, Hayes HD (2010) Is blood thicker than water? A study of stewardship perceptions in family business. Entrepreneurship Theor Pract 34–8:1093–1116. https://doi.org/10.1111/j.1540-6520.2010.00415.x
De Kok JMP, Uhlaner LM, Thurik AR (2006) Professional HRM practices in family owned-managed enterprises. J Small Bus Manage 44–3:441–460. https://doi.org/10.1111/j.1540-627X.2006.00181.x
de Lema DGP, Duréndez A (2007) Managerial behaviour of small and medium-sized family businesses: an empirical study. Int J Entrepreneurial Behav Res 13(3):151–172. https://doi.org/10.1108/13552550710751030
De Massis A, Sharma P, Chua JH, Chrisman JJ (2014) Ability and willingness as sufficiency conditions for family-oriented particularistic behaviour: implication for theory and empirical studies. J Small Bus Manage 52(2):344–364. https://doi.org/10.1111/jsbm.12102

Dekker JC, Lybaert N, Steijvers T, Depaire B, Mercken R (2013) Family firm types based on the professionalization construct: exploratory research. Fam Bus Rev 26(1):81–99. https://doi.org/10.1177/0894486512445614

Dekker J, Lybaert N, Steijvers T, Depaire B (2015) The effect of family business professionalization as a multidimensional construct on firm performance. J Small Bus Manage 53(2):516–538. https://doi.org/10.1111/jsbm.12082

Donaldson L, Davis JH (1991) Stewardship theory or agency theory; CEO governance and shareholders returns. Aust J Manage 16(1):49–64. https://doi.org/10.1177/031289629101600103

Duréndez A, Ruiz-Palomo D, Garcia-Pérez-de-Lema D, Diéguez-Soto J (2016) Management control systems and performance in small and medium family firms. Eur J Fam Bus 6:10–20. https://doi.org/10.1016/j.ejfb.2016.05.001

Dyer WG Jr (1988) Culture and continuity in family firms. Fam Bus Rev 1(1):37–50. https://doi.org/10.1111/j.1741-6248.1988.00037.x

Dyer WG Jr (1989) Integrating professional management into a family owned business. Fam Bus Rev 2:221–235. https://doi.org/10.1111/j.1741-6248.1989.00221.x

El Masri T, Tekathen M, Magnan M, Boulianne E (2017) Calibrating management control technologies and the dual identity of family firms. Qual Res Acc Manage 14(2):157–188. https://doi.org/10.1108/QRAM-05-2016-0038

Eddleston K, Kellermanns FW (2007) Destructive and productive family relationships: a stewardship theory perspective. J Bus Ventur 22(4):545–565. https://doi.org/10.1016/j.jbusvent.2006.06.004

Fama EF, Jensen MC (1983) Separation of ownership and control. J Law Econ 26(2):327–349. Non trovato

Fang HC, Memili E, Chrisman JJ, Penney C (2017) Industry and information asymmetry: the case of the employment of non-family managers in small and medium-sized family firms. J Small Bus Manage 55(4):632–648. https://doi.org/10.1111/jsbm.12267

Filbeck G, Lee S (2000) Financial management techniques in family businesses. Fam Bus Rev 13(3):201–216. https://doi.org/10.1111/j.1741-6248.2000.00201.x

Flamholtz EG, Randle Y (2007) Growing pains: Transitioning from an entrepreneurship to a professionally managed firm. Jossey Bass, San Francisco

Fletcher D, Helienek E, Zafirova Z (2009) The role of family start ups in the emergence of a small business sector in Bulgaria. J Enterprising Cult 17(3):351–375. https://doi.org/10.1142/S0218495809000369

Gedajlovic E, Lubatkin MH, Schulze WS (2004) Crossing the threshold from founder management to professional management: a governance perspective. J Manage Stud 41(5):899–912. https://doi.org/10.1111/j.1467-6486.2004.00459.x

Gilding M (2005) Families and fortunes: accumulation, management succession and inheritance in wealthy families. J Soc 41:29–45. https://doi.org/10.1177/1440783305050962

Giovannoni E, Maraghini MP, Riccaboni A (2011) Transmitting knowledge across generations: the role of management accounting practices. Fam Bus Rev 24(2):126–150. https://doi.org/10.1177/0894486511406722

Gulbrandsen T (2005) Flexibility in Norwegian family-owned enterprises. Fam Bus Rev 18:57–76. https://doi.org/10.1111/j.1741-6248.2005.00030.x

Hall A, Nordqvist M (2008) Professional management in family businesses: Toward an extended understanding. Fam Bus Rev 21:51–69. https://doi.org/10.1111/j.1741-6248.2007.00109.x

Hatum A, Pettigrew A, Michelini J (2010) Building organizational capabilities to adapt under turmoil. J Change Manage 10(3):257–274. https://doi.org/10.1080/14697017.2010.493292

Hiebl MRW (2017) Finance managers in family firms: an upper-echelons view. J Fam Bus Manage. https://doi.org/10.1108/JFBM-07-2016-0014

Hiebl MRW, Mayrleitner B (2017) Professionalization of management accounting in family firms: the impact of family members. Rev Manage Sci 1–32. 10.1007/s11846-017-0274-8

Howorth C, Wright M, Westhead P, Allcock D (2016) Company metamorphosis: professionalization waves, family firms and management buyouts. Small Bus Econ 47:803–817. https://doi.org/10.1007/s11187-016-9761-6
Hwang H, Powell WW (2009) The rationalization of charity: The influences of professionalism in the nonprofit sector. Adm Sci Q 54:268–298. 10.2189/asqu.2009.54.2.268
Jensen MC, Meckling WF (1976) Theory of the firm: managerial behavior, agency costs and ownership structure. J Financ Econ 3:305–360. Non trovato
Johannisson B, Huse M (2000) Recruiting outside board members in the small family business: an ideological challenge. Entrepreneurship Reg Dev 12:353–378. https://doi.org/10.1080/08985620050177958
Kelleci R, Lambrechts F, Voordeckers W, Huybrechts J (2019) CEO personality: a different perspective on the nonfamily versus family CEO debate. Fam Bus Rev s 32(1):31–57. https://doi.org/10.1177/0894486518811222
Kets de Vries MF (1985) The dark side of entrepreneurship. Harvard Bus Rev 8(6):160–167
Lansberg I (1983) Managing human resources in family firms: The problem of institutional overlap. Organ Dyn 12(1):39–46. 23. 10.1016/0090-2616(83)90025-6.
Le Breton-Miller I, Miller D (2011) Commentary: family firms and the advantage of multitemporality. Entrepreneurship Theor Pract 35(6):1171–1177. https://doi.org/10.1111/j.1540-6520.2011.00496.x
Lee KS, Lim GH, Lim WS (2003) Family business succession: appropriation risk and choice of successor. Acad Manage Rev 28(4):657–666. https://doi.org/10.5465/AMR.2003.10899446
Levinson H (1971) Conflicts that plague family businesses. Harvard Bus Rev 49(2):90–98
Lin SH, Hu SY (2007) A family member or professional management? The choice of a CEO and its impact on performance. Corp Gov 15(6):1348–1362. https://doi.org/10.1111/j.1467-8683.2007.00650.x
Lubatkin M, Schulze W, Ling Y, Dino R (2005) The effects of parental altruism on the governance of family-managed firms. J Organ Behav 26(3):313–330. https://doi.org/10.1002/job.307
Mazzola P, Marchisio G, Astrachan J (2008) Strategic planning in family business: a powerful development tool for the next generation. Fam Bus Rev 21(3):239–258. https://doi.org/10.1177/08944865080210030106
McConaughy DL (2000) Family CEOs versus nonfamily CEOs in the family-controlled firm: An examination of the level and sensitivity of pay to performance. Fam Bus Rev 13(2):121–131. 10.1111/j.1741-6248.2000.00121.x.
Miller D (2015) A downside to the entrepreneurial personality? Entrepreneurship Theor Pract 39:1–8. https://doi.org/10.1111/etap.12130
Moores K, Mula J (2000) The salience of market, bureaucratic, and clan controls in the management of family firm transitions: some tentative Australian evidence. Fam Bus Rev 13(2):91–106. 10.1111/j.1741-6248.2000.00091.x
Moya MF (2010) A family-owned publishing multinational: the Salvat company (1869–1988). Bus Hist 52(3):453–470. https://doi.org/10.1080/00076791003721969
Mustakallio M, Autio E, Zahra SA (2002) Relational and contractual governance in family firms: effects on strategic decision making. Fam Bus Rev 15(3):205–222. https://doi.org/10.1111/j.1741-6248.2002.00205.x
Pérez de Lema DG, Duréndez A (2007) Managerial behaviour of small and medium-sized family businesses: an empirical study. Int J Entrepreneurial Behav Res 13(3):151–172. https://doi.org/10.1108/13552550710751030
Prencipe A, Bar-Yosef S, Dekker HC (2014) Accounting research in family firms: theoretical and empirical challenges. Eur Acc Rev 23(3):361–385. https://doi.org/10.1080/09638180.2014.895621
Ray S, Mondal A, Ramachandran K (2017) How does family involvement affect a firm's internationalization? An investigation of Indian family firms. Glob Strategy J 8:73–105. https://doi.org/10.1002/gsj.1196

Reid RS, Adams JS (2001) Human resource management—a survey of practices within family and non-family firms. J Eur Ind Training 25(6/7):310–320
Richards M, Kammerlander N, Zellweger T (2019) Listening to the heart or the head? Exploring the "Willingness Versus Ability" Succession Dilemma. Fam Bus Rev 1–24. 10.1177/089448651983351
Ross S (1973) The economic theory of agency: the principal's problem. Am Econ Rev 63–2:134–139
Rue LW, Ibrahim NA (1996) The status of planning in smaller family owned businesses. Fam Bus Rev 9(1):29–43. https://doi.org/10.1111/j.1741-6248.1996.00029.x
Sacristán Navarro M, Gómez Ansón S (2009) Do families shape corporate governance structures? J Manage Organ 15(3):327–345. https://doi.org/10.1017/S1833367200002650
Salvato C, Moores K (2010) Research on accounting in family firms: Past accomplishment and future challenges. Fam Bus Rev 23(3):193–245. https://doi.org/10.1177/0894486510375069
Schein EH (1995) The role of the founder in creating organizational culture. Fam Bus Rev 8(3):221–238. https://doi.org/10.1111/j.1741-6248.1995.00221.x
Selekler-Goksen NN, Öktem ÖY (2009) Countervailing institutional forces: corporate governance in Turkish family business groups. J Manage Governance 13:193–213. https://doi.org/10.1007/s10997-009-9083-z
Sharma P, Chrisman JJ, Chua JH (1997) Strategic manangement of the future of the family business: past research and future challenges. Fam Bus Rev 10(1):1–36. https://doi.org/10.1111/j.1741-6248.1997.00001.x
Simons R (1995) Levers of control: how managers use innovative control systems to drive strategic renewal. Harvard Business School Press, Boston, MA
Sinha A, Pandey J, Varkkey B (2017) Professionalizing religious family-owned organizations: an examination of human resource challenges. South Asian J Manage 24(2):8–24
Songini L (2006) The professionalization of family firms: theory and practice. In: Poutziouris PZ, Smyrnios KX, Klein SB (eds) Handbook of family business research. Edward Elgar Publishing, UK, pp 269–297
Songini L, Gnan L (2009) Women, glass ceiing, and professionalization in family SMEs. A missed link. J Enterprising Culture 17(4):497–525. https://dx.doi.org/10.1142/S0218495809000461
Songini L, Gnan L (2015) Family involvement and agency cost control mechanisms in family small and medium-sized enterprises. J Small Bus Manage 53(3):748–779. https://doi.org/10.1111/jsbm.12085
Songini L, Vola (2015) The role of professionalization and managerialization in family business succession. Manage Control 35:9–43. https://doi.org/10.3280/MACO2015-001002
Sorensen RL (1999) Conflict management strategies used by successful family businesses. Fam Bus Rev 12(4):325–339. https://doi.org/10.1111/j.1741-6248.1999.00325.x
Speckbacher G, Wentges P (2012) The impact of family control on the use of performance measures in strategic target setting and incentive compensation: A research note. Manage Acc Res 23(1):34–46. https://doi.org/10.1016/j.mar.2011.06.002
Stewart A, Hitt MA (2012) Why can't a family business be more like a nonfamily business? Modes of professionalization in family firms. Fam Bus Rev 25(1):58–86. https://doi.org/10.1177/0894486511421665
Tagiuri R, Davis J (1996) Bivalent attributes of the family firm. Fam Bus Rev 9(2):199–208. https://doi.org/10.1111/j.1741-6248.1996.00199.x
Tessier S, Otley D (2012) A conceptual development of simons' levers of control framework. Manage Acc Res 23:171–185. https://doi.org/10.1016/j.mar.2012.04.003
Tosi HL, Brownlee AL, Silva P, Katz JP (2003) An empirical exploration of decision-making under control and stewardship structure. J Manage Stud 40(8):2053–2071. https://doi.org/10.1046/j.1467-6486.2003.00411.x
Tsui-Auch LS (2004) The professionally managed family-ruled enterprise: Ethnic Chinese business in Singapore. J Manage Stud 41(4):693–723. https://doi.org/10.1111/j.1467-6486.2004.00450.x
Upton N, Teal EJ, Felan JT (2001) Strategic and business planning practices of fast growing family firms. J Small Bus Manage 39(1):60–72. https://doi.org/10.1111/0447-2778.00006

Ward JL (1988) The special role of strategic planning for family businesses. Fam Bus Rev 1(2):105–117. https://doi.org/10.1111/j.1741-6248.1988.00105.x
Ward JL (2004) Perpetuating the family business: 50 Lessons learned from long-lasting, successful families in business. Palgrave Macmillan, Houndmills, England
Yildirim-Öktem Ö, Üsdiken B (2010) Contingencies versus external pressure: professionalization in boards of firms affiliated to family business groups in late-industrializing countries. Br J Manag 21(1):115–130. https://doi.org/10.1111/j.1467-8551.2009.00663.x
Zahra SA, Hayton JC, Neubaum DO, Dibrell C, Craig J (2008) Culture of family commitment and strategic flexibility: the moderating effect of stewardship. Entrepreneurship Theor Pract 32–6:1035–1054. https://doi.org/10.1111/j.1540-6520.2008.00271.x
Zhang J, Ma H (2009) Adoption of professional management in Chinese family business: a multi-level analysis of impetuses and impediments. Asia Pac J Manage 26:119–139. https://doi.org/10.1007/s10490-008-9099-y

The Survival of Family Businesses: The Challenge of Succession

Annalisa Sentuti and Francesca M. Cesaroni

Abstract Family business succession is a key challenge for family firms. On the one hand, it involves several different dynamics and perspectives, and its outcome may compromise the firm's survival if these factors are not adequately considered. On the other hand, succession can be a source of relevant opportunities for the relaunch and renewal of the business, including the possibility to favor, introduce, and support managerialization and professionalization processes, thanks to the involvement of younger generations. In line with this perspective, in this chapter studies on family business succession are presented and discussed, pointing out that handling succession is essential to face challenges and seize opportunities. The involvement of external consultants and advisors can also play a crucial role in reducing risks associated with the succession process and increasing the business's chance of surviving in the long term.

Keywords Family business · Succession · Multidimensionality · Challenges and opportunities · Advisors

1 Introduction

Family business succession is a complex and multidimensional process and can be a very demanding challenge in the business life cycle of family firms. Thousands of companies risk closing down every year because of the troubles associated with the transfer of ownership and management. They are mainly small- and medium-sized family-owned businesses that usually transfer to the next generation within the same family through a family succession process. Even though this is not the only option to guarantee the continuity of the business over time (for an overview of different

A. Sentuti (✉) · F. M. Cesaroni
Department of Economics, Society, and Politics, University of Urbino Carlo Bo, Urbino, Italy
e-mail: annalisa.sentuti@uniurb.it

F. M. Cesaroni
e-mail: francesca.cesaroni@uniurb.it

A. Leotta (ed.), *Management Controlling and Governance of Family Businesses*, Contributions to Management Science,
https://doi.org/10.1007/978-3-030-47741-7_4

succession options, see Zellweger 2017, p. 204), ensuring the survival of the firm by passing it on to the next generation is what distinguishes family-owned businesses from other types of companies (Chua et al. 1999). This is particularly true for first-generation family firms (Gomez-Mejía et al. 2007) as suggested by the perspective of socioemotional wealth (SEW). SEW is defined as "non-financial aspects of the firm that meet the family's affective needs, such as identity, the ability to exercise family influence, and the perpetuation of the family dynasty" (Gomez-Mejía et al. 2007, p. 106). From this theoretical perspective, which has become an influential concept in the study of family businesses, the distinctiveness of family firms is given by having noneconomic objectives (emotional and social needs of the family) that influence their decision-making processes and strategic choices (Gomez-Mejia et al. 2011). Specifically, the priority of the family business is to maintain family control over the company, acting conservatively, and avoiding business decisions that may jeopardize business continuity (Gomez-Mejía et al. 2007). One of the most important non-financial aims, especially in first-generation family businesses, is transgenerational sustainability that prioritizes the survival of the firm by passing it on to the next generation (Astrachan and Jaskiewicz 2008; Zellweger et al. 2010).

For all these reasons, since the Sixties, family succession has been a dominant topic in family business research and practice (Sharma 2004; De Massis et al. 2008).

Family succession is the whole of actions, events, and developments that affect the transfer of managerial control from one family member to another (Sharma et al. 1997, 2001). Therefore, in this process, "both the incumbent who relinquishes managerial control and the successor who takes it over are family members" (De Massis et al. 2008). Consequently, the relationship between incumbent and successor assumes a crucial role for a successful succession (Lansberg 1988). However, incumbent and successor should not be the only actors engaged in the succession process. A wide range of diverse individuals are involved directly or indirectly in this process, and they can be traced back to the other two actors of succession: the family system and the business system. The succession process redefines the family business governance and management over generations, modifying the number, role, and involvement of family members in the ownership, governance, and management of the firm. From the first to the following generations, the number of families involved in the firm may grow, generating an increasing complexity in the governance and management of the business and also in the following succession process. Sometimes, the business passes from the first-generation founder to second-generation brothers and sisters, to cousins and relatives in the third and following generations, making the governance and management of the succession more complex and difficult.

Therefore, it is clear that a succession process involves several different perspectives and dynamics, and if they are not adequately considered, they may compromise the firm's survival (Zellweger 2017). Nevertheless, on the other hand, plenty of research has proven that it can be a source of relevant opportunities for the relaunch and renewal of the firm, introducing innovation and exploiting the potential of the business (Dyck et al. 2002; De Massis et al. 2016; Rondi et al. 2019; Calabrò et al. 2019; Erdogan et al. 2019). From this point of view, succession is also an opportunity to favor, introduce, and support managerialization and professionalization processes, mainly thanks to the involvement of younger generations (Giovannoni et al. 2011; Bracci and Maran 2012; Giovannoni and Maraghini 2013; Busco et al. 2006; Leotta et al. 2017; Bassani et al. 2018; Cesaroni and Sentuti 2019).

In this chapter, studies on family business succession are discussed with this perspective in mind. Namely, in the next paragraph, the main features of family business succession are described, aiming to provide an overview of the multidimensionality and complexity of this process. The third section intends to shed light on succession as a source of opportunities. In the fourth section, based on the main literature on this topic, some suggestions on how to manage succession were provided. In the fifth paragraph, special attention is devoted to the involvement of external consultants and advisors in supporting family business succession. In fact, they can play a crucial role in reducing risks associated with the succession process and increasing the business's chance of survival in the long term. The chapter ends with a brief summary of the main points. In this way, it contributes to the volume by analyzing succession as one of the main challenges in the family business life cycle.

2 Succession in Family Business: A Complex and Multidimensional Process

It is widely recognized that succession is one of the significant challenges for family firms (Handler 1994; Le Breton-Miller et al. 2004). Both the viability of the company in the long term and very often the wealth of the owner family depend on the selection of a competent new leadership able to effectively guide the company.

Numerous scholars agree that the main difficulties of this process are largely due to its remarkable multidimensionality (Gersick et al. 1997). With this term, one refers to the variety of perspectives that must be considered to understand the complexity of the family business.

In order to better comprehend the multidimensionality of the family business, the three-circles model proposed by Tagiuri and Davis (1996) is very helpful. In this model, family firms are conceived as a system consisting of three different subsystems: family, business, and ownership. They are partially overlapping and highly interconnected, causing the occurrence of different problems. In fact, each subsystem is characterized by different goals, rules, expectations, and values, and a variety of issues may result from their interaction and overlapping (Lansberg 1983). Namely, the consequences of the multidimensionality of family firms may arise, especially when they are involved in a succession process (Lansberg 1983; Swartz 1989). According to Handler (1994), "succession is an issue that requires analysis from the perspectives of family, management, and ownership systems in order to adequately understand the perspectives of the different stakeholders."

Therefore, succession has a multidimensional character because it involves the management of aspects that, although deeply interconnected, are substantially different. On the one hand, some issues refer to the ownership and management of the business. On the other hand, we find the conditions that pertain to the sphere of the family and all the family members who are directly or indirectly involved in the succession.

Some authors have proposed dividing the problems that characterize family business and succession, distinguishing between hard and soft issues (Hoover and Hoover 1999; Malinen 2004). Referring to the model by Tagiuri and Davis (1996), hard issues concern technical aspects of a fiscal, legal, financial, equity, and corporate nature, mainly attributable to the inherited issues linked to the asset aspect of the company and the solutions for transferring the ownership to successors. Alternatively, soft issues pertain to the subsystems of the family and the company. They concern the emotional and psychological spheres of the individual subjects and their personal relationships, any conflicts that arise between the different family members involved in the succession process, communication problems between the members of the family and/or company, and problems connected to the transfer of the entrepreneurial role (Cesaroni and Sentuti 2017).

Managing hard issues effectively is necessary to ensure a successful succession. For instance, De Massis et al. (2008) underlined that financial issues, such as the inability to sustain the tax burden related to succession and the inability to find the financial resources to liquidate the possible exit of an heir(s), may play a crucial role in preventing family succession. However, only managing these aspects is certainly not sufficient to guarantee the survival and continuity of the family business. Very often, the complexity of the succession does not derive from problems concerning the transmission of the ownership of the company. This aspect undoubtedly plays a critical role in the success of the succession and, as a result, should not be underestimated. Still, it is not able to fully capture the real complexity of the family succession, which is mainly due to other aspects.

According to Zellweger (2017), within the main sources of complexity in family business succession, first, we can find the involvement of multiple stakeholders (incumbent, successor, the family, the firm, and the society in which the business is established) with differing interests and requests. Second, the incumbent generally assumes a multiplicity of several roles within the business, being simultaneously an "owner, manager, family member, and citizen" (Zellweger 2017, p. 216). Additionally, the complexity is generated by "multiple successions" (Zellweger 2017, p. 216) encompassed in one succession process, which involves not only the transmission of the ownership of the company but also of the board and management roles. That implies that, on the one hand, the next generation progressively takes responsibility for entrepreneurial activity. On the other hand, the senior generation gradually loses its centrality in the life of the company. From this perspective, succession is not a simple act aimed at transferring the business as a legal entity but a medium–long-term process that requires a progressive delegation of government and management roles and functions from predecessor(s) to successor(s) through a mutual role adjustment between them (Handler 1990).

For all these reasons, succession often generates individual and relational problems between the predecessor and successor, the family members, the people involved in the company, and those who belong simultaneously to the two subsystems of the family and the company. Soft issues are decisive. More precisely, the success of the succession can be compromised both by individual and relational factors (De Massis et al. 2008). Individual factors refer to the predecessor and successor and may concern, for instance, the reluctance of the predecessor to withdraw permanently from the company (Levinson 1971; McGivern 1978; Kets de Vries 1993; Sharma et al. 2001) and/or the low motivation, interest, and ability of potential successor(s) (De Massis et al. 2008) and/or his/her/their inadequate preparation (Barnes and Herschon 1976). Relational factors concern problematic relationships between predecessor and successor (Ward 1987; Lansberg 1988; Fox et al. 1996; Davis and Harveston 1998); conflicts, rivalries, or competition in parent–child relationships (Lansberg 1988) or among family members (De Massis et al. 2008); rivalry between the members of the new generation interested in taking over the leadership of the company (Ward 1987); lack of shared values between old and new generations (Tàpies and Fernández Moya 2012); the insufficient and ineffective transfer of knowledge and skills between the predecessor and successor (Cabrera-Suàrez et al. 2001); conflicts between incumbent or potential successor(s) and non-family member managers (Bruce and Picard 2006); lack of trust and support given to the successor by other family members or non-family member managers (De Massis et al. 2008).

Consequently, while managing hard issues concerning financial, patrimonial, legal, and fiscal aspects, we cannot disregard the individual and relational aspects mainly related to psychological and emotional issues that characterize the family businesses and the actors of succession. Nevertheless, at the same time, we should be aware that this process of change is deeply intertwined with the strategic course of the firm, and some authors (Le Breton-Miller et al. 2004) have underlined the need to manage the family succession consistently with the evolution of the business. Thus, factors related to the business, such as its life-cycle stage and the environmental conditions in which the business is embedded, must be considered (De Massis et al. 2008). Consequently, the succession process must be planned and managed, taking into account, for example, the business's economic and financial performance, whether it is in a phase of development, saturation, or decline, and possible changes in market conditions.

To sum up, the succession process calls into question multiple perspectives, which, despite their diversity, are strongly connected. Decisions concerning hard issues related to the ownership transfer inevitably reflect on the family and the business bringing about several soft issues related to the individual and relational level. Therefore, it is of fundamental importance for the success of the succession that the predecessor, who generally plays a central role in the management of the process, has full awareness of the multidimensionality and complexity of the succession as well as the close connection between the perspectives involved.

3 Succession as an Opportunity to Be Seized

Both family businesses and scholars have often considered succession "As if it were a crisis to be overcome" (Dyck et al. 2002, p. 145). This pessimistic conception is also supported by empirical data on the survival of family firms indicated in Chapter "An Overview of Family Business. Profiles, Definitions and the Main Challenges of the Business Life Cycle". Conversely, this contribution focuses on succession as a potential to be seized to maintain or, better, develop business competitiveness and viability.

As some authors and abundant empirical research suggest (Dyck et al. 2002; De Massis et al. 2016; Rondi et al. 2019; Calabrò et al. 2019; Erdogan et al. 2019), if properly managed, succession can generate innovation that can renew the business and consolidate/develop sources of competitive advantage. From this perspective, succession can be an important opportunity for the development and growth of the family business.

Succession as an opportunity to promote change is essential, i.e., vital for the company, when the company is in one or more of the following situations:

- It is a company with high potential to develop but highly based on the family and not oriented to growth due to the choice of the entrepreneur and/or the owner family. Many small businesses have these characteristics, which are typically centered on the figure of the entrepreneur and strongly identify with the family, which remains the main and often the only source of resources (entrepreneurial, managerial, financial, and operational). They may remain unchanged for generations, but it is often the generational shift that initiates a path of growth/development, allowing them to take advantage of the opportunities offered by the market;
- The entrepreneur's life cycle is no longer aligned with the company's life cycle. For instance, it may happen that the company is faced with decisive choices for its competitiveness (e.g., developing new products/markets, growing, internationalizing, investing in new technologies, etc.) and that the entrepreneur does not have the will, sensitivity, or skills necessary to imagine and manage the change required in terms of strategy, structure, and behaviors, as well as to govern the more complex organizational situations that would derive from it;
- It has a stagnation or a decline in performance, perhaps due to wrong strategic choices, the achievement of the descending phases of the company's life cycle (e.g., products/markets are no longer competitive) or the fact that the predecessor, now close to withdrawing, has no longer invested in the development of the company, which, consequently, needs a revitalization of the strategy and a new entrepreneurial spirit;
- It is subject to particular external conditions (e.g., a change in the legislation that impacts the company's product/market mix, a rapid and unexpected change in the market and competitive environment, etc.), which require new skills and a profound revision of the business model.

In all these cases, a change is essential for the continuity and viability of the business. However, the possibility of transforming the succession from a possible threat to a feasible opportunity requires certain conditions, primarily the presence of a new generation with qualified managerial skills (Hall and Nordqvist 2008), which are indispensable to face the complexity associated with change and effectively manage the new strategic paths taken. Only the entry of a new leader who, due to personal aptitudes, acquired knowledge, training, and professional experience, is able to replace the predecessor by providing innovative skills and guide change effectively, can be turning point for the company, the way to exploit its potential, as well as maintain or recover adequate levels of competitiveness. As a result, the ability to innovate and change is essential to seize the opportunities offered by succession.

However, family firms seem to lose their innovativeness throughout generations. Even if some empirical evidence suggests that family firms are particularly innovative (Koenig et al. 2013; Kotlar et al. 2013), other research has pointed out that family firms led by second or subsequent generations are less innovative (Craig and Moores 2006; Beck et al. 2011; Laforet 2013; Kraiczy et al. 2014; Decker and Günther 2017). Maintaining or improving the family firms innovativeness is possible if the successor(s) is (are) able to integrate the succession with the business strategy, or to find the right balance between tradition and innovation in the business formula, because only in this way will they be able to effectively guarantee the competitiveness of the company in the medium-long term.

Recent studies have focused precisely on how family businesses manage to find a compromise between the need to innovate to keep up with the market and the desire to keep the tradition handed down from generation to generation (De Massis et al. 2016; Rondi et al. 2019; Calabrò et al. 2019; Erdogan et al. 2019). For instance, Erdogan et al. (2019) highlight the opportunity offered by intra-family succession to "unlock the family firms innovation potential" (Rondi et al. 2019). Namely, they investigate how long-established family firms manage the paradox between tradition and innovation, namely, the potential contradiction between beliefs and practices that come from the past and the need to renew and update products and production processes to remain competitive. Findings show that current family generations involved in the business may be "imprinted" by the previous family generation, who transmit the family's values, beliefs, practices, and product signs, affecting the innovation of the products and production processes over time and generations (Erdogan et al. 2019).

Succession, however, does not only represent an opportunity to reformulate or innovate products and processes but to introduce 360° change in the company, including the possibility of undertaking professionalization and managerialization paths (on the definition of these concepts, see Chapter "Professionalization and Managerialization in Family Firms: A Still Open Issue)".

The topic of professionalization was limitedly analyzed with reference to the succession processes of family businesses (Chittoor and Das 2007; Songini and Vola 2015; Howorth et al. 2016). The studies conducted have highlighted, first of all, the close links existing between the two phenomena, noting that professionalization can support the company in facing the challenge of succession (Busco et al. 2006; Salvato and Corbetta 2013). At the same time, succession can represent an opportunity to professionalize the family business, favoring the change of management styles and logics (Giovannoni et al. 2011; Giovannoni and Maraghini 2013).

In parallel, some authors (Mazzola et al. 2008; Songini and Vola 2015) suggest how management and control systems can be useful to successors during the succession path. For example, Bracci e Maran (2012) highlight how the succession process is strongly interrelated with the contextual innovation process of managerial tools, which can favor the legitimacy of the successor within the company (Busco et al. 2006). Leotta et al. (2017) have also analyzed a business case, observing that during the succession, and thanks to the successor, a new managerial view was adopted, and new control tools were introduced, such as new information systems and reporting techniques. These tools have also been functional in building the successor's leadership. Finally, Cesaroni and Sentuti (2019), by adopting the actor–network theory, have explored the relationship between management accounting change and the succession process within family firms. Results show that the two processes are deeply interplayed, confirming that the successor may play a crucial role in promoting the introduction of new management accounting systems, and, simultaneously, their adoption is essential for the successor's legitimacy within the family and the firm.

Songini and Vola (2015) have analyzed the relationship among the three phenomena: professionalization (involvement of non-family managers), managerialization (the use of managerial mechanisms, such as strategic planning and management control systems) and family business succession. The longitudinal case study indicates that the involvement of non-family members took place during the succession, choosing former employees of the company, which were preferred to hired external professional. At the same time, they have promoted the adoption of managerial mechanisms that were introduced mostly to cope with firms' and environments' complexity and agency conflicts.

However, family firms and successors are not always able to seize the opportunity to professionalize and managerialize the business. For instance, Bassani et al. (2018) presented an unsuccessful case of professionalization in which the successor hired a general director and other non-family managers during the succession process but was unable to professionalize the firm effectively. In the analyzed case, the main cause of the failure of the professionalization process was the ambiguity of the motivations behind the involvement of external managers. Despite the successor's explicit motivation to professionalize the firm, her implicit and hidden motivations were to reply to her need for personal legitimacy/accreditation. The latter were prevalent and ended up heavily affecting the whole process: when the successor acquired the control of the company, he lost interest in professionalizing the company, with negative consequences in terms of the firm's performance and growth.

The debate on how succession might become an opportunity to introduce innovation in terms of new products and production processes, new services, new markets, new technologies, new materials, and also new managerial culture and new managerial systems, has been gaining momentum. We think that passing from "succession as a crisis to be overcome" to "succession as an opportunity to be seized" is a crucial switch for both family businesses and scholars. A positive approach to succession could strengthen the likelihood of survival across generations, and this may be a key factor in the long-term viability of family firms.

4 Handling the Succession Process

Scholars and professionals agree on the need to plan and handle the succession process effectively because it is essential to face challenges and seize opportunities. However, it is widely recognized that: "there is no one-size-fits-all solution" (Zellweger 2017, p. 203). Every family business succession is unique, given the peculiar features of the three subsystems (family, business, and ownership) and their interconnections in each family firm. Nevertheless, both scholars and professionals have defined, over time, some crucial rules to handle the succession process successfully.

Numerous authors have emphasized, first of all, the need to plan, and with due advance, this process of change (Ward 1987, 2004; Handler 1990, 1992; Kets de Vries 1993; Morris et al. 1997; Sharma et al. 2001; Dyck et al. 2002; Ip and Jacobs 2006; Zellweger 2017).

Yet, the planning of succession is often hindered by some psychological barriers that can restrain the entrepreneur in delineating the right path, such as the change of role and the loss of power, the thought of inactivity, the transience of life and mortality, the fear of triggering jealousy and rivalries among family members, and the difficulty of choosing among the children who will be the successor (Weesie 2017).

Excellent and timely programming, however, allows the incumbent to contain the uncertainty that would arise if the process were left to natural evolution, without outlining the future, without making the necessary decisions and without choosing concrete solutions to give rise to succession. The planning of succession is also necessary to evaluate multiple issues raised by the succession and formulate all the decisions that should be made so that they are consistent with the incumbent and successor's goals and priorities (Zellweger 2017). In particular, the choices will be related to: the succession options (Zellweger 2017); in the case of family succession, the selection (Ward 1987) and the training of the successor (Barnes and Herschon 1976; McGivern 1978; Ward 1987; Morris et al. 1997; Cabrera-Suàrez et al. 2001); his/her career path into the company; the role of the other actors involved (other family members, managers, employees, external interlocutors); the management of business–family relationships (Lansberg 1983; Sharma et al. 2001); how to include the succession in the broader strategic development path of the company.

Therefore, preparing and governing the succession means defining—formally or not—a series of aspects and making the key decisions that will allow the process to evolve in a guided way, without serious (sometimes irremediable) repercussions on their stability and family and business fortunes. That is, it will (Barnes and Herschon 1976; McGivern 1978; Ward 1987; Morris et al. 1997; Cabrera-Suàrez et al. 2001; Zellweger 2017):

- Define the rules for involving the new generation in the family business;
- Designate the successor, identifying who, based on skills, knowledge, attitudes, aspirations, and motivations, will be better than others to take on the role of the new leader of the family business, consistent with the strategic development needs of the company;

- Define the training path of the successor, or all the activities and experiences external and internal to the family business, necessary to help them acquire the knowledge and skills necessary to perform their task when the change occurs in the leader position;
- Decide on the timing of the succession, foreseeing the moment when the successor will officially and effectively take over the leadership role;
- Establish how to manage relationships and communication with other family members, employees and all the main internal or external stakeholders of the family business (banks, key customers, suppliers, etc.);
- Provide, in more complex families, a learning path also for family members who, although not taking on a role in the governing or management bodies of the company, are destined to inherit and maintain a stake in equity and therefore to carry out the shareholder role;
- Outline the asset aspect, identifying and sharing the rules for dividing the ownership of the company among family members, as well as those for the management of family assets.

Therefore, the planning should outline a path divided into several stages, which many authors have helped define and analyze. However, it should be noted that, as anticipated at the beginning of the paragraph, numerous variables may shape the succession process. These variables may relate to the characteristics of the individuals involved (e.g., age, personality, values, training, experiences, leadership style, willingness to delegate by the predecessor side and willingness to wait by the successor's side, etc.), the business (e.g., business sector, uniqueness or multiplicity of business areas, life-cycle stage, size, organizational structure, etc.), and family (e.g., number and gender of new generation components, system of values, presence of one or more candidates for the role of successor, etc.). From the possibility of composing these variables in an infinite number of plausible combinations, it is easy to deduce the impossibility of developing a suitable path to describe all the possible cases that may arise.

From a transversal reading of the various contributions that have deepened the theme of the management of the succession process, mostly published between 1992 and 2000 (Sharma 2004), it is possible to articulate this process in the following phases: maturation of awareness; training of the next generation; the entry path and career of next generation in the family business; the coexistence and leadership transition period; the successor taking the helm at the firm.

The development of awareness is a preparatory phase for starting family succession and mainly concerns the entrepreneur. In fact, it is up to he/she to become fully aware of the will or not, and sometimes of the need, to transmit the business to the sons and/or daughters and the importance of facing the issue considering all the variables that, in some way, will have to be managed. It is good, first of all, that this awareness is acquired prematurely so that each subsequent step can be effectively weighted and the qualities of potential successors can be verified over time. In fact, the entrepreneur's willingness to transmit the business and the entrepreneurial role to sons or daughters does not automatically translate into the motivation and ability of successors to take on this role. Therefore, it is good to always keep in mind the possibility of opting for an alternative solution in which the children do not demonstrate the will, attitude, and necessary skills to take over the leadership role.

The training of the next generation concerns the training process of the successor outside the company. This phase includes a wide range of activities, ranging from family education to the socialization of the entrepreneurial role, from the school path to the possibility of realizing work experiences outside the family business and/or abroad (Barnes and Herschon 1976; McGivern 1978; Ward 1987; Zellweger 2017). These activities are aimed at helping the potential successor to acquire a basic culture, encourage comparison with other young people, develop organizational and analytical skills, and start demonstrating their skills and talents.

The entry path and career of the next generation in the family business aim to help the potential successor acquire the specific knowledge and skills that will serve them to fulfill their task when the change to the leader role occurs. This phase is aimed at the gradual professional development of the successor(s) through periods of permanence in the various functions and taking on various company duties, perhaps alongside key collaborators and/or the entrepreneur themselves. The main goal is acquiring suitable knowledge of the business and the complexity of the entire company system, achieving full awareness of the context.

The coexistence between incumbent and successor, and the leadership transition can last a long time. Its purpose is to allow the transmission of the entrepreneurial role. The challenge for the incumbent and successor, at this stage, is to successfully combine the experience of the senior with the skills of the junior, to jointly develop the company's potential through improvement, renewal, and innovation processes (Zellweger 2017). Generational coexistence must also lead to the mutual adaptation of the roles between the outgoing generation and the emerging generation: as the successor's role gradually grows, that of the predecessor must also decrease (Handler 1990).

The changeover of leader in the company is the final stage of the succession process. The objective of this phase is to transfer the leadership role from one generation to another, allowing the son or daughter, who has demonstrated that they have the necessary qualities, to take over the incumbent at the helm of the company in a definitive way (Ward 1987, 2004).

It is a very delicate phase, often slowed down by a series of resistances to change (Weesie 2017). These resistances can derive from the predecessor, reluctant to abandon their leadership role. In such circumstances, the literature suggests defining a role for the predecessor that does not detach he/she completely from the company (Corbetta 2008). In other cases, other individuals within the company can show such resistances to change. They can assume attitudes and behaviors that go from the non-acceptance of the new entrepreneur to real obstructionism toward his/her work. These expressions can be dictated by the most diverse reasons (Schillaci 1990): fear of diminishing or losing one's power; misunderstanding or non-sharing of the change in plans that the successor intends to carry out; idealization of the past, i.e., the tendency to alter memories by emphasizing previous management and mythologizing the outgoing entrepreneur who becomes, in the collective imagination, a sort of ideal leader, with respect to which the successor, who will never appear to be up to par. To overcome these barriers, the successor must have a thorough knowledge of the context in which he/she will operate, to identify the various sources of resistance and the most appropriate solutions to adopt (e.g., the involvement of key collaborators in change processes, effective communication of current changes, a bottom-up approach to the introduction of organizational and/or managerial innovations).

The legitimacy of the successor has been widely addressed in the literature. Cabrera-Suárez et al. (2001) emphasize, for example, that the succession planning process must also include the acquisition and development of skills and knowledge that give credibility and legitimacy to the successor. Steier (2001), on the other hand, states that legitimization occurs mainly during the entry path and the generational coexistence phase, through the transfer of knowledge and skills from the incumbent to the successor. Finally, other authors, as highlighted in the previous paragraph, highlight the role of managerial control tools for building leadership and legitimizing the successor (Busco et al. 2006; Bracci and Maran 2012; Leotta et al. 2017; Bassani et al. 2018; Cesaroni and Sentuti 2019).

Certainly, in planning and managing the succession, it is necessary to keep in mind that its success does not guarantee—in itself—the continuity of the company, especially if it is not accompanied by a process of innovation and change contextualized to the real needs of the business and integrated with its development path, as previously illustrated. Precisely for that reason, while in the past several authors have analyzed succession by focusing on processes, firm and family features that characterize a successful transfer of ownership and control (Le Breton-Miller et al. 2004), currently scholars are focusing on how innovation can be transmitted across generations (Jaskiewicz et al. 2015; Kammerlander et al. 2015).

5 The Role of External Advisors

In most of the analyses concerning family succession, the primary focus is on the main players in the process—the senior generation, the successor, the family, and the company—and the factors that can favor, or on the contrary hinder, the good outcome of the succession process, ensuring business continuity (Le Breton-Miller et al. 2004). Less interest, on the other hand, is addressed to the external subjects who can facilitate succession and play a decisive role in the progress of this process, even if they are not directly involved (Cesaroni and Sentuti 2016). "External subjects" is an expression used to refer to a broad category of persons, composed of friends or other family members, company collaborators, professionals, consultants, and other subjects outside the company and the family, who are able to reduce the risks of succession and increase the chances of family businesses' survival (Cesaroni and Sentuti 2016).

Naturally, the roles that these subjects can play and the contributions they can offer to facilitate succession are different. In general, the intervention of these subjects could be particularly useful in helping incumbents to deal with succession more consciously and effectively, favoring the entry of successors into the company, preparing the company for succession, and helping the owner family to keep corporate matters separate from family matters. Additionally, external professionals could support family businesses in combining succession with a wider process of revising, redefining, and improving their governance and control systems.

In this chapter, we have focused our attention on the figure and role of a peculiar external individual—the professional advisor. With this term, we are referring to an actor not directly involved in the family business, who has a specific work background and can be hired to provide advice and support the family business in dealing with a wide range of issues (Strike 2012), succession included. In this category, we consider professionals and experts that can provide wide-ranging competencies and knowledge, such as chartered certified accountants, lawyers, notaries, fiscal experts, management consultants, bank operators, industry associations, business brokers, and also family therapists, counselors, psychologists, coaches, mentors, family meeting facilitators, family, mediators, etc. While those included in the first group are generally considered traditional advisors because they offer traditional advisory services such as accountancy, fiscal, and law, those included in the second group are considered "unconventional" advisors, who propose services from psychology and counseling backgrounds such as mediation and conflict resolution (Nicholson et al. 2009).

Their diverse contribution could be very crucial. In fact, due to the multidimensional nature of the succession process, a multidisciplinary approach is needed to handle it effectively (Swartz 1989). However, the multiplicity of expertise required to effectively manage all of these issues is rarely present within the family firm. For this reason, it has been widely recognized that an external advisor can support and favor the succession process by playing an important role in its final success (Morris et al. 1996; Salvato and Corbetta 2013; Strike 2012; Reay et al. 2013; Battisti and Williamson 2015).

Several studies conducted on the role of advisors in supporting family businesses have highlighted the difficulties that many consultants encounter due to problems and situations of conflict that arise within the family (Jaffe et al. 1997). These problems, in fact, often spread beyond family boundaries and end up generating effects that interfere with the management of the business, to the point of hindering the effective performance of the consulting service. These obstacles also occur because advisors are often specialized in business-related problems (mainly those of a strategic, financial, legal, or fiscal nature) but are not prepared or able to deal with the relational aspects of the family businesses. That is why some authors suggest that family business consultants also take into account "the emotional concerns that affected both firm and family" (Strike 2013).

In fact, many of the problems that typically occur in family businesses are the result of the interconnections existing between family, property, and business. Precisely for this reason, these are problems that cannot be effectively solved if faced with a unilateral perspective, i.e., by a single consultant who only takes into account one aspect of the problem and ignores, or is not able to address, those attributable to other subsystems (Lee and Danes 2012). In this regard, Su and Dou (2013) state that: “real issues are often more complicated and interconnected than the issues presented to a single advisor.” Consequently, many of the typical family business problems require the adoption of a multidisciplinary perspective, and this postulates the ability, as well as the availability, of the individual consultant to interact, confront, and collaborate with other professionals, given the inability of a single professional to take care of all the problems (Goodman 1998). In fact, Su and Dou (2013), through a qualitative analysis, have shown that the involvement of a multidisciplinary team increases the degree of precision in identifying the problem, makes it easier to carry out a systematic analysis of the issues, favors the elaboration of a comprehensive, integrated solution, and increases the credibility of the solution provided.

Other authors emphasize that family business consultants should be able to act not only as “content experts” capable of putting their specialized skills to use with problems related to a specific area of the company but should instead be able to act as “process consultants” (Kaye and Hamilton 2004). This role entails possessing the soft skills necessary to manage the problems that arise in the areas of overlap between the three subsystems, thus concerning the relationships between family members and the company. This approach is in line with Tagiuri and Davis’s model (1996). It implies the ability to face the consultancy with the family business with a precise approach, in which particular emphasis is placed on the existing interconnections between family, business, and property. To this end, advisory models based on the theory of systems have proven useful, allowing consultants to “address questions concerning a particular circle, while also considering other perspectives at the same time” (Gersick et al. 1997).

If this approach proves to be useful every time a consulting process is carried out within a family business, it is then indispensable when the family business is involved in a succession process. In fact, the latter is capable of causing very profound changes and challenges at both the family, business, and ownership levels. In fact, many scholars agree that the main difficulties of succession are due to its multidimensional character, which, in order not to jeopardize the company and compromise its continuity, makes the ability to simultaneously take into account the variety of problems that can occur during the various phases of the process fundamental (Le Breton-Miller et al. 2004).

As we said before, the multiplicity of skills needed to deal with and effectively manage all these issues at the same time is rarely present within the company, and this postulates the need to involve a plurality of different individuals, each specialized in dealing with the entire range of problems raised by succession (Swartz 1989). This detail is especially true for the succession from the first to the second generation, which finds the founder, successor, and other family members completely unprepared, all unexperienced, and unaware of the difficulties associated with this phase of the company’s life. That is the reason why it is believed that an external consultant can make an important contribution in favoring the succession process and can have a decisive role in leading it toward a positive conclusion (Morris et al. 1996; Salvato and Corbetta 2013; Strike 2012; Reay et al. 2013; Battisti and Williamson 2015).

As stated by Michel and Kammerlander (2015), the involvement of a consultant can be fundamental in effectively facing all the problems associated with the four phases of the succession process—start-up, preparation, selection, and training.

As noted by Morris et al. (1996), in the literature on family businesses, the involvement of external consultants is considered one of the factors best able to favor a valid conclusion of the succession process (Fox et al. 1996), especially in the case of smaller FBs. Some authors also argue that external professionals can act as facilitators or moderators (Jernigan and Lord 2008).

Swartz (1989) underlines the need to adopt a multidisciplinary approach, and Ip and Jacobs (2006) warn that the dual nature of FBs means that, for the professional, the succession is presented as a "unique, case-by-case process, where a one-size-fits-all mentality is simply inappropriate." This reality implies the need for the consultant to be sensitive to the aspirations and needs of their clients (Westhead 2003) and be able to tune into their needs, even when they are unexpressed. Therefore, the consultants should be able to go beyond the problems explicitly proposed by the client, to identify the deeper issues that the client is facing (Su and Dou 2013).

Despite the recognized multidimensionality of the succession phenomenon, research carried out up to now shows that family businesses mainly resort to "traditional" consultants, primarily chartered accountants and lawyers, involved above all to deal with hard issues (Swartz 1989; Kaye and Hamilton 2004; Bruce and Picard 2006; Nicholson et al. 2009; Sawers and Whiting 2010; Kirkwood and Harris 2011; Barbera and Hasso 2013).

Several scholars have studied the role of the chartered certified accountant in the management of the succession process in depth (Swartz 1989; Kaye and Hamilton 2004). Their role often turns out to be central in the management of family succession, given that this figure represents a fundamental point of reference for obtaining assistance, advice, and support in the crucial phases of the life of the company especially for small and medium family businesses (Reddrop and Mapunda 2015). In fact, several studies have confirmed that the chartered accountant is the figure that is most trusted by the owners of small-medium family businesses, who turn to them to face a series of problems, including those related to succession management (Bruce and Picard 2006).

Jaffe et al. (1997) were the first to observe how the chartered accountant has become entrepreneurs' "trustworthy" consultant, facilitated by the reputation of seriousness and reliability, which won over the members of the family and the family business during often long-lasting professional relationships (Michel and Kammerlander 2015). Nevertheless, several studies have shown that consultancy services provided by accountants are not always able to fully meet the needs and expectations of family business owners (Sawers and Whiting 2010; Cesaroni and Sentuti 2017; Reddrop and Mapunda 2015). As Neubauer (2003) notes, many companies have an accountant they turn to for questions related to succession. However, the accountant, surely able to find optimal solutions as regards, for example, questions of a fiscal nature, does not prove to be as capable in dealing with other issues, more linked to the personal and relational dimension of the succession process. For this reason, many family successions risk being unsuccessful.

Sawers and Whiting (2010) interviewed some small New Zealand companies to understand the role played by accountants in managing the succession process. The analysis provides some useful indications regarding the professional's characteristics that, according to the companies' opinion, condition his ability to manage succession planning effectively. In particular, the existence of a long-term relationship between the professional and the company is important, in addition to the accountant's ability to establish a relationship with their client based on trust and honesty, their competence in providing an objective and impartial point of view on the proposed problems and, finally, their ability to provide useful solutions to manage the succession.

At the same time, previous research reveals some limits concerning the chartered accountant's ability to solve all the problems associated with family succession. According to the companies interviewed, their intervention can be essential to face the more technical aspects—the hard issues—concerning the financial, legal, patrimonial, and fiscal aspects of the succession. At the same time, the idea prevails that the accountant is not the right person to address the soft aspects, concerning psychological and relational dynamics. The research of Nicholson et al. (2009) confirms that, in New Zealand, the main point of reference for family businesses is accountants, followed by lawyers, while recourse to coaches and mentors remains marginal. With regard to the way accountants operate, some authors (Morris et al. 1997) believe that they should work in a network with other professionals and experts in family therapy and succession management, to raise the entrepreneur's awareness of the need to look at succession holistically.

Reddrop and Mapunda (2015) conducted a research to understand the willingness of family businesses to use external consultancy to address the challenges posed by succession. Their analysis confirms the prevalent recourse to the accountant figure but also highlights a feeling of general dissatisfaction with the services received, especially with regard to their ability to deal with and resolve problems of a soft nature. The authors also confirm that empathy and listening skills are the qualities most sought after by accountants. Contrary to what has emerged in previous research, Reddropp and Mapunda believe that the family business does not always use the trusted professional with whom it has slowly developed a medium–long-term relationship. From their study, it turns out that family businesses often look for new consultants, and this search is done mainly through its own network of contacts; the choice often falls on a professional recommended by a colleague or friend, and this suggestion gives instant "vicarious" trust by the company to the consultant.

Recently, Bertschi-Michel et al. (2019) have confirmed the positive impact of external advisors on succession in family-owned SMEs. Specifically, they focus on the concept of the advisor's tertius iungens behavior as the orientation that emphasizes creating or facilitating ties, communication, and collaboration among people (Obstfeld 2005) and, in this case, between predecessor and successor. Bertschi-Michel et al. (2019) proved that, when acting as a tertius jungens, external advisors can be of great help in facilitating communication and collaboration between family members and promoting the achievement of shared objectives. They explore the incumbent and successor's satisfaction with the advisor's services and the post-succession firm performance, also considering the moderating influence of two advisor's characteristics, namely their type and process of involvement. Results also show that incumbent and successor's satisfaction with the advisor increases in the case of formal (versus informal) relationship. Moreover, the ability of an advisor's tertius iungens behavior to positively affect firm performance is stronger when the advisor is involved in the full succession process, and not only in parts of it.

Concerning the Italian context, very little research has investigated this topic. Cesaroni and Sentuti (2016) have questioned the ability of chartered accountants to deal with succession by adopting a multidisciplinary approach, aimed not only at facing hard issues but also understanding the relevance of soft issues. Their analysis—based on a questionnaire addressed to 175 Italian chartered accountants—shows that hard issues are the most recurrent in the professional practice of accountants, who rarely prove to be sensitive and attentive to soft issues such as the problems raised by the relationship and communication processes among family members. Moreover, accountants tend to underestimate the importance of the ability to develop an empathetic relationship with the family business owner and the other members of the family. Furthermore, despite the numerous recommendations coming from the literature regarding the need to collaborate with other consultants with a different background of knowledge and skills, the tendency of Italian accountants to work autonomously, at the very least collaborating with other hard issues experts (mainly notaries, lawyers, and bank officers) prevails. The consequence of this attitude is a possible discrepancy between the family business's expectations and the services provided by the accountants.

Cesaroni and Sentuti (2017) have also investigated the attitude of family businesses toward succession and the possibility of involving external consultants to solve the problems raised by this phase of the company's life cycle. Results have shown that the opinions of family business owners are ambivalent on this issue. On the one hand, the analysis carried out confirms the central role of accountants in helping the family business to face the family succession. On the other hand, however, the authors point out the emergence of various problems related to the relationship between the family firm and accountants, who are not always able to meet the expectations of their clients or provide a truly effective consultancy service. In fact, several family business owners have declared that they are not fully satisfied with the adopted methods and the services received, often judged to be excessively fragmented and not effective. In particular, entrepreneurs complain about the inability of some accountants to fully integrate with the reality of their business and understand the complexity associated with their family nature. At the same time, they judge accountants who are too focused on technical issues, at the expense of relational and personal aspects, which entrepreneurs deem crucial. From the analysis carried out by the authors, it appears that only in one of the cases examined did the interviewed entrepreneur declare that he was fully satisfied with the service received, given the ability of the consultancy company involved to help the company plan and manage all the aspects of the succession. In the analyzed case, the consulting company made use of a multidisciplinary team (composed of an accountant, psychologist, lawyer, and another consultant specialized in succession problems). This team also acted in collaboration with a broader network of experts, who provided additional specialist skills when necessary to deal with particular situations that could not be solved independently by the team.

In summary, the analysis of the literature reveals that entrepreneurs often consider chartered accountants as their main point of reference for dealing with issues related to the succession process. However, they are not always able to fully meet the expectations of family businesses. Despite this centrality granted to the accountant, systematic studies have not yet been carried out on this issue (Strike 2012). Reay et al. (2013) observed the following: "What is missing is a systematic and complete database able to advance the knowledge on the role of consultants and consultancy services." This is especially true with regard to the role of accountants. With few exceptions (Cesaroni and Sentuti 2016; Battisti and Williamson 2015; Reddrop and Mapunda 2015), the existing studies on this topic have neglected accountants' point of view and their opinions regarding the experiences they had in dealing with companies involved in succession processes. The consequence is that many questions are still unanswered, and further investigation is needed to comprehend the issue better.

In conclusion, the shared opinion is that further research is needed to allow a significant advancement of knowledge on the role of external advisors in supporting family succession. In particular, future research should be carried out to investigate the following aspects:

- The advising model adopted by accountants when they are confronted with a family business involved in a succession process;
- The effectiveness of consultancy services offered by a multidisciplinary network compared to that of consultancy services provided by accountants who operate independently or in teams with other hard professionals;
- The family businesses' point of view on the effectiveness of a multidisciplinary network of professionals and experts and its ability to raise the quality level of the advice provided;
- Any existing geographical differences (national and/or regional) regarding the methods adopted by accountants to address the issues raised by the family succession, the main problems they encounter in interactions with family members involved in ownership, and with other family members, and the solutions that they mainly propose to solve these problems;
- The attitude and behavior of small, medium, and large companies toward accountants and the possibility of involving them in the management of succession processes;
- The sensitivity of small, medium, and large companies regarding the soft and hard problems raised by succession.

6 Conclusions

Acknowledging the crucial role of family succession for the longevity and viability of family firms, this chapter has focused on the complexity and multidimensionality of this process of change.

The existing literature on this topic has highlighted that ensuring the survival of the business, passing it down generation to generation, is what distinguishes family-owned businesses from other types of companies. Contextually, available data, and empirical evidence have highlighted that thousands of companies risk disappearing every year because of the problems and difficulties related to family business succession. In other words, combining the willingness to transfer the business through generations with the ability to really do it is not easy. Why?

According to several authors, difficulties are mainly due to the wide range of different actors directly or indirectly involved in this process—first of all, incumbent and successor—also, other family members, the whole business, and its main stakeholders. This implies multiple dynamics and several different perspectives that must be effectively considered in order to manage it successfully.

If handled appropriately, family succession can become a great opportunity for the business. Thanks to the new generation's skills and competencies, firms may be able to exploit its potential, professionalizing the business, adopting new managerial control systems, and introducing products and processes innovations and new business models.

This chapter aimed to offer an overview of the literature on family succession, to shed some light on its complexity but also underline possible opportunities that can be unleashed by succession.

Adopting the three-circles model proposed by Tagiuri and Davis (1996) to explain the multidimensionality of the family business due to the overlapping of family, business, and ownership, we analyzed hard and soft issues concerning succession. Specifically, we emphasized that the family, business, and ownership perspectives are strongly connected and that hard and soft issues are inevitably correlated. Therefore, it is crucial that the incumbent, who generally plays a key role in the management of the process, is fully aware of this complexity to be successful.

Additionally, we would like to suggest that family business owners adopt a positive and proactive approach in dealing with succession, aiming to prevent troubles, seize opportunities, and increase the likelihood of longevity and viability of the firm across generations. To this purpose, we have provided some practical suggestions, based on the main literature on this topic, on how to manage a family succession to overcome the challenge of this process and take chances.

Finally, recognizing that succession requires a multidisciplinary range of knowledge and competencies, which family business owners rarely possess all by themselves, we have devoted special attention to the role of external consultants and advisors in supporting family business succession. Their role could be crucial in dealing with hard and soft issues, reducing risks concerning succession, and increasing the business's chance to survive in the long term. Particularly, we have focused on chartered certified accountants, as they are often a key point of reference for small and medium family businesses. We have discussed their strengths and weaknesses in meeting the expectations of family business owners and emphasized the need for further research to advance knowledge on the role of external advisors in supporting family succession.

References

Astrachan JH, Jaskiewicz P (2008) Emotional returns and emotional costs in privately held family businesses: advancing traditional business valuation. Fam Bus Rev 21(2):139–149. https://doi.org/10.1111/j.1741-6248.2008.00115.x

Barbera F, Hasso T (2013) Do we need to use an accountant? The sales growth and survival benefits to family SMEs. Fam Bus Rev 26(3):271–292. https://doi.org/10.1177/0894486513487198

Barnes LB, Herschon SA (1976) Transferring power in the family business. Harvard Bus Rev 54(4):105–114

Battisti M, Williamson AJ (2015) The role of intermediaries in the small business transfer process. Small Enterp Res 22(1):32–48. https://doi.org/10.1080/13215906.2015.1022129

Bassani G, Cattaneo C, Cesaroni FM, Sentuti A (2018) Management control systems and family business professionalization. The pathway leading to successor's seal of approval. Manag Control 2:15–35. https://doi.org/10.3280/MACO2018-SU2002

Beck L, Janssens W, Debruyne M, Lommelen T (2011) A study of the relationships between generation, market orientation, and innovation in family firms. Fam Bus Rev 24(3):252–272. https://doi.org/10.1177/0894486511409210

Bracci E, Maran L (2012) The role and use of management accounting systems (MAS) in family firms: a case study. Piccola Impresa/Small Bus 3:129–153. https://doi.org/10.14596/pisb.35

Busco C, Riccaboni A, Scapens RW (2006) Trust for accounting and accounting for trust. Manag Account Res 17(1):11–41. https://doi.org/10.1016/j.mar.2005.08.001

Bertschi-Michel A, Sieger P, Kammerlander N (2019) Succession in family-owned SMEs: the impact of advisors. Small Bus Econ, 1–21. 10.1007/s11187-019-00266-2

Bruce D, Picard D (2006) Making succession a success: perspectives from Canadian small and medium-sized enterprises. J Small Bus Manag 44(2):306–309. https://doi.org/10.1111/j.1540-627X.2006.00171.x

Cabrera-Suárez K, De Saa-Perez P, García-Almeida D (2001) The succession process from a resource- and knowledge-based view of the family firm. Fam Bus Rev 14(1):37–46. https://doi.org/10.1111/j.1741-6248.2001.00037.x

Calabrò A, Vecchiarini M, Gast J, Campopiano G, De Massis A, Kraus S (2019) Innovation in family firms: a systematic literature review and guidance for future research. Int J Manag Rev 21(3):317–355. https://doi.org/10.1111/ijmr.12192

Cesaroni FM, Sentuti A (2016) Accountants' role in the management of succession. Empirical evidence from Italy. J Fam Bus Manag 6(3):270–290. 10.1108/JFBM-08-2015-0028

Cesaroni FM, Sentuti A (2017) Family business succession and external advisors: the relevance of 'soft' issues. Small Enterp Res 24(2):167–188. https://doi.org/10.1080/13215906.2017.1338193

Cesaroni FM, Sentuti A (2019) Exploring the relationship between management accounting change and succession process within family firms. Manag Control 1:17–44. https://doi.org/10.3280/MACO2019-001002

Chittoor R, Das R (2007) Professionalization of management and succession performance—a vital linkage. Fam Bus Rev 20(1):65–76. https://doi.org/10.1111/j.1741-6248.2007.00084.x

Chua JH, Chrisman JJ, Sharma P (1999) Defining the family business by behavior. Entrepreneurship Theory Pract 23(4):19–39. https://doi.org/10.1177/104225879902300402

Corbetta G (2008) Learning from practice: how to avoid mistakes in succession processes. In: Tàpies J, Ward JL (eds) Family values and value creation. A Family Business Publication. Palgrave Macmillan, London, pp 9–28. 10.1057/9780230594227_2

Craig JBL, Moores K (2006) A 10-year longitudinal investigation of strategy, systems, and environment on innovation in family firms. Fam Bus Rev 19(1):1–10. https://doi.org/10.1111/j.1741-6248.2006.00056.x

Davis PS, Harveston PD (1998) The influence of family on the family business succession process: a multi-generational perspective. Entrepreneurship Theory Pract 22(3):31–53. https://doi.org/10.1177/104225879802200302

Decker C, Günther C (2017) The impact of family ownership on innovation: evidence from the German machine tool industry. Small Bus Econ 48(1):199–212. https://doi.org/10.1007/s11187-016-9775-0

De Massis A, Chua JH, Chrisman JJ (2008) Factors preventing intra-family succession. Fam Bus Rev 21(2):183–199. https://doi.org/10.1111/j.1741-6248.2008.00118.x

De Massis A, Frattini F, Kotlar J, Petruzzelli AM, Wright M (2016) Innovation through tradition: lessons from innovative family businesses and directions for future research. Acad Manag Perspect 30(1):93–116. https://doi.org/10.5465/amp.2015.0017

Dyck B, Mauws M, Starke FA, Mischke GA (2002) Passing the Baton. The importance of sequence, timing, technique and communication in executive succession. J Bus Ventur 17(2):143–162. 10.1016/S0883-9026(00)00056-2

Erdogan I, Rondi E, De Massis A (2019) Managing the tradition and innovation paradox in family firms: a family imprinting perspective. Entrepreneurship Theory Pract. https://doi.org/10.1177/1042258719839712

Fox M, Nilakant V, Hamilton RT (1996) Managing succession in family-owned businesses. Int Small Bus J 15(1):15–25. https://doi.org/10.1177/0266242696151001

Gersick KE, Gersick KE, Davis JA, Hampton MM, Lansberg I (1997) Generation to generation: life cycles of the family business. Harvard Business Press, Boston, Massachusetts

Giovannoni E, Maraghini MP (2013) The challenges of integrated performance measure-ment systems Integrating mechanisms for integrated measures. Account Auditing Account J 26(6):978–1008. https://doi.org/10.1108/AAAJ-04-2013-1312

Giovannoni E, Maraghini MP, Riccaboni A (2011) Transmitting knowledge across generations: the role of management accounting practices. Fam Bus Rev 24(2):1–25. https://doi.org/10.1177/0894486511406722

Goodman JM (1998) Defining the new professional: the family business counsellor. Fam Bus Rev 11(4):349–354. https://doi.org/10.1111/j.1741-6248.1998.00349.x

Gomez-Mejía LR, Haynes KT, Núñez-Nickel M, Jacobson KJ, Moyano-Fuentes J (2007) Socioemotional wealth and business risks in family-controlled firms: evidence from Spanish olive oil mills. Adm Sci Q 52(1):106–137. https://doi.org/10.2189/asqu.52.1.106

Gomez-Mejia LR, Cruz C, Berrone P, De Castro J (2011) The bind that ties: socioemotional wealth preservation in family firms. Acad Manag Ann 5(1):653–707. https://doi.org/10.5465/19416520.2011.593320

Hall A, Nordqvist M (2008) Professional management in family businesses: toward an extended understanding. Fam Bus Rev 21(1):51–69. https://doi.org/10.1111/j.1741-6248.2007.00109.x

Handler WC (1990) Succession in family firms: a mutual role adjustment between entrepreneur and next generation family members. Entrepreneurship Theory Pract 15(1):37–51. https://doi.org/10.1177/104225879001500105

Handler WC (1992) The succession experience of the next generation. Fam Bus Rev 5(3):283–307. https://doi.org/10.1111/j.1741-6248.1992.00283.x

Handler WC (1994) Succession in family business: a review of the research. Fam Bus Rev 7(2):133–157. https://doi.org/10.1111/j.1741-6248.1994.00133.x

Hoover EA, Hoover CL (1999) Gettingalong in family business: the relationship intelligence. Handbook. Routledge, New York
Howorth C, Wright M, Westhead P, Allcock D (2016) Company metamorphosis: professionalization waves, family firms and management buyouts. Small Bus Econ 47(3):803–817. https://doi.org/10.1007/s11187-016-9761-6
Ip B, Jacobs G (2006) Business succession planning: a review of the evidence. J Small Bus Enterp Dev 13(2):326–350. https://doi.org/10.1108/14626000610680235
Jaffe DT, Lane S, Dashew L, Bork D (1997) The CPA as family adviser. J Account 183(5):42–50
Jaskiewicz P, Combs JG, Rau SB (2015) Entrepreneurial legacy: toward a theory of how some family firms nurture transgenerational entrepreneurship. J Bus Ventur 30(1):29–49. https://doi.org/10.1016/j.jbusvent.2014.07.001
Jernigan M, Lord RB (2008) The mediator's role in the family business. Am J Mediation 2(51):51–63
Kaye K, Hamilton S (2004) Roles of trust in consulting to financial families. Fam Bus Rev 17(2):151–163. https://doi.org/10.1111/j.1741-6248.2004.00010.x
Kammerlander N, Dessi C, Bird M, Floris M, Murru A (2015) The impact of shared stories on family firm innovation: a multicase study. Fam Bus Rev 28(4):332–354. https://doi.org/10.1177/0894486515607777
Kets de Vries MFR (1993) The dynamics of family controlled firms: the good and the bad news. Organ Dyn, 59–71. 10.1016/0090-2616(93)90071-8
Kirkwood J, Harris P (2011) Beyond business: one local government's effort to help business owners with succession planning. Small Enterp Res 18(2):130–142. https://doi.org/10.5172/ser.2011.18.2.130
Koenig A, Kammerlander N, Enders A (2013) The family innovator's dilemma: how family influence affects the adoption of discontinuous technologies by incumbent firms. Acad Manag Rev 38(3):418–441. https://doi.org/10.5465/amr.2011.0162
Kotlar J, De Massis A, Frattini F, Bianchi M, Fang H (2013) Technology acquisition in family and nonfamily firms: a longitudinal analysis of Spanish manufacturing firms. J Prod Innov Manag 30(6):1073–1088. https://doi.org/10.1111/jpim.12046
Kraiczy ND, Hack A, Kellermanns FW (2014) New product portfolio performance in family firms. J Bus Res 67(6):1065–1073. https://doi.org/10.1016/j.jbusres.2013.06.005
Laforet S (2013) Innovation characteristics of young and old family-owned businesses. J Small Bus Enterp Dev 20(1):204–224. https://doi.org/10.1108/14626001311298493
Lansberg IS (1983) Managing human resources in family firms: the problem of institutional overlap. Organ Dyn 112(1):39–46. https://doi.org/10.1016/0090-2616(83)90025-6
Lansberg I (1988) The succession conspiracy. Fam Bus Rev 1(2):119–143. https://doi.org/10.1111/j.1741-6248.1988.00119.x
Le Breton-Miller I, Miller D, Steier LP (2004) Toward an integrative model of effective FOB succession. Entrepreneurship Theory Pract 28(4):305–328. https://doi.org/10.1111/j.1540-6520.2004.00047.x
Lee JH, Danes SM (2012) Uniqueness of family therapists as family business systems consultants: a cross-disciplinary investigation. J Marital Family Ther 38(1):92–104. https://doi.org/10.1111/j.1752-0606.2012.00309.x
Leotta A, Rizza C, Ruggeri D (2017) Management accounting and leadership construction in family firms. Qual Res Account Manag 14(2):189–207. https://doi.org/10.1108/QRAM-09-2015-0079
Levinson H (1971) Conflicts that plague the family business. Harvard Bus Rev 49(2):90–98
Malinen P (2004) Problems in transfer of business experienced by Finnish entrepreneurs. J Small Bus Enterp Dev 11(1):130–139. https://doi.org/10.1108/14626000410519164
Mazzola P, Marchisio G, Astrachan J (2008) Strategic planning in family business: a powerful developmental tool for the next generation. Fam Bus Rev 21(3):239–258. https://doi.org/10.1177/08944865080210030106
McGivern C (1978) The dynamics of management succession. Manag Decis 16(1):32–42

Michel A, Kammerlander N (2015) Trusted advisors in a family business's succession planning process—an agency perspective. J Fam Bus Strateg 6(1):45–57. https://doi.org/10.1016/j.jfbs.2014.10.005

Morris MH, Williams RW, Nel D (1996) Factors influencing family business succession. Int J Entrepreneurial Behav Res 2(3):68–81. https://doi.org/10.1108/13552559610153261

Morris MH, Williams RO, Allen JA, Avila RA (1997) Correlates of success in family business transition. J Bus Ventur 12(5):385–401. https://doi.org/10.1016/S0883-9026(97)00010-4

Nicholson H, Shepherd D, Woods C (2009) Advising New Zealand's family business: current issues and opportunities. Univ Auckland Bus Rev 11(1):1–7

Neubauer H (2003) The dynamics of succession in family businesses in western European countries. Fam Bus Rev 16(4):269–281. https://doi.org/10.1111/j.1741-6248.2003.tb00022.x

Obstfeld D (2005) Social networks, the tertius iungens orientation, and involvement in innovation. Adm Sci Q 50(1):100–130. https://doi.org/10.2189/asqu.2005.50.1.100

Reay T, Pearson AW, Dyer WG (2013) Advising family enterprise: examining the role of family firm advisors. Fam Bus Rev 26(3):209–214. https://doi.org/10.1177/0894486513494277

Reddrop A, Mapunda G (2015) Family businesses: seekers of advice. J Fam Bus Manag 5(1):90–115. https://doi.org/10.1108/JFBM-08-2014-0018

Rondi E, De Massis A, Kotlar J (2019) Unlocking innovation potential: a typology of family business innovation postures and the critical role of the family system. J Fam Bus Strateg. https://doi.org/10.1016/j.jfbs.2017.12.001

Salvato C, Corbetta G (2013) Transitional leadership of advisors as a facilitator of successors' leadership construction. Fam Bus Rev 26(3):235–255. https://doi.org/10.1177/0894486513490796

Sawers D, Whiting RH (2010) Perceived usefulness of business succession planning and chartered accountants' involvement in the process. Small Enterp Res 17(1):87–102. https://doi.org/10.1111/j.1741-6248.2003.tb00022.x

Schillaci CE (1990) I processi di transizione del potere imprenditoriale nelle imprese familiari. Giappichelli Editore, Torino

Sharma P (2004) An overview of the field of family business studies: current status and directions for the future. Fam Bus Rev 17(1):1–36. https://doi.org/10.1111/j.1741-6248.2004.00001.x

Sharma P, Chrisman JJ, Chua JH (1997) Strategic management of the family business: past research and future challenges. Fam Bus Rev 10(1):1–35. https://doi.org/10.1111/j.1741-6248.1997.00001.x

Sharma P, Chrisman JJ, Pablo AL, Chua JH (2001) Determinants of initial satisfaction with the succession process in family firms: a conceptual model. Entrepreneurship Theory Pract 25(3):17–36. https://doi.org/10.1177/104225870102500302

Songini L, Vola P (2015) The role of professionalization and managerialization in family business succession. Manag Control 1:9–43. https://doi.org/10.3280/MACO2015-001002

Steier L (2001) Next-generation entrepreneurs and succession: an exploratory study of modes and means of managing social capital. Fam Bus Rev 14(3):259–276. https://doi.org/10.1111/j.1741-6248.2001.00259.x

Strike VM (2012) Advising the family firm: reviewing the past to build the future. Fam Bus Rev 25(2):156–177. https://doi.org/10.1177/0894486511431257

Strike VM (2013) The most trusted advisor and the subtle advice process in family firms. Fam Bus Rev 26(3):293–313. https://doi.org/10.1177/0894486513492547

Su E, Dou J (2013) How does knowledge sharing among advisors from different disciplines affect the quality of the services provided to the family business client? An investigation from the family business advisor's perspective. Fam Bus Rev 26(3):256–270. https://doi.org/10.1177/0894486513491978

Swartz S (1989) The challenges of multidisciplinary consulting to family-owned businesses. Fam Bus Rev 2(4):329–339. https://doi.org/10.1111/j.1741-6248.1989.tb00002.x

Tagiuri R, Davis J (1996) Bivalent attributes of the family firms. Fam Bus Rev 9(2):199–208. https://doi.org/10.1111/j.1741-6248.1996.00199.x

Tàpies J, Fernández Moya M (2012) Values and longevity in family business: evidence from a cross-cultural analysis. J Fam Bus Manag 2(2):130–146. https://doi.org/10.1108/20436231211261871

Ward JL (1987) Keeping the family business healthy: how to plan for continuing growth profitability and family leadership. Jossey-Bass, San Francisco

Ward JL (2004) Perpetuating the family business. 50 Lessons learned from long-lasting, successful families in business. Palgrave Macmillan, New York

Weesie E (2017) Psychological barriers in business transfers. How to cope with the transfer of SME ownership. Ph.D. Dissertation, Proefschriftmaken.nl

Westhead P (2003) Succession decision-making outcomes reported by private family companies. Int Small Bus J 21(4):369–401. https://doi.org/10.1177/02662426030214001

Zellweger T (2017) Managing the family business theory and practice. Edward Elgar, Cheltenham, UK

Zellweger TM, Eddleston KA, Kellermanns FW (2010) Exploring the concept of familiness: introducing family firm identity. J Fam Bus Strateg 1(1):54–63. https://doi.org/10.1016/j.jfbs.2009.12.003

The Growth of Family Businesses: The Path to Internationalization

Elena Cristiano

Abstract The internationalization of businesses is among the most examined topics in both the economic and management literature. The growing competitive pressures deriving from the emerging countries set new challenges and push, above all, the small- and medium-sized enterprises (SMEs), to search for new paths of international development. In the current economic scenario, the crucial role of SMEs is undeniable, which in most cases are family businesses, in international contexts. Therefore, it is interesting to focus the attention on the identification of the successful strategic factors, which characterize the internationalization models of SMEs, in particular family businesses, and of the internal and external conditions which allow their introduction in the widest international circuits and the admission to advanced forms of internationalization which, besides the simple merchant form, develops through productive delocalizations, openings of the value chain and international reorganizations of the supply chain. The chapter aims at illustrating the connection between the purpose of the family, who is the proprietor of the business, to preserve, enrich, share and acquire the entrepreneurial and management capacities, which are typical of the family business, and the choices concerning the convenience to foreign expansion and the modalities of entry in the markets. In this way, it is highlighted that the choice of pursuing the internationalization strategy, as well as the modality through which it is possible to carry out it, is influenced not only (in any case not exclusively) by the business dimensions, but also rather by the peculiarities of the family business.

Keywords Family business · Internationalization · Strategic alliances · Delocalization · International growth

---

E. Cristiano (✉)
Department of Business Economics and Law, University of Calabria, Rende, Italy
e-mail: elena.cristiano@unical.it

A. Leotta (ed.), *Management Controlling and Governance of Family Businesses*,
Contributions to Management Science,
https://doi.org/10.1007/978-3-030-47741-7_5

1 Introduction

The topic of the international competitiveness of businesses is extremely current, especially in the light of the recent changes in the world economy. The growing competitive pressures deriving from the emerging countries set new challenges and push, above all, the small- and medium-sized enterprises (SMEs), to search for new paths of international development. The internationalization of businesses is among the most examined topics in both the economic and management literature: the first one deals with the reasons with reference to the opening towards foreign markets, whereas the second one is more focused on knowing the implications of the presence of a business out of the domestic context where it works. The prevailing literature of *International Business* and *Strategic Management* has mainly dealt with the problems concerning big businesses (Johanson and Vahlne 1977; Cantwell and Piscitello 2000). Only starting from the second half of the 90s of the past century, studies at issue, contextually to studies with regard to *Entrepreneurship*, have equally, if not more, focused on the processes of internationalization of the smallest businesses (Lu and Beamish 2001), in most cases family businesses. In the past, the insufficient interest in the study of the dynamics of the international growth of the family business was due to the fact that, for a long time, family business has been considered an organizational form of transition, prevailing in the initial phase of the business life cycle, and destined to evolve in the managerial model in order to allow significant rates of growth and profitability. Such concept attributed some typical features to the family business, thus identifying it with the small-medium-sized business, characterized by slow rates of growth and by a centralized and scarcely formalized organizational structure, based on self-financing policies and mechanisms of internal succession, which was often well-established in advantageous local contexts (e.g. industrial districts and clusters), which was implicitly little innovative in technological terms, and generally less oriented towards the international expansion, if compared to the managerial business. In time, the studies on the dynamics of the business growth have contradicted this point of view, thus highlighting the presence of strongly dynamic family businesses, which have succeeded in acquiring, rapidly and with an international echo, strategies of strong international expansion, which have been successfully pursued. Despite the dynamism shown by these businesses also on an international level, there are some factors which cannot be ignored: there are financial, information, organizational, strategic, management, entrepreneurial difficulties and limitations that businesses encounter when operating according to some multinational prospects and that, in most cases, impede the accumulation of knowledge on international markets and the formation of a global culture. This may allow the development of the exploratory model, but it does not facilitate the passage towards more complex models of internationalization, which require the management of a division of labour at an international level. In the current economic scenario, the crucial role of SMEs is undeniable, which in most cases are family businesses, in international contexts. Therefore, it is interesting to focus the attention on the identification of the successful strategic factors, which characterize the internationalization models of SMEs and of the internal and external conditions which allow their introduction in the widest international circuits and the admission to advanced forms of internationalization which, besides the simple merchant form, develops through productive delocalizations, openings of the value chain and international reorganizations of the supply chain. Generally, the issues of internationalization concern the reasons (why), the convenience or not to the expansion abroad (if), the modalities of entry in the markets (how), the timing of choices (when) and the degree of internationalization (how much). With reference to family businesses, such aspects follow particular dynamics, thus considering their peculiarity, and they have different configurations according to how ownership and management interact between them. Moreover, considering different approaches according to which internationalization may be examined (economic, process-related, relational, of resources and capacities), the family business represents an interesting context of analysis with reference to the approach of resources and capacities. Therefore, this chapter aims at illustrating the connection between the purpose of the family, who is the proprietor of the business, to preserve, enrich, share and acquire the entrepreneurial and management capacities, which are typical of the family business, and the choices concerning the convenience to foreign expansion and the modalities of entry in the markets. In this way, it is highlighted that the choice of pursuing the internationalization strategy, as well as the modality through which it is possible to carry out it, is influenced not only (in any case not exclusively) by the business dimensions, but also rather by the peculiarities of the family business. Starting from the study of the elements which characterize the family business, it is possible, more conveniently, to understand and analyse the expansion paths on foreign markets. In this perspective, particular attention is given to the *Social Emotional Wealth* (SEW) theory which, starting from the theory of the behaviour (first and foremost the agency theory), affirms that family businesses, which are owned and managed by the family, evaluate their choices and, consequently, the relating decisions on the protection of the family assets, to be intended in a wide sense. Family assets are the result of all the values that the family shares with and wants to transmit to the business and which inevitably influence its management and control (the overlapping between family and business). As all the other businesses, also the family ones should guarantee their own growth by catching the international opportunities, by enlarging, in such way, their basis of market, knowledge and skills. Anyway, if compared to the other businesses, family businesses might encounter greater difficulties to undertake internationalization paths for the high costs deriving from such choices and for the complexity of the management of activities, which are carried out in different markets, also at a geographical level. Another limitation that family businesses might encounter in undertaking the internationalization of their activity is represented by the shortage of capital to be destined in this respect. In this case, it might be necessary that the family assigns a share of ownership in order to be able to access the capital necessary to make the investment on foreign markets. In any case, the family is not always willing to give away a share of ownership which, however, would change the structure of the business in terms both of management and administration. In the absence of adequate skills inside the family, who owns and manages the business, moreover, it might be necessary to hire non-family managers in order to manage the path to internationalization more adequately. Nevertheless, it is often possible to encounter resistance with regard to this decision, and this might represent a further obstacle for fulfilling such path. An opportunity of growth for the family business, as the opening towards foreign markets is, may be represented by the entry of the new generations, a typical process of family businesses. Therefore, there are different typical elements of the family business (governance, organizational culture, management practices, succession) which may, in different ways, influence the choice of the internationalization process and the modalities through which it may be pursued.

2 Family Management and the Process of Internationalization: A Review of Literature

The understanding of the strategies for the internationalization of the family business may not disregard the dynamics existing between the *family,* which owns/controls the business, and its members, thus including those who are part of the business, even if they are not family members. Therefore, above all, it is necessary to identify the subjects who have the leadership and control of the business, and, especially, it is necessary to distinguish them on the basis of their membership or not to the proprietor family. Moreover, it is useful to understand the generation to which the subjects of the management and of the governance belong and the relationship with the founder/proprietor family. The symbiosis between family and business, which is the basis of the peculiar organizational culture and of its management practices, influences the modalities of definition and fulfilment of the business strategies, and therefore, it has to be considered in the analysis of the processes of internationalization. Since family businesses are characterized by a greater cohesion and shared strategic point of view, by minor conflicts and greater stability of the organizational culture, they tend to pursue defensive strategies which emphasize the production efficiency and the conservation, differently from what occurs for non-family businesses and without a "parental" control of the management, which tend more to seize innovations and explore new fields. The widespread attitude of aversion to risk might impede from catching entrepreneurial opportunities with greater aggression and, so, inhibit the pursuit of strategies of growth abroad. For this reason, the level of internationalization of family businesses might result lower if compared to other business contexts. As a proof of the negative influence of the family ownership on the choices of internationalization, there are numerous studies which highlight how the family nature of the business inhibits the tendency to pursue paths of opening towards foreign markets, even more if there is the presence of minority shareholders, who make pressure on the decision-makers, thus limiting the autonomy in long-term choices (Arregle et al. 2017). Nevertheless, with the succession of the new generations, in particular from the second on, such tendency seems, in some cases, to be lessened, thus highlighting a greater propensity to the reinforced internationalization, if there are local cooperation agreements, joint ventures or export groups (i.e. alliances) or forms of capital investment in the business activities carried out by another organization or by a remarkable shareholder, who is a non-family member (Fernández and Nieto 2006). The process of internationalization may be also limited by factors, which are both internal, such as the attitude of the top management and the internal organization of the business, and external, such as the competitive environment (Gallo and Pont 1996). Nonetheless, recent observations of the phenomenon show that the ownership and the involvement of the family positively influence the choices of the internationalization process (Zahra 2003) and that the international performance of family businesses is as profitable as the one made by similar non-family businesses (Carr and Bateman 2009); analogously, it is observed that the tendency to the internationalization of family businesses is high and, in not few cases, also greater than the internationalization of non-family businesses (Chen et al. 2014; Muñoz-Bullón and Sanchez Bueno 2012; Piva et al. 2013). Other more recent studies have highlighted a positive correlation between the family business and internationalization in the presence of managers, who are external to the family in the top management team, with an effect which is inversely proportional to the intensity with which the objectives of the SEW theory are mirrored on the business strategic management. This result is, however, in line with the aversion to the risk, which is typical of the family business (Vandekerkhof et al. 2015). Finally, other studies show that the interaction between the greater family ownership and the institutional ownership positively influences the decisions of internationalization (Chen et al. 2014).

A third group of studies, finally, has not highlighted significant differences between family business and non-family business with regard to the tendency to start the process of internationalization, though it may be observed that greater resistance is encountered in family businesses, which the family is not only the proprietor of, but also the manager of (George et al. 2005; Schmid et al. 2015). Moreover, in different examples of Chinese family businesses, it may be observed a positive connection between internationalization and growth and a negative connection between internationalization and earning power, though the earning power decreases in the presence of a substantial support by the corporate governance (Lu et al. 2015).

In this respect, from the synthesis of the research studies, some not univocal results may be observed with regard to the behaviour of the family businesses in the choices of internationalization and the reasons may be attributed to different elements. Firstly, the heterogeneity of these businesses has to be considered in relation to the ownership, governance and management, thus distinguishing them for their attitude to the diversification in *family-owned* and *family-managed* businesses (Arregle et al. 2012; Chrisman et al. 2005). In this respect, it is useful to underline that the decision of internationalizing is influenced by the interaction between the potential incoming business, with its internal elements, and the context where it is integrated, which is the source of contacts and information and so of competitive advantage. Given the distinctive characteristics, for the family business, such theory is still more significant.

3 The Process of Internationalization

The opening of businesses towards international markets represents one of the main strategies of growth for businesses, through which “a firm expands the sales of its goods or services across the borders of global regions and countries into different geographic locations or markets”.[1]

The choices relating to the fact if it is opportune to internationalize are typically oriented to evaluate opportunity and/or necessity, an evaluation in which numerous variables come into play. Among them, there is the pursuit of different forms of economy (economy of scale, economy of experience, learning economy) and of market power, with the consequent increase in the total share and the diversification of the risk (Gande et al. 2009); the access to not available resources, in terms of quantity and/or quality, or which are very expensive at a domestic level (Niosi and Tschang 2009); the cost abatement (Andersen 1997); the search for innovation (Prange and Verdier 2011); the greater return on capital employed in R&D (Kafours et al. 2008); the acquisition of new knowledge or advantages of location (Cafferata 1993); the improvement of performances (Hitt et al. 1997). In relation to such opportunities, different difficulties exist, among which the costs of coordination of the activity of expansion abroad, which increase when there is an increase also of the expansion of the geographical and cultural distance between the country of origin and the country of destination of the investment, considering also the uncertainty which characterizes it. In fact, the incoming business might be in the condition of having to face problems relating to cultural, institutional, juridical and logistical differences of the host country (the liability of foreignness). In order to reduce the effect of such local complexity, the incoming business might have necessity to legitimize it at a local level, also through actions of partnership. In doctrine, there are different approaches in the study of the internationalization process. The first one (the Foreign Direct Investment) explains such phenomenon through the *eclectic* paradigm, according to which the choice of the form and of the location of destination of the opening towards international markets is based on the costs of transactions, with the convenience to “internalize” the most expensive ones and those with a greater risk degree. In contrast to such approach, there is the model Uppsala (the *processual* school), which affirms that international expansion may occur through an incremental process which positively feels the effect of the cognitive improvement and of experience deriving from a greater and greater learning and involvement in the foreign activity. In this way, the risk and uncertainty are reduced, since, at least in an initial phase, there is a movement towards nearer locations, both culturally and geographically, in order to have the possibility to acquire greater familiarity when operating in international contexts. The greater acquired acknowledgement allows businesses to move also towards more distant locations. A third reference approach, which is based on a relational approach (the social network), intends internationalization as the product of the intercurrent relationships between the business stakeholders and the external network, which it is part of and from which it obtains important resources and information. Therefore, the

[1] Hitt et al. (2007, p. 251).

opportunity to diversify a business depends on the intensity with which the business influences the context where its activity is carried out. The three approaches, which have been previously synthesized, have represented the basis of the development of the management literature at issue, which has examined the processes of internationalization, thus analysing, at different levels, the connections among the factors which favour/limit them. A first level of analysis focuses on the cultural background and on the international experience of each individual manager (the individual level) and on the diversity of structure and dimensions of the team of top managers (the group level). Such analysis aims at understanding the influence (either encouraging or limiting) of the individual peculiarities of each decision-maker, including those present inside the team, with regard to the typologies of the business strategic choices, thus including the internationalization. As far as the managerial team is concerned, among the examined aspects, there is one element which is very important: the dimensions which might have a direct and positive correlation with the choices of the internationalization process, which is as greater as its structure is wider and more heterogeneous. A second level of analysis focuses on the distinction between factors, which are internal and external to the business, thus distinguishing them in relation to the incidence on the decisions to internationalize. The factors, which are internal to the business (the *firm-specific* factors), are the dimensions, the age, the strategy, the organizational procedures, the degree of diversification of the product and of innovation. The factors, which are external to the business, are typically distinguished into two groups, that is, they are referred to the sector (the *industry-specific* factors), such as the level of the demand and the competitive structure; to the country (the *country-specific* factors), such as the cultural, juridical, political-economic, institutional characteristics. In the first group the structure of the sector represents, for sure, the most important factor with regard to the choice of internationalization, since its constitutive elements (the presence of barriers at the entry/exit, the presence of the competing businesses and their degree of concentration; the market power relating to competitive businesses; the current and potential level of demand; the presence of businesses which form the value chain) influence the advantage or not to invest in a specified sector. In the second group (the *country-specific* factors), the factors are distinguished on the basis of the country either of origin of those businesses which internationalize, or of destination of the internationalization (the *target*). In relation to the first of the two factors, generally, businesses coming from the most developed countries, which have greater international experience, have a greater institutional support, also at a financial level[2]; vice versa, businesses coming from emerging countries have less resources available and, above all, limited experience of internationalization, especially with regard to the dynamics of specific institutional contexts. As regards, the country of the concerned internationalization, the element which will mostly influence the success of the process, is represented by the affinity between the culture of the incoming business and the culture of the targeted country and, above

[2]In this respect, policies and instruments supporting internationalization, carried out by various bodies (MED the Ministry of Economic Development, FTI, Foreign Trade Institute, CIPE, the Interministerial Committee for Economic Planning) may be considered.

all, the opening and containment capacity of the market of products offered by the incoming business. In this ambit, burocratical variables are particularly remarkable, especially at a normative and regulatory level, of the targeted country; the burocratical costs which the incoming business shall have to bear in order to deal with the new location; the political, economic and financial-monetary stability; the local policy, which is followed *vis-à-vis* the investments coming from abroad.

3.1 Internationalization and Performances

One of the motivations according to which businesses expand their market beyond national borders concerns the improvement of their performances. It is for this reason that it is necessary to carry out an accurate analysis both of the resources, which are available inside the business, of the opportunities that it may have, and of the modalities through which such activity may be carried out. In the past, the studies at issue highlighted a positive correlation between the process of internationalization and performances, thus considering the scope and degree of the internationalization. Such assertion derives from the observation of the increase of the market power and of the various economies, which are pursued following the most important presence of the businesses in various countries, in terms both of the degree of internationalization (the degree of internationalization, DOI), an expression of the turnover made by the business beyond the national borders, and of the scope of the firm international business, measured by the number of countries (Zahra 2003; George et al. 2005; Naldi and Norqvist 2008) or by geographical macro-regions (Cerrato and Piva 2012) towards which the business exports or in which it sells its products and by the number of foreign branches (Sherman et al. 1998). Most recently, studies have highlighted that as the international diversification grows, businesses increase their experience, thus accessing to new resources and knowledge and succeeding, in this way, in reducing the high costs connected to such activity (the learning effect). Nevertheless, experience has shown that for very low or very high levels of international diversification, the connection among the variables becomes negative, since the costs of coordination are not compensated by the benefits which derive from the international expansion. In the light of such observations, it may be understood how the topic of internationalization is complex, since there are many connections to be considered, there are different levels of analysis and there are numerous factors to be taken into consideration. Such complexity grows if, in particular, family businesses are considered: compared to the other typologies of businesses, they have peculiar characteristics, which magnify the effects of the factors which influence the choices of internationalization.

3.2 Location, Timing, Degree and Forms of Internationalization

The *location* of the investment abroad is represented by the country where the business opts for destining its activity of internationalization. Such choice is influenced by some factors, which are external to the business and specific of the sector (the *industry-specific* factors) and of the country (the *country-specific* factors), which often determine also the choice of the modality, through which the business accesses the foreign market, and of the investment timing. The choice of the location is strictly connected to the degree of attractiveness of the sector, which is expressed through the market potential, represented by its dimensions and by its growth potential, and through the risk of the investment. The attractiveness of the sector shows the probability that market can either develop, with the passing of time, a greater absorption of the offered products, or offer market inputs at lower costs or, in any case, lower than those that the incoming business would bear in the country of origin. The risk of the investment shows the uncertainty, which is perceived by the incoming business with regard to the location, considering also the current and potential political-economic conditions of the country of destination. The degree of the attractiveness of the sector of destination of the expansion abroad grows when the perception of the stability of the location increases. Many evaluations for the choice of the *location* can be useful also for the choice relating to the *timing* of entry, that is, the most adequate choice of the time within which the process of entry in the foreign market may be carried out. It is strictly connected to the choices of the location and of the modality of entry in the foreign country, and it is influenced by factors that are internal and external to the business, the first ones being prevailing. Among the internal factors, there are the particularly important resources and capacities, which the incoming business has; among the external factors, there are the environmental conditions and the structure of the sector. Finally, there are some firms, which were born as internationalized (the *born global* firms) or which pursue strategies of internationalization in the early years of their activity (the *early internationalizing* firms), thus obtaining the competitive advantage for the rapidity of the action (the first mover of the advantage). The choices of timing are generally distinguished in early choices (rapid choices) and in delayed choices (cautious choices). The early choices are made in the presence of opportunities to be rapidly seized on, and therefore, they need reassuring information with regard to the risk of the investment and of a greater flexibility (the modality of non-equity entry). Instead, the delayed choices are made after an accurate analysis of the elements which determine the investment, such as the growth potential of the location, the benefits deriving from the investment and the costs of entry. The tendency towards the one or the other choice shall also depend on the availability of the business resources and on the purpose for which the activity of expansion abroad is carried out. The timing depends also on the choices of the location which, it is not excluded, may be also more than one at the same time. In this case, the timing might vary according to the effect that it has on the factors (internal and external factors) of the competitive advantage. For example, it might be more opportune, in some locations, to make a rapid entry in order to seize on, in advance, compared to the competing undertakings, the opportunities offered by the foreign market of destination and delay the entry in the location, where there are greater uncertainties connected to the risk of the investment. As a matter of fact, businesses with acquired international experience are more inclined to make choices of early entry in the foreign markets, also if they have to accept a higher risk.

A further element to be analysed is the degree of internationalization which, just for its determination, detects in what measure foreign sales relate to the domestic ones. In some cases, it may represent also a valid support tool in the evaluations of the effect of the foreign activity on business performances.

The degree of internationalization (DOI) may be measured in terms of the correlation between foreign sales and total sales *(Foreign sales/Total sales).* Such indicator (FSTS) is the most widespread in the literature (Zahra 2003; Fernandez and Nieto 2006; Gomez-Mejia et al. 2007; Calabrò 2013; Oesterle et al. 2013), both for the facility to find and elaborate information and for a matter of comparability among the results deriving from different studies. Other indicators concern the correlation between foreign assets and total assets, or FATA (Foreign assets/Total assets); the correlation between foreign employees and total employees, or FETE (Foreign employees/Total employees); the correlation between foreign subsidiaries and total subsidiaries (Foreign subsidiaries/Total subsidiaries). The international business scope of the enterprise is measured through the number of countries (Zahra 2003; George et al. 2005; Naldi and Norqvist 2008) or geographical macro-regions (Cerrato and Piva 2012), where the enterprise exports or sells its own products, and through the number of foreign branches (Sherman et al. 1998). The evaluation of the degree of internationalization of the business has to be made on the whole, thus combining the results of various indicators. Nevertheless, it is not always possible to have all the demanded data available, and therefore, sometimes it is not possible to exactly indicate the scope of the international activities carried out by the business.

In the implementation of the process of international growth, it is important to consider the modality of entry in the foreign market, which shall be chosen in relation to the kind of proprietary asset which is intended to be established. In other words, it is necessary to identify the most adequate instrument in relation to the degree of control/autonomy to have on the/to leave to the subsidiary. The modalities of entry in foreign markets are generally distinguished into two groups, that is, *equity* and *non-equity* groups. In the first group, there are the most expensive and complex instruments, that is, the property subsidiaries (i.e. the *greenfield investments*), acquisitions and some types of alliances (the *joint ventures* and alliances called the *swaps,* which consider crossed exchanges of shares). Such instruments are used in case of more durable investments, which are not flexible and at a high risk and which, therefore, are accurately expected and planned. In the second group, there are the less expensive instruments, such as exports and some kinds of alliances which have forms of collaboration on a basis which is not based on shares, but it is contractual (i.e. the franchising and the licensing contract). Exports represent the instrument which is more widely used especially in the initial phase of the expansion abroad and, frequently, in the countries which are less far from those of origin, both for cost reasons and for plausible cultural affinities. They may be managed by the exporter or directly through structures abroad through which he/she exercises the control both on the local distribution and on the marketing or, indirectly, by entrusting the local intermediaries with the commercial management of the exported products (a solution which is preferred by small and medium-sized businesses). Such instrument of internationalization is generally adopted by those businesses which do not own sufficient resources for the use of more expensive instruments, even if at a higher degree of control; they have limited, if not absent, experience in international markets, and for this reason, they prefer to explore the opportunity of growth abroad before making more expensive and engaging investments; they intend to minimize the risk, thus preferring more flexible instruments which allow to modify, at any time, the strategic choice; they want to enter the foreign market rapidly, aiming at increasing the volume of sales in order to increase the market power, the possible scale economies and the action range, without using, in any case, a considerable number of resources. Exports, even if they are expensive, do not allow to control the activity abroad directly and to learn knowledge at a local level. The businesses, which intend to have a greater control, to defend their competitive advantage and increase their knowledge on the location in order to obtain/increase advantages of location, should address their choice towards more complex instruments. A first step might be represented by alliances, that is, by an agreement between two businesses or among more businesses which have the same interest. In this case, the common interest might be represented by the expansion towards a foreign country and the alliance might be either among more businesses of different origins, all having the purpose of internationalizing their activities, or among foreign businesses and a local business, the involvement of which might allow to access the local contacts and its specific knowledge of the targeted location. Alliances may be classified on the basis of the objectives of the collaboration (i.e. the exploration of new resources, the exploitation of the innovation); on the basis of the geographical origin of the partners (domestic or international); on the basis of the proprietary structure (equity and non-equity); on the basis of the core business of the partners (who are connected in different phases and in the same phases of the value chain); on the basis of the duration of the agreement (temporaneous or permanent). In the presence of a certain degree of uncertainty and in order to implement the entry in the new market, the incoming business might be willing to share the risk of the investment with a partner business, usually a local one, thus forming an alliance through which two or more businesses have a share (equal or different in relation to the respective assets) of the third business (the so-called *joint venture*). *Joint ventures* are subject to the risk of a possible conflict among partners also in relation to the objectives and strategies to be followed, since they are not established by a decision-maker. Such instrument is preferred by the businesses, which need to know the location well through what the local partner knows about it, which are willing to obtain the support of the new location through the agreement with the local partner, which have the possibility to enter the market with a certain rapidity, thus demolishing the barriers at the entry. A modality which implies, for the incoming business, higher levels of commitment and of use of resources is represented by the acquisitions through which the incoming business (the purchaser) acquires the majority block of shares of a targeted business (the targeted one), which has its registered office in the country of the internationalization process. Through the acquisitions, the purchaser business has the possibility to access the local knowledge of the targeted business in order to improve its innovative capacity and/or its competitive advantage; to overcome the barriers at the entry through the control of products and customers of the targeted business; to diversify the total risk of the business; to increase its own market power, thus entering new businesses or new geographical areas. Finally, a further form of internationalization is the *greenfield* investment, through which a business creates a subsidiary or a proprietary branch, via which it may enter the foreign market without the support of a local or foreign partner. Such investment has the highest degree of control, and therefore, it is the most expensive, and it needs more time to be made and reduces, at the minimum, the flexibility of the investment. Its adoption is opportune when the incoming business needs to defend its own proprietary advantage, without risking the imitation and diffusion; it intends to avoid the transfer of knowledge, which is typical of alliances and acquisitions and the sharing of the decision-making power; it wants to let the subsidiary be the basis from which the expansion towards other foreign markets may be implemented (Fig. 1).

Generally, the cost of the modality of entry shall be as much higher as greater the degree of control to have on the subsidiary shall be. The choice of the instrument to be used for entering foreign markets shall also depend on the degree of flexibility which is intended to keep in the investment in such activity. If there is the possibility to give up or modify the investment, at any time (flexibility), it is then opportune to use less engaging instruments or *non-equity* instruments (i.e. *exports or licensing contracts*) or *equity* instruments at reduced shareholding (i.e. *swap alliances or joint ventures*). Each type of the used investment has advantages and disadvantages. The high-control instruments allow a greater accordance of the objectives of the subsidiary with those of the incoming business, against, nevertheless, greater costs, uses of resources and risks. Vice versa, the instruments at more reduced control have minor costs, uses

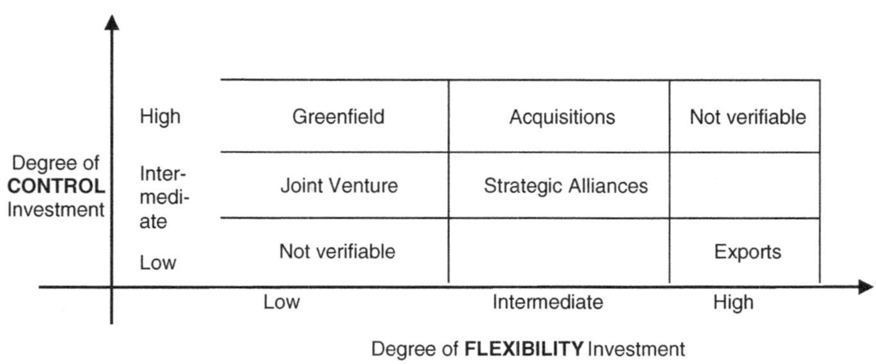

Fig. 1 Classification of the modalities of internationalization

of resources and risks for the incoming business, but they leave broader autonomy margins to the subsidiary, thus facilitating any opportunistic behaviours.

4 The Strategies for Internationalization and the Family Business

As for all the other typologies of business, also for family businesses, the choice to access foreign markets may represent a condition of convenience or of necessity which, in any case, is influenced by the emotional and business needs connected to the use of resources and capacities. In describing how such choices are finally made, inside family businesses, it is necessary to consider different configurations of ownership and management.

In the *family-centred* business, the need for preserving the internal entrepreneurial and managerial capacities prevails over any other choice, the choice of the expansion beyond national borders included. Since it is a need which often is more emotional than business-type, often the decision not to expand towards foreign markets prevails, in order not to compromise some capacities, which are considered critical for the survival of the family business, such as the knowledge of the territory, the acceptance of a lower risk profile and the capacity of seizing opportunities only inside the national territory. In this ambit, internationalization is not seen as an opportunity of growth: the international experience is represented by sporadic episodes of export for orders coming from foreign customers. Instead, when business needs are prevailing, if compared to the emotional needs, it is possible that the proprietor family makes more favourably the decision to open to foreign markets, if from these markets the business may have fundamental benefits. In the *market-oriented* family business, the needs connected to the entrepreneurial and managerial capacities are different, since the managerial ones prevail over the entrepreneurial ones, given the presence of subjects, who are external to the family in the proprietary configuration. Moreover, business needs seem more markedly to be present, whereas the emotional dimension tends to vanish. In these conditions, the tendency to a growth on foreign markets is greater. The family business considers any opportunity of competitive growth positively and, therefore, is more favourable to an expansion abroad which may be useful to this end. Should not the *market-oriented* family business have the specific managerial capacities, there would be a greater opening to acquisition processes of new skills which are added to the family's ones in its possession. In the *investor-centred* family business, instead, the needs connected to the capacities are further different, if compared to the two configurations, which have been previously illustrated. The presence of a non-family partner, who is important and decisive for the destiny of the family business, significantly orients the choice whether it is convenient to follow the internationalization process or not. In the hypothesis of an investor, who enters the family group in replacement of other family proprietors, the situation is not dissimilar from the situation of *family-centred* businesses, even if the external partner is for sure more qualified and may have further capacities and skills, which the family business needs. The case is different when the investor enters the family group, thus generating equity for the growth. In this situation, since the objective of the business fast growth is a priority if compared to other alternatives, the choice if undertaking or not the process of internationalization is strongly influenced by such desire of growth. There is a further case, when the investor enters the family group in order to lighten or solve a situation of crisis inside the business. In these situations, the need for survival prevails and the family business considers the international expansion an opportunity to be exploited in order to solve such crisis. The choices relating to the modalities of entering foreign markets and the decisions of internationalization of the value chain are strongly influenced, once again, by the family configurations and by the needs connected to the managerial and entrepreneurial capacities, which are necessary to maintain the profile of family business. In the *family-centred* model, the emotional need to keep the control on the acquired and fundamental capacities to compete might, once the path to internationalization has been chosen, lead to the choice of the modality of exports rather than of a policy of direct investments which may jeopardize the control of the critical resources. Actually, the path to internationalization, which is mostly performed by family businesses, above all by the Italian ones, is represented by the export with all its limits, also the limits concerning the knowledge of the targeted market, which derive from it. In its turn, export is almost always practised in the indirect modality, through the recourse to an intermediary, in order to reduce the risks connected to the entry in a foreign market. The direct export, nevertheless, is more widespread in those cases in which the family business, once its familiarity with the foreign country has been acquired, does not intend to renounce the direct control of the capacities and resources which it considers as critical in order to compete. In the *market-oriented* model, the dominance of managerial positions leads family businesses, which decide to internationalize, to pursue even more aggressive modalities of entry in foreign markets. Among these modalities, the choice often relapses on the opening of a sale branch or a production branch directly in the foreign country where the family business has chosen to operate, in most cases it is a branch which is controlled by one of its own managers. In this way, the emotional need to not lose the control well conciliates with the business need to seize opportunities where the foreign market allows to do it. A further element to be taken into consideration in the case of family businesses is the way through which such activity is financed, that is, through its own resources, modalities of partnership or acquisitions. Once again, with regard to such choices, the nature of the real needs and the business financial liquidity are significant. For example, if the business has adequate financial resources and does not intend to lose the control of the new acquired capacities, it shall opt for acquisitions or for its own direct investments. In those cases in which the business need is prevailing, a further opportunity has to be taken into consideration, the opportunity of a partnership with foreign subjects in which the benefits of the collaboration shall be considered more positively than the risks of damage of control. In the *investor-centred* model, the variety of proprietary configurations, which is possible inside the model for the different nature and different roles of the private investor, may open a still wider spectrum of entry modes, according to how the external partner considers the contribution or not of a foreign partner as important, the strategic modality of an exclusive entry, the advantage to perform a cheap-money acquisition, the critical importance of some partnerships, which are already consolidated. In these cases, it is not infrequent that the investor contributes with some further entrepreneurial and managerial capacities which the family business is more lacking in, and so, the choices relating to the instruments to be adopted for internationalization are mostly influenced by the business needs and less by the emotional ones.

Consequently, the presence of the family in the property and/or in the business supervisory bodies, with its prevalently conservative nature, influences the choices of modality of entry in foreign markets. In a SEW prospect, such presence shall lead family businesses to make more traditional and less risky choices; such tendency weakens in the presence of young generations which might be more inclined to riskier forms of internationalization, such as acquisitions or joint ventures, and/or to hire external professionals, who are capable to support such choice.

In short, the greater presence of the family in the business ownership and/or in the control bodies facilitates the adoption of more complex instruments of internationalization, equity-type, such as the greenfield. Vice versa, such tendency is reduced with the presence, in the business, of, at least, a successor and/or non-family managers.

5 The Process of Internationalization as the Driving Force of the Change of the Family Business

As it is known, family businesses are identified for their conservative nature, which is unfavourable to the risk. There is a conflict between the desire to transfer, to the future generations, the benefits deriving from the activity of the business in which the *family* has invested its own assets on one side and the necessity to adequate to the new market prospects, which more and more orient businesses to investments beyond national borders. Generally, the processes of expansion and of the international expansion in particular imply the necessity to be equipped with new assets which, once the peculiarities have been considered, expose the family business to new forms of debt, to a loss of the control and to the influence of non-family members with regard to the strategic management. Moreover, often it is necessary to resort to skills which are external to the business which inevitably determine a further loss of the control of the decisions. All these factors might inhibit the process of growth through the expansion abroad or orient the choice of the location towards countries, which are culturally close. Therefore, often the internationalization process implies some changes, which, for family businesses, turn out to be more complicated. The change, which is more frequently adopted in order to introduce innovative elements, is the replacement of the management: a replacement that, in a non-family business, might occur without particular blows, whereas it becomes more difficult in a family business. In a family business, it could be represented by the succession to the control of a new generation composed of younger family members, who are capable of reconsidering the business, which has been adopted until then. But not always the new generations have the same incentives or, simply, the same capacities, which led the predecessors to success. Therefore, in these cases, in the presence of a strong motivation to expansion, it shall be necessary to hire non-family managers (who are also descendants from the founders), that is, subjects who have adequate know-how and experience and with a wider and more innovative point of view. This openness reduces the rigidity which is typical of the family business, often created also by the entrepreneur's attitude, who, with the passing of time, since he/she feels more responsible *vis-à-vis* the family and the descendants, increases his/her natural aversion to the risk. Also, the composition of the Board, often characterized by the excessive presence of the family's members, may represent an obstacle to internationalization just for its conservative nature. In order to overcome such obstacle, it would be beneficial to introduce, inside such governance authority, some non-family members, who are capable of offering alternative orientations to the management's choices and of generating new knowledge and information. Therefore, in short, in the presence of a strong conservative nature, in order to be able to undertake paths of international growth, it shall be necessary to create a culture which considers the change and the periodical transformation of the business model, thus encouraging the openness to ideas coming from outside or from new generations. The management of the change, in fact, may depend on the ability shown by the family business to know how to open the administration structure to non-family members. According to some studies (i.e. George et al. 2005; Cerrato and Piva 2012; Calabrò 2013), in fact, there is a correlation between the path to internationalization and the introduction of a CEO or of non-family proprietors, just as the introduction of non-family members in bodies, as the case of the Board is. The introduction in the governance of non-family members positively influences the change management, since they may help the business in the processes of expansion abroad, thus providing for not only advice and assistance, but, sometimes, also for contacts with other businesses with which it is possible to work together and access new channels of information and support. Considering the complexity of the management of the internationalization path, in family businesses, there is now the tendency to hire, inside the Board, non-family members who may contribute to the process of expansion abroad, thus providing for additional knowledge, experience and abilities that the founder or the top management might not have in that particular moment. On the contrary, studies have shown that the absence, in the Board, of non-family members reduces the possibility to undertake paths of international growth, thus limiting the access to important resources to this end and thus increasing the aversion to the risk. Some authors, by showing the positive effects on the choices of expansion deriving from their support, distinguish the non-family members on the basis of their background and experience. They highlight the role of the *business experts*, that is, of those who, having already developed similar paths for their own businesses, provide support to the business, or of the *support specialists*, that is, those who support the business, providing either legal knowledge or contacts with the capital market. Such opening determines the transformation of the traditional family business into a family business which is managed by professional managers, who are responsible for the decision-making process. Nevertheless, it is opportune that the family practises, in any case, an effective supervision *vis-à-vis* the external managers not for limiting the degree of freedom through which they decide, but rather for avoiding that they work in their exclusive interest.

In the process of internationalization, an important role is played by the relationships that the business succeeds in developing with the context where it operates. The quantity and the quality of the contacts, which a business has inside the network where it is located, allow it to come into contact with new businesses with which it may establish new relationships of business. The contacts, both at an organizational and individual level, of small- and medium-sized businesses, in general, are based on the previous forms of experience and on the trust relationship, which has developed in time (the family capital). In the prospect of the SEW theory, such relationships are considered as essential in the consideration of the strategies of expansion, since the business does not feel threatened but, on the contrary, reassured by the support and information obtained by its own relational contacts. Family businesses often develop strong and stable relationships with customers, suppliers, banks and stakeholders, and such attitude should foster network relationships, which are favourable to foreign expansion. Nevertheless, it may be observed that family businesses tend to remain anchored to their own bonds, as it is proved by the fact that they prefer forms of partnership with other family businesses with which they have cultural and organizational affinities. Instead, it is opportune that family businesses do not remain isolated, since networks allow them to know new opportunities/threats, thus reducing the uncertainty relating to the new location, a potential target of an international investment. In the absence of a network, for example, the opportunities for the international expansion might be underestimated since they might not be considered as occasions of growth or simply because they are not in line with the business culture.

6 The Choices of Location, Timing and Degree of Internationalization in the Family Business

The identification and choice of the location is one of the most delicate choices for the family business which decides to start the path to expansion abroad. The less risky solution for the traditional family business is the choice of a location, which is as similar as possible to the country of origin. Opportunities of foreign investment in more distant locations and, therefore, which are potentially riskier, may be seized in family businesses, which are managed either by younger generations, who are freer and less conservative, and, for this reason, less influenced by the principles of the SEW theory; or by non-family managers, who have greater know-how and experience in international markets and contacts of networks, which are useful in this respect. The physical distance and the risk of the investment are factors which influence a lot the choice of the location of the family business: family businesses, of course, follow an incremental process in internationalizing them, thus preferring bordering countries, which are more similar, from a cultural point of view, in the first phases, for expanding; subsequently, they prefer more distant countries, which are presumably less similar. Internationalization is considered one of the main corporate strategies of growth of the family business, and therefore, at the beginning, the family business prefers to seize the opportunity to affirm its own competitive (and beyond national borders) advantage in bordering countries, where its reputation of reliability and the network relationships have greater possibilities to rank successfully. The *distance* of the location is not only geographical, but it is expressed also by the differences in the values, tastes and preferences which are expressed by consumers, by the institutional, juridical, infrastructural differences. The greater distance causes greater uncertainty and, consequently, a perception which is higher than the risk of the foreign investment. Considering the conservative nature of the founder or generations which are closer to him/her, there will be a propensity for locations which are very similar to the locations of origin. In short, it may be observed that the greater the presence of the family in the business ownership and/or in the supervisory bodies shall be, the smaller the tendency to enter a location at a political and financial high risk shall be. The presence, in the business, of at least one successor and/or of non-family managers, vice versa, facilitates the entry in a political and financial high-risk location.

Also, the identification of the timing of entry by a family business is influenced by the business conservative nature, and therefore, there shall be a propensity for the delayed entry. In fact, unlikely, an early timing shall be chosen, since it is mainly risky. Such choice shall be made most likely in businesses which are managed by younger generations, who are more inclined to risk and/or by managers skilled at international activities, on condition that the family business does not prefer to adopt a strategy of external observation of a rival before investing abroad. In short, the greater the presence of the family in the business ownership and/or in the supervisory bodies shall be, the slower the timing of entry shall be. The presence inside the business of at least a successor and/or non-family managers, vice versa, promotes the adoption of a faster timing. Similar considerations may be made as far as the degree of internationalization is concerned: the greater the presence of the family in the business ownership and/or the supervisory bodies shall be, the smaller the degree of internationalization shall be, whereas the presence inside the business of at least a successor and/or of non-family managers facilitates its boost.

7 Conclusions

In the current competitive context, the expansion abroad represents an opportunity of growth for the business, and often, it allows its survival. Family businesses, even if they keep their own *social emotional endowment* unchanged, may not ignore such new scenario and have to consider the possibility to open both to new investors and to the entry of non-family members in the Management Board. Similarly, the active involvement of the new generations is opportune, and they may bring new vitality to the family business. It is undeniable that the strategy of internationalization may be excessively challenging for a family business, since internationalizing means to modify objectives, culture and structure. The family, who is about to undertake a process of internationalization, inevitably finds itself to deal with a paradox, that is not investing in order not to risk the family's assets excessively or investing in order to keep and increase them. The reinterpretation of the choice of internationalizing on the basis of the emotional needs of the owner family offers a mapping of the behaviours of the family business, which is useful to contextualize different aspects through which the phenomenon appears in the empirical analysis. Such mapping allows to highlight the relationship between the ownership-administration and business behaviours and to trace the path for the future empirical tests, in which the choices of internationalization of the family business take into consideration some small/medium configurations. The debate on the involvement of the new generations in the business, which is seen as a particular *event* in the life cycle of the family business, allows to integrate the studies on the international entrepreneurship in the ambit of the studies on family businesses. The use of theoretical meanings such as altruism, trust (competence and integrity-based) in the decisions relating to internationalization and the use of the stewardship theory, as a theoretical basis for the study of the internationalization of family businesses, contributes to explain the reason according to which some family businesses have difficulties pursuing international paths of growth, whereas the others adopt international strategies of success. The studies, which have been conducted, highlight an intrinsic complexity and a deep diversity which characterize the family businesses, which internationalize in terms of timing, choice of the targeted markets and modalities of internationalization. These aspects seem to vary in relation to the particular phase of the life cycle in which the family business is, to the degree of generational involvement, to the founder's point of view and to other specific characteristics of family businesses.

Therefore, the implementation of the international growth process implies the change of some organizational and cultural aspects and a greater awareness of the economic agents (the ruling family) of the family business on different fronts, from the importance of the involvement of the new generations in the business dynamics to the importance of the opening to external professionals. In both cases, it is opportune to establish an open dialogue which promotes the understanding of the main criticalities and opportunities which arise from the choice of letting the activities be international. The development of interpersonal dynamics, which are based on altruism and trust, increases the tendency to share the risks connected to the decisions of internationalizing the business (and the family). In this way, the main decision-makers of family businesses accrue their awareness on what are the factors which may be present in the decision-making dynamics relating to the processes of internationalization. Moreover, such changes have to be associated with a greater capacity of finding not only the managerial resources but also the financial resources, which are necessary to a greater extent in order to implement the expansion abroad. In this sense, family businesses have to be willing to accept the entry of new investing partners, who are also non-family members. Finally, the path to internationalization should be supported also by financial incentives, given that foreign competitiveness is a fundamental objective of economic policy.

References

Andersen O (1997) Internationalization and market entry mode: a review of theories and conceptual frameworks. MIR: Manag Int Rev 37:27–42

Arregle JL, Duran P, Hitt MA, Essen M (2017) Why is Family firms' internationalization unique? A meta–analysis? Entrepreneurship Theory Pract 41(5):801–883. https://doi.org/10.1111/etap.12246

Arregle JL, Naldi L, Nordqvist M, Hitt M (2012) internationalization of family-controlled firms: a study of the effects of external involvement . Gov Entrepreneurship Theory Pract 360(6):1115–1143. https://doi.org/10.1111/j.1540-6520.2012.00541.x

Cafferata A (1993) La transizione dell'impresa multinazionale. Sinergie 32:17–28

Calabrò A et al (2013) The influence of ownership structure and board strategic involvement on international sales: the moderating effect of family involvement. Int Bus Rev 22:509–523. https://doi.org/10.1016/j.ibusrev.2012.07.002

Cantwell J, Piscitello L (2000) Accumulating technological competence: its changing impact on corporate diversification and internationalization. Ind Corp Change 9(1):21–51. https://doi.org/10.1093/icc/9.1.21

Carr C, Bateman S (2009) International strategy configurations of the world's top family firms. Manag Int Rev 49(6):733–758. https://doi.org/10.1007/s11575-009-0018-3

Cerrato, D., Piva, M. (2012). The Internationalization of Small and Medium-Sized Enterprises: The Effect of Family Management, Human Capital and Foreign Ownership. Journal of Management Governance, 16, pp. 617-644. https://doi.org/10.1007/s10997-010-9166-x

Chrisman J, Chua J, Sharma P (2005) Trends and directions in the development of a strategic management theory of the family firm. Entrepreneurship Theory Pract 29:555–575

Chen, H.L., Hsu, W., T., Chang, C.Y. (2014). Family Ownership, Institutional Ownership, and Internationalization of SMEs. Journal of Small Business Management, 52 (4):771-789, DOI: 10.1111/jsbm.12031

Fernández Z, Nieto MJ (2006) Impact of ownership on the international involvement of SMEs. J Int Bus Stud 37(3):340–351. https://doi.org/10.1057/palgrave.jibs.8400196

Gallo MA, Pont CG (1996) Important factors in family business internationalization. Family Bus Rev 8:83–97. https://doi.org/10.1111/j.1741-6248.1996.00045.x

Gande A, Schenzler C, Senbet LW (2009) Valuation effects of global diversification. J Int Bus Stud 40(9):1515–1532. https://doi.org/10.1057/jibs.2009.59

George G, Wiklund J, Zahra A (2005) Ownership and the internationalization of small firms. J Manag 1:31(2):210–233. https://doi.org/10.1177/0149206304271760

Gomez Mejia LR, Makri M, Kintana ML (2007) Diversification decisions in family-controlled firms. J Manag Stud 47(2): 223–252. https://doi.org/10.1111/j.1467-6486.2009.00889.x

Hitt MA, Hoskisson RE, Kim H (1997) International diversification: effects on innovation and firm performance in product diversified firm. Acad Manage J 40(4):767–798

Hitt MA, Ireland RD, Hoskisson RE (2007) Strategic management: competitiveness and globalization. Concepts and cases, 7th ed. Thomson South-Western, Mason, OH, USA

Johanson J, Vahlne JE (1977) The internationalization process of the firm: a model of knowledge development and increasing foreign market commitments. J Int Bus Stud 8(1):23–32. https://doi.org/10.1057/palgrave.jibs.8490676

Kafouros MI, Buckley PJ, Sharp JA, Wang C (2008) The role of internationalization. Explaining Innov Perform Technovation 28(1):63–74. https://doi.org/10.1016/j.technovation.2007.07.009

Lu JW, Beamish PW (2001) The internationalization and performance of SMEs. Strateg Manag J 22(6–7):565-580. https://doi.org/10.1002/smj.184

Lu J, Liang X, Shan M, Liang X (2015) Internationalization and performance of chinese family firms: the moderating role of corporate governance. Manag Organ Rev 11(4):645–678. https://doi.org/10.1017/mor.2015.32

Muñoz Bullón F, Sánchez Bueno MJ (2012) Do family ties shape the performance consequences of diversification? Evidence from the European Union. J World Bus 47(3):469–477. https://doi.org/10.1016/j.jwb.2011.05.013

Naldi L, Norqvist M (2008) Family firms venturing into international markets: a resource dependence perspective. Front Entrepreneurship Res 28(14), Article 1

Niosi J, Tschang FT (2009) The strategies of Chinese and Indian software multinationals: implications for internationalization theory. Ind Corp Change 18(2):269–294

Oesterle MJ, Richta HN, Fisch JH (2013) The influence of ownership structure on internationalization. Int Bus Rev 22:187–201

Piva E, Rossi Lamastra C, De Massis A (2013) Family firms and internationalization: an exploratory study on high-tech entrepreneurial ventures. J Int Entrepreneurship 11(2):108–129

Prange C, Verdier S (2011) Dynamic capabilities, internationalization processes and performance. J World Bus 46(1):126–133. https://doi.org/10.1016/j.jwb.2010.05.024

Schmid T, Ampenberger M, Kaserer C, Achleitner AK (2015) Family firm heterogeneity and corporate policy: evidence from diversification decisions. Corporate Gov Int Rev 23(3):285–302. https://doi.org/10.1111/corg.12091

Sharma P et al (1997) Strategic management of the family business: past research and future challenges. Family Bus Rev 10(1):1–35. https://doi.org/10.1111/j.1741-6248.1997.00001.x

Sherman HD Kashlak RJ, Joshi M P (1998) The effect of the board and executive committee characteristics on the degree of internationalization. J Int Manage 4(4):311–335

Sharma P (2004) An overview of the field of family business studies: current status and directions for the future. Family Bus Rev 17(1):1–36. https://doi.org/10.1111/j.1741-6248.2004.00001.x

Vandekerkhof P, Steijvers T, Hendriks W, Voordeckers W (2015) The effect of organizational characteristics on the appointment of nonfamily managers in private family firms: the moderating role of socioemotional wealth. Family Bus Rev 28(2):104–122. https://doi.org/10.1177/0894486513514274

Zahra SA (2003) International expansion of U.S. manufacturing family businesses: the effect of ownership and involvement. J Bus Ventur 18:495–512. https://doi.org/10.1016/S0883-9026(03)00057-0

Investment Decisions in Listed Family Firms: Risk Aversion and Emotional Attachment

Claudia Frisenna and Davide Rizzotti

Abstract A critical concern of family firms' behavior is the low propensity to invest and grow. Indeed, because of the undiversified nature of their investments and the unwillingness to dilute corporate control, family owners have incentives to influence investment decisions, limiting investment spending on long-term projects. This study aims at analyzing how a different board structure impacts on investment decisions. In particular, this study investigates whether board monitoring and the CEO's emotional attachment might affect investment spending within family firms. Building on agency and stewardship constructs as complementary frameworks, we suggest that both board monitoring and the presence of an emotionally involved CEO may be positively associated with the level of investments in long-term projects.

Keywords Family-oriented behavior · Agency theory · Stewardship theory · Board independence · Family CEO

1 Introduction

Family firms constitute the oldest and most prevalent form of the organizational structure all over the world. As highlighted by La Porta et al. (1999), family-controlled firms dominate the economic landscape worldwide. The presence of family-owned firms is significant both in USA and in Europe. For instance, researchers show that about 35% of the S&P 500 are family firms (Anderson and Reeb 2004). In Europe, the percentage of family firms is around 70–80% (Prencipe et al. 2014).

Despite their economic relevance, for several reasons, including economic and ideological preconceptions, the governance literature has mainly focused on listed widely held corporations typical of the Anglo-Saxon context, disregarding some

C. Frisenna (✉) · D. Rizzotti
Department of Economics and Business, University of Catania, Catania, Italy
e-mail: claudia.frisenna@unict.it

D. Rizzotti
e-mail: rizzotti@unict.it

A. Leotta (ed.), *Management Controlling and Governance of Family Businesses*, Contributions to Management Science,
https://doi.org/10.1007/978-3-030-47741-7_6

peculiarities of listed family firms that may impact on small investors in two opposite ways.

In particular, on the one hand, small investors are exposed to the potential risk of wealth expropriation, since family owners tend to consider the firms as a private asset and to make corporate decisions that give priority to the maximization of the family interests rather than the firm's one (Morck and Yeung 2003; Young et al. 2008).

On the other hand, small investors can benefit from the emotional attachment of family owners and executives to the firm, and the sense of identification of family members to the firm and the relative reputational concern.

In this chapter, we examine the underinvestment problem, one important concern of family firms. In order to deal with the problem, we integrate the agency perspective with the stewardship perspective, to consider both the role of monitoring and the impact of the emotional attachment of top executives on investment decisions.

2 Definitional Concerns

Definitely, the appropriate definition of the family firm is the main critical issue in family business research, and the debate on how to define a family firm is far from been conclusive (Chrisman et al. 2003; Klein et al. 2005; Mroczkowski and Tanewski 2007). Conceptually, scholars agree that family firms are those in which the family owner exerts influence on a firm's behavior (Gomez-Mejia et al. 2011). Clearly, such a broad definition creates challenges in achieving homogeneous operational definitions. Essentially, it is possible to identify two distinct operational approaches, aimed not only at distinguishing family firms from non-family firms, but also at capturing the heterogeneity existing within family firms, namely the "involvement approach" and the "essence approach". The involvement approach focuses on the power of the family to influence corporate decisions, assuming that it depends on the degree of family involvement in the ownership, or/and in the management of the firm (Gomez-Mejia et al. 2011; Prencipe et al. 2014).

The essence approach recognizes family involvement as a necessary but not sufficient condition to detect the essence of the family dimension and its several facets. According to this approach, the essence of family firms depends on whether the family's identity and the firm's identity are embedded in each other, and it varies according to the way in which core firm values and culture overlaps with those of the family (e.g., Astrachan et al. 2002).

Undoubtedly, the essence approach generates more than a few issues for empiricists who rely on large archival data.

As a consequence, the involvement approach is mostly used in quantitative research (Prencipe et al. 2014). The indicators generally used to operationalize family's influence are the percentage of family ownership and/or the presence of family members in managerial or governance positions. According to the definition employed, scholars identify family firms as "family owned," "family controlled" and "family owned and managed," thereby trying to detect the heterogeneity of family firms (Gomez-Mejia et al. 2011).

However, concerns arise with respect to the different criteria adopted to separate family firms from non-family counterparts, especially with respect to the minimum threshold of family ownership, which appears to be highly context-specific. For instance, in the US context a threshold of 5% may be considered sufficient to identify family firms, while in the European context, in which stock ownership is highly concentrated, the minimum threshold to detect the family dimension should be at least 25% (Gomez-Mejia et al. 2011). In Italy, for example, family owners averagely hold more than 50% of corporate stock ownership (Prencipe et al. 2011).

In sum, it seems that a standard operational definition of family firms is far from being identified, and it would probably also be unsuitable. Therefore, the choice of the operational definition should be contingent on the research's objects and settings (Gomez-Mejia et al. 2011).

Since the object of investigation of this study regards large listed family firms, the definition of family firms follows the involvement approach. Two main reasons motivate its adoption. First, the involvement approach is particularly suitable in studies that build on agency constructs, which focus on potential risks of expropriation rising from the concentration of ownership in the hands of a dominant family (Prencipe et al. 2014). Second, the adoption of the involvement approach allows empirical researchers to exploit the large number of publicly available data on stock ownership and board composition (Prencipe et al. 2014).

In conclusion, this study defines a firm as family owned if the person who established or acquired the firm, or their families, or descendants hold at least 50% of the decision-making rights mandated by their share capital. This definition is the most adopted operationalization of family businesses (Salvato and Moores 2010), as it ensures that the family has the power and the incentives to affect corporate decisions, regardless of the presence of the family members in the governance structures.

3 Peculiarities of Listed Family Firms

In listed family firms, the presence of a large number of small investors, generally passive and external to strategic management decisions, leads to peculiar critical concerns.

On the one hand, small shareholders may face risks of expropriation, since family owners tend to consider the firms as a private asset to transfer to future generations (Anderson and Reeb 2004; Gomez-Mejia et al. 2011; Berrone et al. 2012). The desire to maintain corporate control for a long term may lead the controlling family to make corporate decisions that give priority to the maximization of the family interests rather than the firm's one (Morck and Yeung 2003; Young et al. 2008). Moreover, because of high information asymmetries, the control family could extract the wealth brought into the company by minority shareholders, appropriating it through operations in clear conflict of interest (tunneling), such as selling family members of company assets at unprofitable prices for the company, recognizing excessive wages to family member managers or setting transfer prices that benefit the family (Johnson et al. 2000). The existence of conflicts of interests between family owners and minority shareholders is largely examined in the agency theory and generally defined as Type II problem, in order to distinguish it from the conflicts of interests between owners and managers typical of widely held firms.

On the other hand, small investors can benefit from the emotional attachment of family owners and executives to the firm and the sense of identification of family members to the firm and the relative reputational concern. This peculiar feature is generally emphasized in the stewardship theory, according to which family executives tend to feel a strong sense of commitment to the firm, its employees and all stakeholders, and are motivated to do their best for the sustainability of the firm in the long run (e.g., Miller and Le Breton-Miller 2005; Miller and Le Breton-Miller 2006a, b; Le Breton-Miller et al. 2011).

4 Underinvestment Problem and the Role of Board of Directors

A critical concern of family firms' behavior is the low propensity to invest and grow. Indeed, because of the undiversified nature of their investments and the unwillingness to dilute corporate control, family owners have incentives to influence investment decisions, limiting investment spending on long-term projects (Anderson et al. 2012; Lins et al. 2013).

Most of prior studies suggest that investment decisions in family firms are moved by family-oriented particularistic interests. In particular, evidence shows that family-controlled firms tend to be more conservative and to face severe financial constraints, which lead to underinvestment problems, low growth and stagnation (Anderson et al. 2012; Chrisman and Patel 2012).

In an agency perspective, there are two main reasons that lead family firms to face severe growth's threats, namely the willingness to protect the family control over corporate decisions and the risk aversion due to the high financial involvement (La Porta et al. 1999).

First, the desire to defend their controlling position may lead to financial constraints and underinvestment problems. Indeed, family owners are reluctant to dilute family holding, and they are likely to rely on internal-generated resources or private wealth (Sirmon and Hitt 2003; Fernandez and Nieto 2006; Andres 2011). The unwillingness to accede to external funds impedes growth ambitions and leads to pass up investment opportunities, with consequences in terms of limited corporate dimensions and stagnation (Morck and Yeung 2003; Sirmon and Hitt 2003; Allio 2004).

Second, family owners are highly financially involved and most of the family's wealth is often invested in the single firm (Gómez-Mejía et al. 2007). The undiversified nature of family holding leads family owners to be risk averse and to prefer the preservation and stability of the family's wealth, at the expense of growth and expansion (Schulze et al. 2001; Graves and Thomas 2006; Lee 2006).

Therefore, because of both the desire to defend their controlling position and risk aversion, family owners have incentives to limit investment spending. Moreover, because of their controlling positions, family owners have also the power to affect investment decisions, exerting their influence to force the firm to pursue the family's interest, such as the prevention of investment spending, at the expense of minority's interests (Demsetz and Lehn 1985; Anderson et al. 2003).

Prior empirical evidence mostly confirms the agency assumption. For instance, Anderson et al. (2012) find that, compared to non-family counterparts, family firms devote fewer resources to both R&D spending and capital expenditures.

While the relationship between family ownership and investment spending has been widely investigated, literature provides limited insight into whether different board structures may have any impact on investment decisions.

This gap constitutes not only an empirical issue, but mostly it constitutes a theoretical concern in family business studies. Actually, the two main theoretical frameworks to understand the relationship between board composition and family firms' behavior lead to conflicting insights (Le Breton-Miller et al. 2011).

Agency theory underlines that because of managerial entrenchment, family owners have the power to limit investment spending, since managers act with the aim to defend family's interests, thereby adopting investment spending rules based on family's risk preferences rather than market-based criteria (Anderson et al. 2012). Following the agency perspective, one could expect that an effective board monitoring is needed in order to weaken the link between family and executives, particularly when the top manager is a family member.

Nevertheless, agency theory misses to consider the importance of the emotional involvement in the firm management, typical of family firms.

The bright side of the emotional attachment rising from the family involvement in the corporate management is highlighted, instead, in the stewardship theory (Davis et al. 1997; Miller and Le Breton-Miller 2006a, b). In particular, the stewardship framework suggests that because of the emotional involvement, managers' decisions are moved by higher-level needs, such as the willingness to ensure the continuity and the growth of the firm, even in spite of financial risks and personal sacrifices (Miller and Le Breton-Miller 2006; Miller et al. 2008). Therefore, following the stewardship perspective, one could expect that the presence of a CEO emotional involvement is needed in order to mitigate family-oriented particularistic behavior, thereby leading to higher investment spending, apart from the board monitoring.

In the following subsections, we describe how an effective board monitoring, on the one hand, and an emotionally involved CEO, on the other, may reduce the underinvestment problem.

4.1 The Role of Board Monitoring

According to the agency perspective, the board of directors constitutes the main control device to mitigate conflict of interests between family owners and minority shareholders. To be effective, the board must be able to provide an independent judgment, not affected by the controlling family's influence. Therefore, the safeguard of minority investors' interests is mainly entrusted to independent directors, who should act to prevent family opportunism on the behalf of minority shareholders (e.g., Shleifer and Vishny 1986, 1997; Anderson and Reeb 2004; Park and Shin 2004). Most of prior studies support the view that board independence is able to reduce agency conflicts. For instance, Miller and Le Breton-Miller (2006a, b) point out that the inclusion of independent directors prevents minority's wealth expropriation. Similarly, Anderson and Reeb (2004) show that independent-dominated boards prevent from the risk of expropriation and reduce family opportunism, leading to higher firm performance.

As regards investment decisions, the way in which independent directors may prevent family opportunism is by reducing risk aversion of family owners and financial constraints deriving from the unwillingness to dilute family control.

Clearly, independent directors cannot intervene directly on the risk preferences of the controlling family. However, independent directors may reduce the influence of the controlling family over investment decisions, by weakening managerial entrenchment in several ways. For instance, independent directors may affect the CEO's selection process, inducing the appointment of non-family-affiliated executives (Anderson and Reeb 2004). Moreover, independent directors may provide an objective monitoring over CEO performance, ensuring a prompt replacement of a poorly performing CEO (Weisbach 1988). The evaluation and monitoring of independent directors may induce top executives to act in the firm's interest rather than in the family's interest. For instance, managers may have higher incentives to undertake profitable projects, thus reducing underinvestment problems deriving from the family's risk aversion.

Board independence may affect the level of investment spending in family firms also relaxing financial constraints. Indeed, independent directors are likely to be networked with financial institutions, and therefore, they contribute to provide the relational capital able to facilitate the acquisition of financial resources (Stearns and Mizruchi 1993; Clarysse et al. 2007). Moreover, capital providers enjoy benefits deriving from the monitoring of independent directors over corporate decisions, which is reflected in a lower cost of debt. Accordingly, prior studies show that board independence is associated with lower cost of debt and higher credit rating (Anderson et al. 2004; Ashbaugh-Skaife et al. 2006).

Therefore, board independence may reduce family opportunism and underinvestment problems by weakening managerial entrenchment and by relaxing financial constraints.

According to the above discussion, the following proposition is proposed:

Proposition 1 Within family firms, board independence is positively associated with the level of capital expenditures.

4.2 The Role of CEO Emotional Involvement

The main corporate decisions, such as the development and the implementation of investment strategies, are made by the chief executive officer. Therefore, both the CEO skills and the level of CEO's commitment constitute key drivers of investment decisions and firm's future prospects (Adams and Ferreira 2007; Song and Thakor 2006; Malmendier and Tate 2005).

Family involvement in the top executive position may constitute an important driver of the family firm's growth, due to the critical role played by the emotional attachment and reputational concerns of top managers in strategic planning.

Theoretically, the stewardship constructs suggest that a high degree of emotional attachment may lead managers to act as stewards of their firms, making decisions on the basis of higher-level needs, which go beyond the economic private interest. In particular, stewards' decisions are moved by the aim to ensure the continuity and the growth of the firm, being also willing to accept financial risks and personal sacrifices (Miller and Le Breton-Miller 2006; Miller et al. 2008).

Therefore, in the stewardship perspective, the emotionally involved CEO should act in the firm's interest, trying to assure growth and success for their businesses. In this perspective, the strong commitment toward growth should lead to longer investment horizon and lower risk aversion (Miller and Le Breton-Miller 2006).

Yet, the degree of emotional attachment varies according to the strength of the bind between the CEO and the firm. In particular, the level of emotional attachment with the firm should be significantly higher for family member CEOs than for external professional managers (Miller and Le Breton-Miller 2006a, b).

In this latter case, the borderline between agency and stewardship perspectives becomes much thinner. Actually, the controlling family usually appoints affiliated professional managers on the basis of personal relationships, in order to protect its interests (Morck and Yeung 2003; Young et al. 2008; Prat et al. 2010). While, on the one hand, the closer relationship between the family and the executives could lead to a higher commitment to the firm (Miller and Le Breton-Miller 2006a, b), on the other hand, executives have incentives to preserve the trust of the family owners, in order to keep their position for a long time (Volpin 2002; Brunello et al. 2003). In such a case, the CEO loyalty is built toward the family, rather than toward the firm. Therefore, professional CEOs are likely to favor investment decisions according to the family's risk aversion, rather than market-based criteria (Morck and Yeung 2003; Anderson et al. 2012).

Conversely, the emotional attachment and the sense of intimate belonging to the firm are particularly emphasized in family CEOs (Miller and Le Breton-Miller

2006a, b; Berrone et al. 2012; Gómez-Mejía et al. 2007). Since their name, identity and reputation are inextricably tied to the firm, they tend to develop a strong sense of personal identification and belonging to the firm, which creates incentives that go beyond the economic self-interest (Miller and Le Breton-Miller 2005; Berrone et al. 2012). In particular, they tend to act as farsighted stewards of their firms and are more likely to feel a high commitment to the firm's growth and continuity (Miller and Le Breton-Miller 2006a, b). As a consequence of their emotional commitment to the firm's growth, family executives may be willing to accept risks and to undertake long-term investment projects, both on fixed assets and innovation (James 1999; Le Breton-Miller et al. 2011). In addition to the prevention of risk aversion, the quest for firm's growth and continuity leads family CEOs to overcome financial constraints rising from the desire to keep the control in the hand of the family, by developing strong long-term relationships with lenders, which facilitate access to debt financing (Anderson et al. 2003; Miller and Le Breton-Miller 2006b; Prencipe et al. 2008; Micelotta and Raynard 2011).

While the high emotional involvement provides family CEOs the incentives to act as farsighted stewards of their firms, the longer tenure and kinship relationships with other family owners give them the ability and discretion to influence corporate decisions, overcoming potential conflicts with other family owners (Miller and Le Breton-Miller 2006a, b).

According to the above discussion, we formulate the following proposition:

Proposition 2 Within family firms, the presence of a family CEO is positively associated with the level of capital expenditures.

4.3 Conclusions

In this chapter, we examine the underinvestment problem, one important concern of family firms trying to understand how a different board structure impacts on investment decisions.

Building on agency and stewardship constructs as complementary frameworks, this study investigates whether board monitoring and CEO's emotional attachment might affect investment spending within family firms. In particular, we suggest that both board monitoring and the presence of an emotionally involved CEO may be positively associated with the level of investments in long-term projects.

This study contributes to the literature in four ways.

First, this study adds to the debate on board independence in family firms. Actually, some family business scholars claim that the outside directors' oversight might be unnecessary or even detrimental in the context of family firms, since it may discourage attitude toward stewardship (e.g., Lee and O'Neill 2003; Corbetta and Salvato 2004; Jaskiewicz and Klein 2007). While showing that the presence of a family CEO may mitigate agency conflicts with small investors, this suggests that a greater power balance and a higher representation of independent directors may prevent family opportunism, encouraging executives to act in the firm's interest.

Second, this study enriches the recent debate on the heterogeneity of family firms' behavior (Chua et al. 2012; Chrisman et al. 2012). In particular, this study suggests that the different degree of CEOs' emotional commitment may be a crucial determinant of the heterogeneity of family firms' behavior.

Third, this study contributes to the debate on professionalization in family firms (e.g., Stewart and Hitt 2012), by warnings that the family dimension and its non-economic features can have some bright sides, which deserve to be protected when models of professionalization are proposed.

Finally, this study provides a theoretical contribution, stressing that the adoption of agency and stewardship framework in a complementary way allows researchers to extend the body of knowledge of family businesses' behavior (Le Breton-Miller et al. 2011).

References

Adams RB, Ferreira D (2007) A theory of friendly boards. J Financ 62(1):217–250. https://doi.org/10.1111/j.1540-6261.2007.01206.x

Allio MK (2004) Family businesses: Their virtues, vices, and strategic path. Strat Leadership 32(4):24–33. https://doi.org/10.1108/10878570410576704

Anderson RC, Reeb DM (2004) Board composition: balancing family influence in S&P 500 firms. Adm Sci Q 49(2):209–237. https://doi.org/10.2307/4131472

Anderson RC, Duru A, Reeb DM (2012) Investment policy in family controlled firms. J Bank Financ 36(6):1744–1758. https://doi.org/10.1016/j.jbankfin.2012.01.018

Anderson RC, Mansi SA, Reeb DM (2003) Founding family ownership and the agency cost of debt. J Financ Econ 68(2):263–285. https://doi.org/10.1016/S0304-405X(03)00067-9

Anderson RC, Mansi SA, Reeb DM (2004) Board characteristics, accounting report integrity, and the cost of debt. J Acc Econ 37(3):315–342. https://doi.org/10.1016/j.jacceco.2004.01.004

Andres C (2011) Family ownership, financing constraints and investment decisions. Appl Financ Econ 21(22):1641–1659. https://doi.org/10.1080/09603107.2011.589805

Ashbaugh-Skaife H, Collins DW, LaFond R (2006) The effects of corporate governance on firms' credit ratings. J Acc Econ 42(1):203–243. https://doi.org/10.1016/j.jacceco.2006.02.003

Astrachan JH, Klein SB, Smyrnios KX (2002) The F-PEC scale of family influence: a proposal for solving the family business definition problem1. Fam Bus Rev 15(1):45–58. https://doi.org/10.1111/j.1741-6248.2002.00045.x

Berrone P, Cruz C, Gomez-Mejia LR (2012) Socioemotional wealth in family firms: theoretical dimensions, assessment approaches, and agenda for future research. Fam Bus Rev 25(3):258–279. https://doi.org/10.1177/0894486511435355

Brunello G, Graziano C, Parigi BM (2003) CEO turnover in insider dominated boards: the Italian case. J Bank Financ 27:1027–1051. https://doi.org/10.1016/S0378-4266(02)00244-3

Chrisman JJ, Patel PC (2012) Variations in R&D investments of family and nonfamily firms: behavioral agency and myopic loss aversion perspectives. Acad Manag J 55(4):976–997. https://doi.org/10.5465/amj.2011.0211

Chrisman JJ, Chua JH, Pearson AW, Barnett T (2012) Family involvement, family influence, and family centered non-economic goals in small firms. Entrep: Theory Pract, 36(2): 267–293. https://doi.org/10.1111/j.1540-6520.2010.00407.x

Chrisman JJ, Chua JH, Litz R (2003) A unified systems perspective of family firm performance: an extension and integration. J Bus Ventur 18(4):467–472. https://doi.org/10.1016/S0883-9026(03)00055-7

Chua JH, Chrisman JJ, Steier LP, Rau SB (2012) Sources of heterogeneity in family firms: An introduction. Entrep Theory Pract 36(6):1103–1113. https://doi.org/10.1111/j.1540-6520.2012.00540.x

Clarysse B, Knockaert M, Lockett A (2007) Outside board members in high tech start-ups. Small Bus Econ 29(3):243. https://doi.org/10.1007/s11187-006-9033-y

Corbetta G, Salvato CA (2004) The board of directors in family firms: one size fits all? Fam Bus Rev 17(2):119–134. https://doi.org/10.1111/j.1741-6248.2004.00008.x

Davis J, Schoorman R, Donaldson L (1997) Towards a stewardship theory of management. Acad Manag Rev 22:20–47. https://doi.org/10.5465/amr.1997.9707180258

Demsetz H, Lehn K (1985) The structure of corporate ownership: Causes and consequences. J Polit Econ 93(6):1155–1177. https://doi.org/10.1086/261354

Fernandez Z, Nieto MJ (2006) Impact of ownership on the international involvement of SMEs. J Int Bus Stud 37:340–351. https://doi.org/10.1057/palgrave.jibs.8400196

Gomez-Mejia LR, Cruz C, Berrone P, De Castro J (2011) The bind that ties: socioemotional wealth preservation in family firms. Acad Manag Ann 5(1):653–707. https://doi.org/10.5465/19416520.2011.593320

Gómez-Mejía LR, Haynes KT, Núñez-Nickel M, Jacobson KJ, Moyano-Fuentes J (2007) Socioemotional wealth and business risks in family-controlled firms: evidence from Spanish olive oil mills. Adm Sci Q 52(1):106–137. https://doi.org/10.2189/asqu.52.1.106

Graves C, Thomas I (2006) Internationalization of Australian family businesses: a managerial capabilities perspective. Fam Bus Rev 19(3):207–224. https://doi.org/10.1111/j.1741-6248.2006.00066.x

James HS (1999) Owner as manager, extended horizons and the family firm. Int J Econ Bus 6(1):41–55. https://doi.org/10.1080/13571519984304

Jaskiewicz P, Klein S (2007) The impact of goal alignment on board composition and board size in family businesses. J Bus Res 60(10):1080–1089. https://doi.org/10.1016/j.jbusres.2006.12.015

Johnson S, La Porta R, Lopez-de-Silanes F, Shleifer A (2000) Tunneling. Am Econ Rev 90(2):22–27. https://doi.org/10.1257/aer.90.2.22

Klein SB, Astrachan JH, Smyrnios KX (2005) The F-PEC scale of family influence: Construction, validation, and further implication for theory. Entrep Theory Pract 29(3):321–339. https://doi.org/10.1111/j.1540-6520.2005.00086.x

La Porta R, Lopez-de-Silanes F, Shleifer A (1999) Corporate Ownership Around the World. J Financ 54(2):471–517. https://doi.org/10.1111/0022-1082.00115

Le Breton-Miller I, Miller D, Lester RH (2011) Stewardship or agency? A social embeddedness reconciliation of conduct and performance in public family businesses. Organ Sci 22(3):704–721. https://doi.org/10.1287/orsc.1100.0541

Lee J (2006) Family firm performance: Further evidence. Fam Bus Rev 19(2):103–114. https://doi.org/10.1111/j.1741-6248.2006.00060.x

Lee PM, O'Neill HM (2003) Ownership structures and R&D investments of US and Japanese firms: agency and stewardship perspectives. Acad Manag J 46(2):212–225. https://doi.org/10.5465/30040615

Lins KV, Volpin P, Wagner HF (2013) Does family control matter? International evidence from the 2008–2009 financial crisis. Rev Financ Stud 26(10):2583–2619. https://doi.org/10.1093/rfs/hht044

Malmendier U, Tate G (2005) CEO overconfidence and corporate investment. J Financ 60(6):2661–2700. https://doi.org/10.1111/j.1540-6261.2005.00813.x

Micelotta ER, Raynard M (2011) Concealing or revealing the family? Corporate brand identity strategies in family firms. Fam Bus Rev 24(3):197–216. https://doi.org/10.1177/0894486511407321

Miller D, Le Breton-Miller L (2006a) Family governance and firm performance: agency, stewardship, and capabilities. Fam Bus Rev 19(1):73–87. https://doi.org/10.1111/j.1741-6248.2006.00063.x

Miller D, Le Breton-Miller I (2005) Managing for the long run: lessons in competitive advantage from great family businesses. Harvard Business Press.

Miller D, Le Breton-Miller I (2006b) Priorities, practices and strategies in successful and failing family businesses: An elaboration and test of the configuration perspective. Strat Organ 4(4):379–407. https://doi.org/10.1177/1476127006069575

Miller D, Le Breton-Miller L, Scholnick B (2008) Stewardship versus stagnation: an empirical comparison of small family and non-family businesses. J Manag Stud 45(1): 51–78. https://doi.org/10.1111/j.1467-6486.2007.00718.x

Morck R, Yeung B (2003) Agency problems in large family business groups. Entrep Theory Pract 27(4):367–382. https://doi.org/10.1111/1540-8520.t01-1-00015

Mroczkowski NA, Tanewski G (2007) Delineating publicly listed family and nonfamily controlled firms: An approach for capital market research in Australia. J Small Bus Manage 45(3):320–332. https://doi.org/10.1111/j.1540-627X.2007.00215.x

Park YW, Shin HH (2004) Board composition and earnings management in Canada. J Corp Financ 10(3):431–457. https://doi.org/10.1016/S0929-1199(03)00025-7

Prat A, Bandiera O, Guiso L, Sadun R (2010) Italian managers: fidelity or performance. In: Boeri T, Merlo A, Prat A (eds) The ruling class: management and politics in modern Italy. Oxford: Oxford University Press. https://doi.org/10.1111/j.1468-0335.2012.00927.x

Prencipe A, Bar-Yosef S, Dekker HC (2014) Accounting research in family firms: theoretical and empirical challenges. Eur Account Rev 23(3):361–385. https://doi.org/10.1080/09638180.2014.895621

Prencipe A, Bar-Yosef S, Mazzola P, Pozza L (2011) Income Smoothing in Family-Controlled Companies: evidence from Italy. Corp GovAnce: Int Rev 19(6):529–546. https://doi.org/10.1111/j.1467-8683.2011.00856.x

Prencipe A, Markarian G, Pozza L (2008) Earnings management in family firms: evidence from R&D cost capitalization in Italy. Fam Bus Rev 21(1):71–88. https://doi.org/10.1111/j.1741-6248.2007.00112.x

Salvato C, Moores K (2010) Research on accounting in family firms: past accomplishments and future challenges. Fam Bus Rev 23(3):193–215. https://doi.org/10.1177/0894486510375069

Schulze WS, Lubatkin MH, Dino RN, Buchholtz AK (2001) Agency relationships in family firms: theory and evidence. Organ Sci 12:99–116. https://doi.org/10.1287/orsc.12.2.99.10114

Shleifer A, Vishny RW (1986) Large shareholders and corporate control. J Polit Econ 461–488. https://doi.org/10.1086/261385

Shleifer A, Vishny RW (1997) A survey of corporate governance. J Financ 52(2):737–783. https://doi.org/10.1111/j.1540-6261.1997.tb04820.x

Sirmon DG, Hitt MA (2003) Managing resources: linking unique resources, management, and wealth creation in family firms. Entrep Theory Pract 27(4):339–358. https://doi.org/10.1111/1540-8520.t01-1-00013

Song F, Thakor AV (2006) Information control, career concerns, and corporate governance. J Financ 61(4):1845–1896. https://doi.org/10.1111/j.1540-6261.2006.00891.x

Stearns LB, Mizruchi MS (1993) Board composition and corporate financing: the impact of financial institution representation on borrowing. Acad Manag J 36(3):603–618. https://doi.org/10.5465/256594

Stewart A, Hitt MA (2012) Why can'ta family business be more like a nonfamily business? Modes of professionalization in family firms. Fam Bus Rev 25(1):58–86. https://doi.org/10.1177/0894486511421665

Volpin PF (2002) Governance with poor investor protection: evidence from top executive turnover in Italy. J Financ Econ 64(1):61–90. https://doi.org/10.1016/S0304-405X(02)00071-5
Weisbach MS (1988) Outside directors and CEO turnover. J Financ Econ 20:431–460. https://doi.org/10.1016/0304-405X(88)90053-0
Young MN, Peng MW, Ahlstrom D, Bruton GD, Jiang Y (2008) Corporate governance in emerging economies: a review of the principal–principal perspective. J Manage Stud 45(1):196–220. https://doi.org/10.1111/j.1467-6486.2007.00752.x

Governing Family Businesses: A Research Map

Gaia Bassani, Cristiana Cattaneo, Elena Cristiano, and Antonio Leotta

Abstract The chapter aims at developing a theoretical framework of the family business challenges intended to ordering the topics discussed in the previous chapters, namely managerialization and professionalization, succession, internationalization, and relations with financial markets. These topics are seen as challenges a family business has to deal with by managing specific relations between actors distributed in space and time. From this point of view, governance is considered as a unifying topic since its structures need to be assessed in order to facilitate the management of all the other challenges. The concept of governance here proposed is drawn from the management control studies focused on lateral relationships.

Keywords Governance · Professionalization · Managerialization · Internationalization · Succession · Financial market · Management accounting and control system

1 Introduction to a Map of Family Business Topics

Given the relevance of family businesses, the need to know their specific features, discussed in Chapter "An Overview of Family Business. Profiles, Definitions and the Main Challenges of the Business Life Cycle" of the present volume, is aimed

G. Bassani (✉) · C. Cattaneo
Department of Management, Economics and Quantitative Methods, University of Bergamo, Bergamo, Italy
e-mail: gaia.bassani@unibg.it

C. Cattaneo
e-mail: cristiana.cattaneo@unibg.it

E. Cristiano
Department of Business Economics and Law, University of Calabria, Rende, Italy
e-mail: elena.cristiano@unical.it

A. Leotta
Department of Economics and Business, University of Catania, Catania, Italy
e-mail: antonio.leotta@unict.it

A. Leotta (ed.), *Management Controlling and Governance of Family Businesses*, Contributions to Management Science,
https://doi.org/10.1007/978-3-030-47741-7_7

at dealing with the main challenges which represent the principal topics about these firms. These challenges have been discussed in the previous Chapters "Professionalization and Managerialization in Family Firms: A Still Open Issue", "The Survival of Family Businesses: The Challenge of Succession", "The Growth of Family Businesses: The Path to Internationalization", and "Investment Decisions in Listed Family Firms: Risk Aversion and Emotional Attachment", referring to managerialization and professionalization, succession, internationalization, and relations with financial markets. In the present chapter, we propose to interpret such challenges as originated from the dialectics between family and non-family members, family and business interests, old and new family generations, domestic and foreign market dynamics, and family firm CEO and financial investors. The dialectical view of family business challenges proposed in this chapter leads to considering their management as a search for alliances between the actors involved in all the challenges. Growth and development of a family firm take place through their market expansion, which entails an increase of the firm organizational complexity. Managerialization and professionalization of the family firm are the main challenges family and non-family members have to deal with by merging family with professional and managerial values and principles. Family firm's market expansion is often accompanied with the entrance into one or more foreign markets. This often constitutes a relevant chance for the firm to grow. The uncertainty related to foreign markets and the shortage of capital to be devoted in this respect, joint with the usually low willingness of family owners to make such kind of investments, represent the main features of the internationalization strategies. The need of the family firm to invest in acquiring the new market knowledge may be satisfied by hiring a new external advisor, or a new professional manager, with expertise in the new market. Moreover, for the family firm to reinforce its presence in the new market, an international partnership may be developed, which may require that the family assigns a share of ownership to the new partner. Thus, the main internationalization challenges stem from the need of the family members to develop alliances with non-family actors (potential advisors or professional managers, potential partners, and so on) for entering the new market and improving the firm position. Other challenges are specific of the listed family firms, which need to design corporate governance mechanisms aimed at assuring financial investors that their expected return will be satisfied. The support of investments through financial markets often requires the design of appropriate governance architectures which favor the alliance of the firm with financial investors. In line with these arguments, the described challenges will be considered as problems to be solved by searching for alliances among actors distributed in space.

The family firm survival and development in time, on the other hand, need a trans-generational transfer of the family vision of the business. An alliance between the incumbent and the successors, old and new generations, is the key for the family business to survive and develop over time. This is the case where the actors to be allied are distributed over time.

Therefore, governing a family firm needs a continuous search for alliances to be held in space and time. Put it other ways, the search for alliances needs: the construction of networks distributed in space, referring to challenges such as managerialization and professionalization, internationalization, and relations with financial markets; and the construction of networks distributed in time, for the challenge of succession. These arguments entail that governing a family firm cannot be reduced to the traditional domain of business governance, namely to a search for appropriate governance structures and incentive mechanisms aimed to align the owner's and the management's interests. Rather, governing a family firm needs to be conceived of as a continuous and dynamic search for composing the different interests of the actors mentioned above (Van der Meer-Kooistra and Scapens 2008), namely a continuous process of constructing networks of allies around managerialization and professionalization, internationalization, relations with financial markets, and succession challenges. Moreover, we see all these challenges to be strongly interrelated. Indeed, as suggested by Chittoor and Das (2007), professionalization and succession challenges are linked with each other, being professionalization a way to deal with the challenge of succession (Busco et al. 2006; Salvato and Corbetta 2013), on the one hand, and being succession a way to professionalize a family business (Giovannoni et al. 2011; Giovannoni and Maraghini 2013), on the other. Similarly, internationalization is favored by a successful process of managerialization and is supported by good relations with financial investors. This interdependence among all the challenges suggests conceiving of governance in the broader sense of governing the interdependent networks around a family business.

This chapter proposes a conceptual framework that shed light on the role of governance in managing the family business networks. The framework draws on the contributions about family business challenges discussed in the previous chapters and is intended to highlight the main links between the topics. Thus, the conceptual framework we develop from the literature aims to categorize and describe topics relevant to the study, and maps relationships among them (Rocco and Plakhotnik 2009). Specifically, we refer to family business challenges conceiving of family businesses as networks distributed in time and space (Justesen and Mouritsen 2011). The interdependence between all the networks distributed in time and space needs to conceive of their governance as a process characterized by interdependence, flexibility, and continuous learning (Van der Meer-Kooistra and Scapens 2008). Given the need to study governance as a way to compose the different interests related to a network distributed in time and space, we conceptualize governance in the family business context drawing on the concept of "systems package" proposed by Malmi and Brown (2008) in the management control area. This concept "points to the fact that different systems are often introduced by different interest groups at different times" (Malmi and Brown 2008, p. 291; Leotta and Ruggeri 2012, p. 431).

We review some relevant studies on family business governance drawing on this theoretical lens in order to highlight how the other scholars have dealt with governance as a way to govern the challenges under discussion. The concept of governance that results from our review can be judged as useful if it helps family businesses to manage their challenges. This depends on how scholars dealing with governance have clear maps of family business topics as challenges. Thus, mapping governance studies on family businesses requires packaging the maps of all the family business challenges.

The contribution of this chapter is twofold. First, it proposes a conceptualization of family business governance that seems to be more appropriate to the specifics of this kind of firms. Drawn on the extant management control literature, this conceptualization of governance could stimulate future research as it offers useful theoretical lenses for interpreting case evidence. Second, this chapter proposes that the most relevant topics on family business challenges can be composed into a unitary picture that highlights the main linkages among the topics. By linking the main topics, we propose to map the research path already followed in the present volume and the one that still needs to be followed.

The remainder of the chapter is structured as follows. Section 2 discusses managerialization and professionalization, internationalization, and relations with financial markets as family business challenges to be dealt with by developing alliances between actors distributed in space. Section 3 discusses succession as a challenge which involves actors distributed in time. Section 4 proposes composing all the challenges previously discussed into two kinds of interdependent networks of actors distributed in space and time, respectively, and considers the package of the two kinds of networks as the subject of the family business governance. Taking account of the interdependence between the two kinds of networks, we propose reviewing governance studies drawing on the concept of "governing systems package." This concept leads our review highlighting how family business governance studies have dealt with governance as a way to manage interdependence. Section 5 is an attempt to draw a unitary map of research that can be a guide for future research (map for research).

2 Mapping Family Business Topics as Networks Distributed in Space: The Challenges of Managerialization and Professionalization, Internationalization and Relations with Financial Markets

2.1 Mapping Managerialization and Professionalization: Family and Non-family Members as a Network Distributed in Space

Managerialization and professionalization have received great attention from family business academics, entrepreneurs, and practitioners. Both processes are interrelated with the business life cycle, performance, development, and survival of every family business (Dyer 1989; Stewart and Hitt 2012). As described in Chapter "Professionalization and Managerialization in Family Firms: A Still Open Issue", managerialization pertains to the presence of formal management control systems in businesses

(Songini and Vola 2015). Although surviving challenging markets and economic contexts calls for an increasing amount of information, family businesses appear less formalized in terms of management control than non-family ones (Cattaneo and Bassani 2015; Hiebl and Mayrleitner 2017).

Moreover, the introduction and use of formal management accounting and control systems cause internal issues, such as the acknowledgement of merit and the non-family managers' empowerment through a clear process of delegation. When family members have a poor reputation, the coexistence of family and non-family managers undermines the familiar context of the business. Reputation, competence, proactiveness, and risk-taking behavior intertwine with rewards. The principle of merit should guarantee the right rewards to family and non-family managers (without prejudice) according to the above criteria.

Some studies have suggested the introduction and use of performance evaluation systems as a guarantee of transparent and appropriate rewards (Chua et al. 2009; Dekker et al. 2013; Sinha et al. 2017; Ward 2004). Personal performance measured by these systems usually benefits from a tight relationship with the performance of the business as a whole, and this relationship drives its members in the correct strategic direction. Although the presence of a formally acknowledged system might mean that family members receive discretionary rewards (Sinha et al. 2017), the principle of merit, if it is part of the business's culture, should guarantee that discretionary rewards are exceptions, not a routinized process; and, as with all exceptions, the human resource manager should be able to justify it.

Performance evaluation systems are not the only formal systems mentioned in the family business literature. Empirical evidence of where managers have used strategic planning (Dekker et al. 2013; Ward 1988) shows that family and non-family members or entrepreneurs and managers are able to delegate tasks. Rue and Ibrahim (1996), for example, scanned more than a hundred family businesses with the aim of recognizing strategic planning functions and roles. Their results revealed a high degree of sophistication in corporate performance objectives and an appropriate presence of monitoring systems, albeit with periodic signs of deviation. Family business researchers who have focused on the strategic process espouse the benefits of strategic planning (Ward 1988) and have offered opinions on how it should be implemented.

Strategic planning and performance evaluation systems provide valuable information to manage and drive businesses. Boards of directors constantly use these systems. Many authors (Mustakallio et al. 2002; Songini 2006; Yildirim-Öktem and Üsdiken 2010; Zhang and Ma 2009) have identified the board of directors as an important mechanism of governance and formal management in family business. The presence of non-family professionals in a family business is usually related to the existence of formal management accounting and control systems. But this is not a rule. Occasionally, non-family professionals sit on the board of directors (Dekker et al. 2013). At other times, they may sit on the board, but there are no other formal systems in place that guarantee the principle of merit or the presence of delegation processes.

The presence of non-family professionals in a family business is a process usually known as professionalization (Dekker et al. 2013; Stewart and Hitt 2012). But, as we read in Chapter "Professionalization and Managerialization in Family Firms: A Still Open Issue", this is only part of the story. Family and non-family professionals professionalize the business (Dyer 1989) when they gain legitimacy and authority through their brilliant scholarly and experiential background and personality (see Kelleci et al. 2019 for details). The multidimensional process of professionalization, as described in Chapter "Professionalization and Managerialization in Family Firms: A Still Open Issue", involves different factors, such as people, culture, and firms and systems. The systems that guarantee the decentralization of authority, the principle of merit, and so on are the systems we mention during the managerialization process. Thus, the two processes are intimately intertwined and the boundaries are confused.

2.2 *Mapping Internationalization: Domestic and Foreign Markets as a Network Distributed in Space*

It is undeniable that the specific characteristics of the family business, that is, its peculiar organizational culture and managerial practices, founded on symbioses between the family and the business, are intangible factors that influence, in different ways, the pursued strategies (Corbetta and Montemerlo 1999; Zahra 2003). Moreover, these factors have to be considered in the analysis of the internationalization processes. The family-dominated managerial teams have higher levels of cohesion and shared strategic consensus and, at the same time, less conflicts than the non-family managerial teams (Ensley and Pearson 2005). Nevertheless, they are also characterized by a risk aversion which might impede the possibility of taking opportunities of growth deriving from the investment in foreign markets. Given their peculiarity, family businesses need particular structures and governance mechanisms with the purpose of governing the complexity of different and coexisting subsystems (i.e., the family and the business) (Calabrò et al. 2009). Notably, the governance structure influences the businesses' internationalization choices (Zahra 2003). Scholars have different motivations when they analyze and examine in-depth the factors which lead such businesses, with different sizes and ownership structures, toward international paths: primarily the globalization of markets and the entrepreneurial practices. Moreover, just as for many businesses, also family businesses have perceived that undertaking successful international paths represents a fundamental instrument for their dimensional and organizational growth (Claver et al. 2007). Expanding the activities abroad allows to renew both the family system and the business system through new employment opportunities for the controlling family's members and through new opportunities of business sustainability for the future generations (Zahra 2003). Internationalizing one's own business (and also the family) positively contributes to the business performance (Claver et al. 2008).

Internationalization is a complex decision, accompanied by a fundamental and often irreversible business transformation process, which concerns the financial structures, the organizational and technical structure, the positioning on the market, the management of human resources. Internationalization, understood as the exchange of goods between different countries, is a process by which the supply chains or value chains that characterize the entire production cycle that goes from production to final consumption expand in space. This occurs both when a company uses raw materials, patents, or components that come from other countries in one place; and when a company feels the need or the opportunity to relocate part or all of its production to another country; or even when a company that produces in one place brings its products to consumers located in other geographic markets.

The businesses' expansion beyond the national boundaries is conditioned by the availability of the resources necessary for this purpose, and often, it is pursued through different ways (direct and/or indirect exports, strategic agreements, joint ventures, foreign direct investment or FDI). Each way has some advantages in terms of risk diversification, of the increase in the bargaining power of the suppliers, of the distributors and clients, of the use of economies of scale and of range of action, and of the generation of learning economies.

In this perspective, this spatial expansion is noted, as if the links of the supply chains in which the various economic activities are divided unfolded in space in search of an optimal location, creating ever wider and more complex intertwining on one side between series of participant producers from different countries, their own role in the same production process, scattered in space and, on the other, a dense fabric of relationships between producers and consumers belonging to different countries. The new communication and transport systems that facilitate the movement of goods and services in space are the result of the search for competitive advantages by companies operating in these fields of activity. The spatial expansion of the production chains can be induced by the deliberate choices and actions of the companies engaged in seeking a competitive advantage, either through the supply on cheaper foreign markets or the location of productions in places at lower cost or with the sale of products on a large scale to acquire critical masses which minimize unit costs. For the purposes of the internationalization strategy, it is important to identify the elements that, on the demand side or on the supply side, or on both sides, reward the enlargement or the narrowing of the space on the cost or revenue front. Moreover, it is important the monitoring and reviewing of all the dynamics of the demand, the technologies, and the behaviors of current or potential competitors.

The internationalization strategy therefore constitutes a subspecies of the spatial expansion strategy that companies still face in their development path. The theoretical basis of internationalization strategies is the way of positioning oneself with respect to the space that sees the company cross-national borders to access, on the side of factors of production or product, to other countries. Interpreting the internationalization strategy as a cross-border projection of the most general geographic expansion strategies offers various advantages from the interpretative point of view. There are many elements that must be assessed in this dimension in order for the international expansion process to take place successfully, such as the obstacle of borders and customs that gives internationalization elements of additional risk compared to strategies; internal geographical expansion; the currency boundaries that constitute a potential risk factor capable of altering the convenience points of spatial choices and often in forms and intensities difficult to predict; the regulatory and jurisdictional discontinuity that entails difficulties, and therefore costs of adjustment to the new operating conditions and risks in the level of protection of rights with respect to the activity carried out in the country of origin; the linguistic barriers that influence the entire information process; and discontinuity in the context. In some cases, when you cross borders, not much changes: neither the language, nor the legislative structure, nor the work habits, nor the methods of consumption or the ways of life. In this case, internationalization ends up being a simple geographical extension of the company's business. But in other cases, everything changes: the ways of conducting business, the distribution systems, the organization of production, the rules of competition. In these cases, territorial expansion ends up encountering a context so different from the starting one that it can be seen as a real diversification.

Internationalization almost never ends in a simple movement along the geographic axis, but often involves a revision of the entire corporate strategic structure. Internationalization is the result, in continuous evolution of a process that leads to the progressive spatial extension of the company's value chain beyond national borders. The concept of process underlines the evolutionary and dynamic nature of the phenomenon, while the concept of space is to be understood in a broad sense: The extension of the activities can take place in a regional, continental, global space. Internationalization is the result of the interaction of a variety of circumstances and motivations that impact on corporate life with different times and importance. In the history of a business, internal and external pressures interact and condition each other, so it is often difficult to trace the process of international expansion to a single cause. It should also be stressed that in order for the company to embark on an international journey it is necessary that these stimuli meet positive attitudes on the part of the company owners and management. Internationalization in a non-occasional way is a complex process that requires the utmost commitment by the company over a medium–long period. It is clear that without the support of top management and a positive attitude toward the theme of international growth, there is little chance of lasting success in this activity, even in the presence of facilitating internal and external stimuli. In family businesses, these aspects take on particular relevance, given the peculiarity of their governance.

The coexistence of divergent systems, which evolve and change in the different phases of the life cycle (Calabrò et al. 2009; Zahra 2003), the presence of the family's members, with a different level of the risk perception and of propensity to risk, may influence the decision to undertake international activities. From the analysis of the literature on the internationalization of family businesses, it may be observed that they tend to internationalize their own activities only after having strengthened their positions in the reference national markets (Fernandez and Nieto 2005; Graves and Thomas 2006). Moreover, there is not a shared opinion on the effects that the characteristics of the controlling family/families have on the international activities. Actually, many family businesses find themselves solving the conflict deriving from the motivation to pursue the opportunities beyond the national boundaries (the propensity toward an external growth through internationalization), on the one hand, and the wish to keep the centralized control in the business on the other hand (the risk aversion and the choice of low-risk entrepreneurial projects, focused on the domestic market). The internationalization of a business may be the result of specific "events" (Bell et al. 2001); in the case of family businesses, the generational passage and the subsequent involvement of the new generation in the business may help family businesses have success (Sharma et al. 1997), through carrying out of numerous activities (i.e., the creation of new products/services, the identification of new international market areas, the launch of factories and foreign branches, etc.), just as it is indicated in the studies on the international entrepreneurship. Many other studies examine the factors which encourage (e.g., the medium, long-term orientation, the entrepreneurial orientation, etc.) or inhibit (e.g., the risk aversion, the absence of support by governance authorities, etc.) the international activities of family businesses (Gallo and Sveen 1991; Gallo and Pont 1996; Zahra 2003; Fernandez and Nieto 2005; Graves and Thomas 2008). The studies carried out in such ambit lead to not univocal results, and there is a motivation for that: the existence of conflicting opinions on the risk profile of family businesses. According to some scholars, the marked risk aversion (Sharma et al. 1997; Hall et al. 2001), the resistance to change, the rigidity in the leadership styles, the limited financial capacities, the difference in the objectives, the conflicting relationships among the different family's members (Ward and Dolan 1998) which, in many cases, characterize family businesses, make them less prone to seize the opportunities of growth in international markets. Nevertheless, there are also empirical argumentations and results which evoke other possible developments. Some scholars (Corbetta and Salvato 2004), in fact, suggest that family businesses, contrary to what has been previously expressed, are very often good at undertaking entrepreneurial activities (e.g., the opening-up toward international markets), which are characterized by a high level of risk (Zahra 2005; Naldi et al. 2007). The factors which may influence such choice are represented by the open and direct communications, the propensity to manage the conflicts of the family's members, the consideration of the different entrepreneurial points of view, altruism and mutual trust (the prospect of the *stewardship theory*). In particular, the existence of altruism (Zahra 2003) and of mutual trust (Calabrò and Mussolino 2013), by creating an organizational culture which favors the taking on of specific risks related to the implementation of strategies of international growth, influences the decision to become international. Moreover, the risk perception characterizing the complexity of specific strategy options is reduced by the direct involvement of the family's members in such decision-making process (Zahra 2003).

2.3 Mapping Relations with Financial Markets: Family Business and Financial Investors as a Network Distributed in Space

The need to follow a path of development and growth can lead family firms to overcoming their financial constraints accessing financial markets. Different challenges come out from the decision to access financial markets. An important challenge involves the family, which may risk losing the corporate control over the firm. The aptitude of the family owners to maintain their control over the business entails that the demand for fund-raising is mostly addressed to small financial investors, who can behave as small shareholders, outside the corporate control of the firm. The main interest of minority shareholders is to gain a financial benefit from their shares. So, for the family to attract small financial investors it needs to ensure them that the CEO is able and willing to act in the business interest. The presence of family members in the firm CEO is often perceived as symptomatic of the CEO aptitude to take decisions led by particular interests, such as family interests, not in line with the business success. As discussed in Chapter "The Growth of Family Businesses: The Path to Internationalization", this small financial investors' perception can be a further constraint of financial resources for the family firm development, leading to the so-called under-investment problem. As discussed in Chapter "The Growth of Family Businesses: The Path to Internationalization", the extant literature recognizes two opposite theoretical arguments that can be mobilized to interpret such a problem and deal with it. The two theoretical lenses are agency theory and stewardship theory, and are already outlined in the abovementioned chapter. Explicitly, agency theory underlines that managers act with the aim to defend family's interests, thereby adopting investment spending rules based on family's risk preferences rather than market-based criteria (Anderson et al. 2012). The stewardship framework, instead, suggests that because of the emotional involvement, managers' decisions are moved by the willingness to ensure the continuity and the growth of the firm, even in spite of financial risks and personal sacrifices (Miller and Le Breton-Miller 2006; Miller et al. 2008). In this part of the book, and consistently with the purpose of the present chapter, the two theoretical lenses, just mentioned, are considered as two different views on how the small financial investors perceive the family-owned businesses. An underlying assumption, which needs to be made explicit for this discussion, is that from a small financial investor's point of view, a family-owned business, like any other kind of business, is just an investment opportunity. Therefore, as such, the decision to invest in such businesses is valued according to the financial return one can reasonably expect. Following this behavioral assumption, agency and stewardship theoretical lenses can be discussed as two opposite lenses that a financial investor can use to predict her expected returns from a family business investment. Through these two theoretical lenses one can reflect on the role the investor can require for the CEO and for the board of monitoring within the family firm. From the agency perspective, the board of monitoring constitutes the main control device to prevent or mitigate conflict of interests, since it is supposed to weaken the linkages between family and executives. It does so by entrusting to independent directors the safeguard of the minority shareholders' interests. Conversely, from a stewardship perspective, the presence of the family CEO, where emotional attachment and a sense of belonging to the firm characterize investment decisions, is sufficient to safeguard the minority shareholders.

To sum up, the two opposite reasonings, related to the agency and the stewardship theories, suggest two opposite governance architectures which regulate the relationships between family and executives, within the family firm, in the aim of ensuring the alliance of the firm with financial investors. In line with these arguments, the challenges coming from the need of the firm to attract small financial investors should be dealt with by an appropriate management of relationships between family and non-family members, within the firm, and between family business and small financial investors, within the financial market. Both the kinds of relationships need to be managed in a system view; therefore, they need to be considered as parts of a network of actors distributed in space.

3 Mapping Family Business Topics as Networks Distributed in Time: The Challenge of Succession

The difficulty of family businesses to survive beyond the first generation makes succession one of the most critical family business challenges. In the extant family business literature, succession is viewed as a process that transfers leadership (Sharma et al. 2001), ownership (Le Breton-Miller et al. 2004), and knowledge (Daspit et al. 2016) between two family member categories, namely the incumbent and the successor or successors, if more. Being leadership, ownership, and knowledge the subjects of transition, any succession process involves actors that need to align their values, interests, and backgrounds, respectively. Moreover, although the transition of leadership, ownership, and knowledge occurs between two categories of family members, non-family members also are involved in the succession process and can influence it. About this point, studies of family business succession have dealt with the relevance of stakeholders and the external environment for a succession process. Specifically, as noticed by Lam (2011), three streams of research can be distinguished on how succession studies have considered the multi-actor and dynamic nature of succession. A first stream of research focuses on the issues related to stakeholders including business founders, their successors, and other stakeholders such as family members and professional managers (Janjuha-Jivraj and Woods 2002; Sharma and Irving 2005; Shepherd and Zacharakis 2000; Stavrou 1999). A second stream of research focuses on the process of succession by examining the interdependence between stakeholders and the external environment of the family business (Churchill and Hatten 1987; Malinen 2001; Morris 1996; Royer et al. 2008; Scholes et al. 2010; Sharma et al. 2003; Tatoglu et al. 2008; Westhead 2003). Finally, a third stream of research focuses on the issues related to succession planning (Bigliardi and Dormio 2009; Le Breton-Miller et al. 2004; Motwani et al. 2006; Sharma et al. 2003). Although some studies conceptualize succession as an instantaneous happening, most of the scholars agree with Le Breton-Miller et al. (2004) in describing succession as a process that has to be examined through a three-phase model (Lam 2011; Daspit et al. 2016). "In Phase 1, ground rules for the process are established and communicated, potential successors are identified, and a succession plan is created. In Phase 2, the abilities of potential successors are assessed and training is provided for development. The power transfer occurs in Phase 3 with the incumbent stepping down and the chosen successor assuming the role of top manager" (Daspit et al. 2016, p. 46).

Thus, the extant literature conceptualizes succession as a multi-phase process involving a number of stakeholders who interact along the process. In addition to that, the variety of the actors involved has been distinguished considering the different roles played by each actor along the process. As Lam (2011) noticed, the attitude toward the succession differs when the incumbent talks as the father or the business owner. In line with this argument, the succession process has been conceptualized as a multi-role adjustment process that involves individuals, social context, and ongoing social interaction (Lam 2011).

The multi-actor nature of the succession process has led some study to focus on the main succession problems from a static perspective, describing these problems as factors hindering succession. For instance, some propositions derived from empirical research state: "(a) positive parent–child relationship between the founder or incumbent and the successor enhances the development of successor leadership" (Cater and Justis 2009, p. 117). In our view, such a proposition sounds as an obvious statement. What makes a parent–child relationship positive or negative is the relevant issue that a study like that has left unexplored. Another example is the study by De Massis et al. (2008) on factors impeding intra-family succession. The study offers a list of impeding factors, classifying them into individual, relational, financial, and contextual factors. Besides the contribution given by this classification, factors such as low ability of potential successor, conflicts in parent–child relationship, and so on quite obviously prevent succession to occur. Following such an approach, most of the studies do not sufficiently highlight the antecedents of the described factors. They do not look into the very core of the problem investigated. According to us, the very question of "what makes family succession successful or unsuccessful" is left open.

In line with the view of succession as a process, we posit that the above question needs to be addressed by investigating on how the different actors involved interact according to the various roles they can play. Because the number of actors and roles may be ample, and this can make the investigation more complex, in the present section we focus on intra-family succession and suggest addressing the issue of what makes intra-family succession successful by assuming the relationship between the incumbent and the successor as part of a network composed of the main actors involved in this relevant change. In line with the extant literature, according to which succession entails the transfer of at least leadership from the incumbent to the successor, and drawing on Leotta et al. (2017), who described a succession project as a leadership construction process, we argue that the exit of a succession process depends on the extent to which the successor is recognized as a leader by the actors and family and non-family members, who interact with him or her. Therefore, a succession project falls when the successor lacks leadership aptitude. Miller et al. (2003) conducted an exploratory, inductive study aimed at looking into those problems in failing succession. They found at the core of such problems an inappropriate relationship between an organization's past and present. The attitude of the successor toward the past was distinguished into conservative, rebellious, or wavering, where the successor, respectively, was attached to the past, rejected the past, or incongruously blended past and present. Drawing on this study, we highlight the relevance of temporality in the study of intra-family succession. The temporal dimension was the subject of a special issue of Family Business Review (Sharma et al. 2014) which was inspired by an earlier special issue of Academy of Management Review (Godman et al. 2001). Drawing on Ancona et al. (2001), Sharma et al. (2014) discuss the conception of time, and the categories of relationships of activities to time and of organizational actors to time. This latter category, which seems to us the most relevant for the present study, was declined into temporal perception and temporal personality. As Ancona et al. (2001) specify: "By perception of time we mean the understanding and knowledge about time acquired through the senses" (Ancona et al. 2001, p. 518). Temporal personality, instead, is defined as: "the characteristic way in which an actor perceives, interprets, uses, allocates, or otherwise interacts with time" (Ancona et al. 2001, p. 519).

Drawing on the studies mentioned above, we argue that in examining the network of actors involved in the succession process, the temporal dimension is one of the most relevant aspects that can contribute to explain the problems occurring during a succession process. Some family business studies have adopted temporal categories as distinctive features of family businesses. Zellweger and Sieger (2012), drawing on three in-depth qualitative case studies, highlight the relevance of temporality. They examine the boundaries of the entrepreneurial orientation construct when applied to the context of long-lived family businesses. The cases show that these firms have been successful over time, even with moderate or low levels of overall corporate entrepreneurship. Particularly relevant to the challenge of succession, the temporal dimension has been adopted by Davis and Harveston (1999). They conducted a quantitative study on the effect of the so-called generational shadow on the organizational conflict that disturbs a succession process. They define generational shadow as "a prior generation's excessive and inappropriate involvement in an organization, possibly causing social disruptions in the organization (e.g., Harvey and Evans 1995)" (Davis and Harveston 1999, p. 311). Davis and Harveston (1999) add to the earlier study by Harvey and Evans (1995) the different effects of generational shadow on organizational conflicts distinguishing situations where succession was not completed from situations of complete succession.

Besides the management literature, management accounting studies seem to better suit with the temporal categories mentioned earlier. Considering succession as one of the main organizational changes a family business can experience, the stream of the literature of management accounting change is of help as it relies on temporal categories. Mainly, studies on management accounting change can be discussed from two points of views which show the linkages between succession and managerialization topics: on the one hand, considering how the dialog between the incumbent and the successors can favor the success of management accounting change, letting family members to seize the opportunity to managerialize the firm; and on the other hand pointing out how enacting a managerialization and professionalization process can support family members in preparing succession, or completing it.

The study by Giovannoni and Maraghini (2013) moves from the first perspective. It offers a result that highlights the positive role of the founder, counterbalancing the negative effect described as generational shadow by Davis and Harveston (1999), as discussed earlier. Their study examines the integration of performance measurement systems as a process of accounting change consisting of restructuring the current system by the implementation of an integrated report which provided a comprehensive picture of the firm's performance. This process of change involved all organizational actors in designing the performance indicators, setting targets for each measure, and assessing performance. In this context, the integration was achieved through the coordinating role of the founder, who directly monitored the progresses made in the various areas and intervened to resolve any problem. The direct intervention of the founder acted as an additional mechanism complementing the integrating role of performance measurement system.

Other studies point out how managerialization and professionalization can positively influence the exit of a succession process. Giovannoni et al. (2011) explore management accounting changes during succession preparation. They highlight that management accounting practices reinforced the influence of the founder, transferring his or her knowledge of the business across generations and to the family and non-family professional managers (Kelly et al. 2000). Management accounting practices facilitated internal communication and interaction, as well as the diffusion of a common vision of the business across generations.

In addition to Giovannoni et al.'s (2011) conclusions, management accounting innovations can support succession process acting on social mechanisms, such as trust between old and new generations, and trust between successors and the rest of the organization establishment. Bracci and Maran (2012), drawing on the institutional framework of management accounting change, investigate the role of management accounting innovations in building or dismantling trust and creating new organizational routines in family successions. In doing so, this study broadens its focus on the larger network of actors involved in a process of succession, especially in the case of successions beyond the second and the third generations, where successors are not brother and sisters but cousins from several families. More specifically, the study by Bracci and Maran shows that in the succession process the introduction of management accounting practice can rebuild conditions of trust and legitimacy among the successors, and between the successors and the rest of the organization establishment (Busco et al. 2006). The study by Bracci and Maran thus highlights the complexity of the network involved in a succession process, examining how management accounting practice can mediate in the relationships between successors, and between successors and the rest of the organization establishment. The centrality of trust and the role of management accounting innovation in building or dismantling trust in the successors are related to the gap of knowledge and experience of the successors, as perceived by the incumbent and the rest of the organization establishment. The temporal perception that the incumbent and the rest of the organization have about the experience of the successors seems to us to be a relevant category for understanding such dynamics. The development of trust can be seen, in fact, as a way to overcome the temporal disadvantage of the younger generation as perceived by the other actors.

Considering the roles of both professionalization and managerialization in a succession process, Songini and Vola (2015) conducted a longitudinal case study which showed that non-family professional managers have a positive role, as well as family and firm governance mechanisms. A larger network of allies is thus observed, composed of humans, such as professionals, and non-humans, such as governance and managerial mechanisms.

In summary, time and its categories have been acknowledged as specific features of the family firm strategy and of its succession process. The still poor management accounting literature acknowledges implicitly the relevance of time in the succession process. The role of management accounting practices has been highlighted as integrating the values between the founder and the rest of the family organization (Giovannoni and Maraghini 2013); transferring knowledge across generations (Giovannoni et al. 2011); and building trust in successors (Bracci and Maran 2012). We see these three roles of management accounting practices as closely related to the transfer of knowledge and leadership, which are two of the three subjects of transition enacted by a succession process. The transfer of ownership, indeed, still needs to be examined by management accounting studies.

Moreover, in highlighting the facilitating role played by management accounting practices in a succession process, the studies discussed above base their reasoning on the implicit assumption of the different positions in time of the actors involved. It is because the founder, the successors, and the rest of the organization establishment are actors distributed in time that their values and knowledge need to be integrated and transferred.

4 Packaging the Maps: Governing Family Businesses to Manage Interdependent Networks

4.1 Interdependence Among All the Challenges

As discussed previously, family businesses face many challenges in the course of their existence; these can lead to growth and continuity in the business or to failure. In general, any firm (family or non-family) has to manage the above-described phenomena.

Professionalization (through family or non-family members) becomes often a way to enhance competencies and skills necessary in a changing environment and to support the firm in managing its growth and complexity. In the same way, managerialization gives the firm tools to manage better and monitor factors that assure continuity. Internationalization is a way to enlarge the business geographically and to exploit new opportunities, often through a profound change in the business model of the firm. The opening-up of financial markets is often the only way to obtain the resources necessary to feed the growth of a firm, or to assure continuity. Succession is an issue in any firm when the founder takes the decision to leave, and others have to take it into the future.

However, as shown in the entire volume, and specifically in this chapter, these challenges have further problematic aspects for family businesses. Moreover, they cannot be considered as occurring independently of each other.

For example, internationalization asks for specific skills and competencies in operating beyond national boundaries. Internationalization, as discussed in paragraph 2.2, implies the management of different laws, systems, cultures, resources, and languages, and involves the entire structure and organization of the firm. Family-owned businesses do not have univocal attitudes toward internationalization, and these depend on many factors. Some authors suggest that family businesses view internationalization as a way of enforcing long-term continuity. In contrast, some family businesses see it as a risky means of growth (Ray et al. 2017). Undoubtedly, such a profound change needs human resources with experience in international contexts and the use of more sophisticated tools. In this sense, the involvement of professionals and the start of managerialization processes can moderate risk and allow a better monitoring of those contexts (Moya 2010).

Moreover, sometimes succession and internationalization are intertwined, because the enlargement of the firm's borders is seen as an opportunity to create space for a new generation of members, avoiding overlapping of areas of influence and conflicts between successors. Moreover, the successor can be the initiator of the process, giving a new direction to the firm's growth, and exploring and pursuing an international path. In this way, the successor can put his/her personal imprint on the business, providing a different point of view to that of his/her predecessors.

As internationalization usually absorbs many financial resources, it naturally links to the opening-up of financial markets, in some cases abroad. The firm must take the opportunity to grow internationally yet not cede control to outsiders. Moreover, when the opening-up of financial markets involves international investors, the firm must face new regulations, financial investors' expectations, mechanisms of governance, and so on. Moreover, the multi-local presence of a business should be appreciated during investment-raising negotiations. Thus, an international presence suggests to investors that the business is a viable proposition.

Professionalization and managerialization can be effective levers in the succession process. During their stages of growth, family businesses face different degrees of professionalization and succession (Giovannoni et al. 2011) and both processes can occur simultaneously. When family members or non-family members professionalize (Dyer 1989), some may take part in the succession process. Similarly, when family and/or non-family members succeed and manage the thorny path of change, the succession process could lead to professionalization. Thus, as with succession (De Massis et al. 2008), professionalization may involve family insiders and outsiders.

Professionalization can support the process of succession when both family and non-family members are present. In fact, the literature acknowledges the importance of the role of outsiders (i.e., non-family professional managers) during intra-family succession (Salvato and Corbetta 2013). Some non-family members might benefit from the long experience of incumbency and thus be in a position to support the establishment of the new generation of owners. Selecting the right successor is far from straightforward. In recognizing the importance of continuity, Chittoor and Das (2007) suggest choosing a professional manager who has already worked in a family business.

Furthermore, managerialization might involve the introduction of a managerial accounting and control package managed by non-family professional managers. Harris and Ogbonna (2007) described the implementation of managerial accounting and control in family businesses as a way to manage complexity and to transfer family ownership to a non-family external team. Songini and Vola (2015) highlighted interdependence in strategic planning, managerial accounting and control, and non-family professional managers within the succession process.

Even if the relationship between professionalization, managerialization, and succession is deeply studied, other linkages have to be considered. For example, access to financial market asks for the presence of a planning and control system, an adequate governance and organizational structure, as well as a clear strategy. Consequently, the process of managerialization is a prerequisite for accepting the challenge of obtaining financial resources from the markets, giving robustness to the firm's plan, and for moderating the contrasting forces of family and market expectations. The presence of professionalism with experience in relation to financial investors (who may sometimes be institutional investors) makes access to markets easier. We have already discussed the relationship between professionalization, managerialization, and internationalization.

Finally, succession and the opening-up of financial markets can be closely related. For example, the succession process can involve several family members with different views of the firm's growth or members who are not interested in being part of the firm. In such circumstances, the new structure of the firm might need an injection of financial resources to maintain stability and support growth.

To sum up, each relationship contained within the challenges faced by the family business is biunivocal relationships and can be represented in a matrix showing how all the topics are intertwined (Fig. 1).

As has been considered in the previous paragraphs, each of the above challenges can be read as a network of actors distributed in space (professionalization and managerialization, internationalization, access to financial markets) or in time (succession). Moreover, the topics do not necessarily always have a one-to-one relationship. On the contrary, they are often simultaneous, giving rise to more complex relations and a dynamic building of the networks described earlier. For example, the distributed network in succession that involves incumbent and successor could cross the network distributed in space of managerialization with regard to family and non-family members. If, at the same time, the firm needs to access financial markets to support a succession or internationalization, more networks are joined, as it (or more especially the family member who is the chief financial officer) becomes involved with investors, eventually international investors, or domestic and international markets. This has an effect also on the network of family and non-family

	Professionalization and managerialization	Internationalization	Relations with financial markets	Succession
Professionalization and managerialization		Provide competences and tools to manage international markets	Managerialization is often a prerequisite for a presence in financial markets. Professionals with competence in relationships with financial investors make access to the market easier	Professionalization and managerialization facilitate the succession process
Internationalization	Stimulate need for professional and management tools to support and monitor internationalization		Ask for financial resources, often obtained abroad also	Create opportunity for family members, mitigating contrast among family members
Relations with financial markets	Ask for expert in relationship with financial markets and a more managerial firm	Support internationalizazion, through access to financial resources		Can facilitate succession processes, making easier individual choice of family members
Succession	Ask for more competencies and tools available for the successor	Can open new market opportunities	Can initiate a growth process that need financial resources	

Fig. 1 Relationships between topics

members because professionals and management accounting tools become part of the topic of succession and international and financial markets.

In our view, all these topics and the dynamic evolving of networks could be read and managed using governance systems. In general, the authors have suggested considering all topics as interrelated processes that interfere with multiple phases of the organizational life cycle. Among the interrelations of the network of involved stakeholders (i.e., family and non-family members, incumbents and successors, family business and investors, domestic and international markets), the governance package is continually re-established.

4.2 *The Governance Systems Package for Managing Interdependencies*

Corporate governance is a significant, wide, complex, and problematic concept characterized by numerous features. From a broad perspective, corporate governance has been defined as a system "of constraints that shape the ex-post bargaining over the quasi-rents generated by the business" (Zingales 1998); "of ways in which suppliers of finance to corporations assure themselves of getting a return on their investment" (Shleifer and Vishny 1997); and "of laws, rules, and factors that control operations in a company" (Gillan and Starks 1998). Corporate governance, as a system of bodies and functions by which companies are controlled and directed (Cadbury 1992; OECD 1999), includes all the individual or collective bodies (the shareholders' meeting, the board of directors, the managing director, the director-general, the manager) that preside over decision making.

In terms of entrepreneurship, in small and medium-sized enterprises the system of governance represents a fund of resources, since governance authorities are composed of financial capital-bearing subjects and of human capital, in terms of entrepreneurship, know-how and managerial skills, decision making, and interpersonal skills. Moreover, it is an instrument to organize the same resources, since it presides over the means of allocation and coordination of resources.

The economic literature provides numerous definitions of corporate governance, which is certainly a focus of interest and heated debate (Forestieri 1998; Pugliese 2008; Tricker 1998). In fact, over the years, the concept of corporate governance has evolved through various papers (Airoldi and Forestieri 1998; Bruni 2002; Coase 1937; Coda 1997; Daily et al. 2003; Ells 1960; Huse 1996; Monks and Minow 2004; Rhodes 1996; Shleifer and Vishny 1997; Williamson 1979). The definitions differ in terms of both the increasing presence of greater numbers of stakeholders in the process of governance (shareholders, managers, employees, the state, consumers, investors, and so on), and the broad and multiple corporate bodies or mechanisms which are highly significant for business governance (the board of directors, managers, the board of statutory auditors, and so on).

Family-owned businesses can be different to non-family ones (Zahra 2003) in terms of objectives, ethics, size, financial structure, international structures and strategies, and corporate governance (Chrisman et al. 2005). One of the distinctive features of family businesses is owner-managership (Zahra 2003). Anglo-Saxon public companies have an almost total division between ownership and control. This is not the case in family businesses. Generally, the owners, who are family members, are also involved at different levels in the management of the firm (Calabrò et al. 2013).

The correct composition and implementation of governance systems are acknowledged in the literature as an important condition for continuity (Charkham 1994; Ward 1991). Definitions of the representative bodies of the economic entity, of their tasks and working modalities, are necessary to identify the primary stakeholders and their interrelationships. The useful theories relating to these bodies are divided into three main groups: hierarchical, pluralist, and partnership (Montemerlo 2000). Hierarchical theories (managerial theory, agency theory, and transaction cost theory) have in common the concept according to which the family business is governed in the interest of a well-defined category of subjects, being either owners or managers. In particular, agency theory focuses on aligning the divergent objectives in relation to both the relationships between ownership and management, and to the relationships with the stakeholders. It focuses on the conflict of interest between the "principal" (the ownership) and the "agent" (the management), and it attributes the task of monitoring management actions to the governance structure, to avoid opportunistic behaviors that may lead to reduced performance. Within the ambit of family businesses, the overlap of roles and the connection between share ownership and governance ensure that all shareholders deal with business management; moreover, because of the relationships between the ownership and management, which are limited not only to the working environment, conflicts are avoided and agency costs are reduced. In transaction cost theory, the family business has a privileged position, since it may be managed by a single person who represents the authority, or better, the controlling body, and this reduces organizational costs.

Partnership theories consider as primary stakeholders those who confer risk capital and those who work in the business; they represent a real patrimony when single contributions cannot be distinguished any longer (Aoki 1984). These theories can certainly apply to family businesses, who, to survive and develop, acknowledge the need for contributions by both categories of primary stakeholders. In this respect, it is necessary to implement synergistic relationships, which allow the common and efficient use of skills, knowledge, and financial means.

Pluralist or integration theories focus particularly on business continuity. Among others, the stakeholder theory, the theory of property rights, and the stewardship theory are included here. The stakeholder theory sets forth the idea that it is up to higher management to understand the current and prospective stakeholders' interests and to keep the evolution of their relationships under control (Freeman 1984). The theory of property rights is based on the hypothesis that business control and ownership coincide. The stewardship theory supposes that the management is trustworthy and able to act in the interest of all business members (Donaldson and Davis 1991).

To understand the dynamics of family businesses, it is useful to examine the hypotheses underlying the stewardship theory, which make reference to compliant behaviors, in which the interests of the different stakeholders are aligned with those of the business (Corbetta and Salvato 2004; Eddleston and Kellermanns 2007; Eddleston et al. 2008). When compared with the agency theory, which suggests opportunistic behavior by economic agents, the stewardship theory is better adapted to the particular nature of family businesses (Fama 1980; Jensen and Meckling 1976). In fact, in family firms there are different levels of altruism in line with the hypotheses of the stewardship theory, such as long-term orientation, the presence of systems of values shared between the family and the business, the direct identification of the family with the business (Davis et al. 1997), the reciprocity relationship, the participatory decision-making process, and the shared control of the business governance system (Eddleston and Kellermanns 2007).

Therefore, the attention given to governance has to be focused on traditional issues (succession, strategy, and organization) to tackle them more in-depth, systematically, and more extensively, and with regard to three aspects: ownership, management, and family. Governance decisions concern not only the choice of business strategies, the definition of the plan and budget objectives, and the approval of financial statements, but also the choice of business leaders, directors and top management supervisors, the establishment of the governance bodies, the definition of the organizational structure in terms of system and operational mechanisms, and choices concerning the process of generational turnover. The role of governance is important and delicate also in relation to decisions concerning the professionalization of the board of directors and of the owners, a problem which has long been debated, especially with regard to the lack thereof. The significant involvement of the owners ensures that the board of directors is composed mainly of family members, who may be strongly resistant to the introduction of non-family members. This is an issue that also arises in medium-sized and large businesses.

Moreover, it may happen that, in those cases in which the directors are also shareholders or top managers, the board of directors does not work efficiently (Corbetta and Tomaselli 1996; Gnan and Montemerlo 2008). In both instances, a business might not completely benefit from the roles played by the board of directors, namely monitoring and supporting strategic management, key skills supply, and management of the relationships between the owning family and the wider business world (Montemerlo 2009).

According to the agency theory, the role of the board of directors' monitoring vis-à-vis (both family and non-family) management is played through the agents' monitoring; Each "principal" (family shareholders and not managing shareholders) has to invest his/her own resources to guarantee that his/her own "agents" (family or non-family managing director and other top managers) pursue the goals for which they were appointed and not their own. Studies have proven that the overlap between ownership and management (a feature of family businesses) on the one hand reduces traditional agency costs and on the other creates other agency costs, since it induces the business manager to engage in prejudicial behavior for the benefit of family shareholders (Schulze et al. 2001). The basis of this behavior is not actually selfishness, but altruism vis-à-vis the family members, in which the business leader attempts to advance the career of unsuitable family members, to remunerate them for poor performance, and so on (Chua et al. 2003; Schulze et al. 2003).

As far as the role of support for strategic management and supply of key skills is concerned, reference should be made to studies dealing with the relational aspects, in particular those that discuss the stewardship theory, which ascribes a function of support on the part of the board of directors for higher management in favor of all stakeholders. It also stresses resource dependence, wherein the board of directors provides key resources for business continuity and development (Brunetti and Corbetta 1998; Corbetta and Salvato 2004). The role of support for the management involves the mediation of the relationships between the owner family and business concerns, particularly generational turnover, and the relationships and communications among the family shareholders and between them and the management. Agency theory highlights how monitoring, which is carried out in a shareholders' or a board of directors' meeting, allows for the protection of shareholders' interests. Stewardship theory focuses on the board of directors' contribution to the process of succession, that is, in keeping the business in the hands of the family and leading the most competent members to the top management positions. Independently of the theoretical approach, studies have emphasized the importance of the board of directors' needs and modality of professionalization, the most important being the introduction of outsider advisors (coming from neither the owners nor the managers). These advisors may contribute to the monitoring role, to the role of support for strategies and the supply of resources, and to the role of support for the management in their negotiation of the relationships between the owner family and other businesses (Ward 1991). The effectiveness of the board of directors may be fully expressed only through the effective functioning of the whole system of governance (Braun and Sharma 2007). For this purpose, it is necessary to professionalize the ownership setup and to integrate the formal bodies into informal structures and mechanisms (Melin and Nordqvist 2000).

5 Reassembling All the Family Business Challenges Through the Governing Systems Package: Drawing a Unitary Map of Research

So far, we have discussed studies on managerialization and professionalization, internationalization, and relations with financial markets and succession, considering these topics related to the main challenges to be dealt with by an appropriate governing systems package. Particularly, we have argued that dealing with managerialization and professionalization, internationalization, and relations with financial markets requires managing relations among actors that are distributed in space. Rather, dealing with succession requires managing relations among actors distributed in time. We also have argued that the relations among these actors are interdependent and need to be managed through governance mechanisms other than hierarchy. Indeed, we see the relations among the actors in all the challenges as lateral relations that present the characteristics conceptualized by Van der Meer-Kooistra and Scapens (2008). Drawing on two illustrative cases, the authors highlight "(…) that lateral relations are characterized by interdependence, complexity and continuous change" (Van der Meer-Kooistra and Scapens 2008, p. 366). In the family business settings, we see the characteristic of interdependence to be relevant, since we recognize a reciprocal interdependence between the actors involved in all the challenges discussed above. We also see the characteristic of complexity to be relevant, but complexity seems to assume a different meaning along the various challenges. In managerialization and professionalization, complexity is due to a difference between the technical backgrounds of family members and non-family professional managers. In internationalization, there is difference between domestic and foreign or international markets, in terms of structures and dynamics. In entering financial markets what matters is the different business perspectives between family business CEO and financial investors. All of these are differences between actors distributed in space. In succession, instead, complexity is due to a difference between the leadership aptitude and values, and the business experience and time perceptions of the incumbent and the successor. It is the difference between actors distributed in time. We see the characteristic of continuous change, that is an obvious requirement for all the challenges. So, it seems less relevant for characterizing the relations engaged to deal with all the challenges.

Considered the characteristics of interdependence and complexity according to the meaning just clarified, the relations engaged during all the challenges need to be dealt with by means of a governance systems package "(…) that emphasise exchange of knowledge, co-operation as well as competition, flexibility as well as standardisation and shifts in the leadership role" (Van der Meer-Kooistra and Scapens 2008, p. 366). All of these are problems that have to be dealt with during all the challenges. The spatial and temporal distribution of the network of actors involved in professionalization and succession problems highlights the a-centered and a-static nature of such a network (Quattrone and Hopper 2001). Hierarchy is not appropriate for such problems as the changes they require arise as emergent. As Van der Meer-Kooistra and Scapens propose: "(…) minimal structures are needed to 'regulate' the lateral relations, but these structures must leave room for manoeuvre to enable the parties to react to new situations as they arise (…)" (Van der Meer-Kooistra and Scapens 2008, p. 366). The authors discuss four types of structure: economic, institutional, social, and technical. They propose a definition of each of the four structures. The economic structure consists of the specific economic arrangements made by the parties, such as the performance measures and efficiency norms. The institutional structure comprises the external legal and other regulations, together with the internal organizational arrangements, the type of contracts, and the formal nature of the relationship. The social structure refers to the social ties between the parties. The technical structure governs the technical aspects of the transactions and of the production and information processes (Van der Meer-Kooistra and Scapens 2008).

We suggest reassembling all the challenges by means of these four types of structure that represent the basic categories of the governing systems package. Figure 2 shows our conceptual framework.

As will be discussed briefly, economic, institutional, social, and technical structures can allow the governing systems package to align interests, values, and knowledge among the actors involved in the processes related to all the challenges. The studies discussed in the previous sections can be mapped along these four types of structure in order to appraise the extent to which the extant literature on family firms has covered the issues related to each of the challenges previously discussed from a governance perspective. Rather than linking the studies discussed above to each of the four structures, we find interesting to interpret these studies highlighting how they combine issues related to the four types of structure.

The role of the social structure can be highlighted in managerialization and professionalization studies. Problems of parental altruism could be solved through the implementation of informal personnel controls (Dekker et al. 2013), while the leaders' mental model could be detected from an analysis of the belief systems (Stewart and Hitt 2012). A need for social and technical structures is noticed by other studies that refer to problems such as the leaders' mental model of the business (Chua et al. 1999; Stewart and Hitt 2012) and their competences and skills to manage the development paths. Problems in the relationship between family and non-family members are identified in idiosyncratic family values and behaviors (Hall and Nordqvist 2008; Lee et al. 2003; Sacristán Navarro and Gómez Ansón 2009). They can be interpreted as a call for a governance systems package more pronounced on social structures. While the role of the institutional structure has been highlighted by Chittoor and Das (2007), Gedajlovic et al. (2004), and Dekker et al. (2015), discussing the authority decentralization and delegating decision power as part of the professionalization process, other studies seem to emphasize the combined function of economic, institutional, and social structures. Formal strategic planning helps the separate highlighting of the business and family's goals (Rue and Ibrahim 1996; Sharma et al. 1997). The principle of merit is monitored by reward and compensation systems (Ward 2004) among which there are payment systems based on incentives

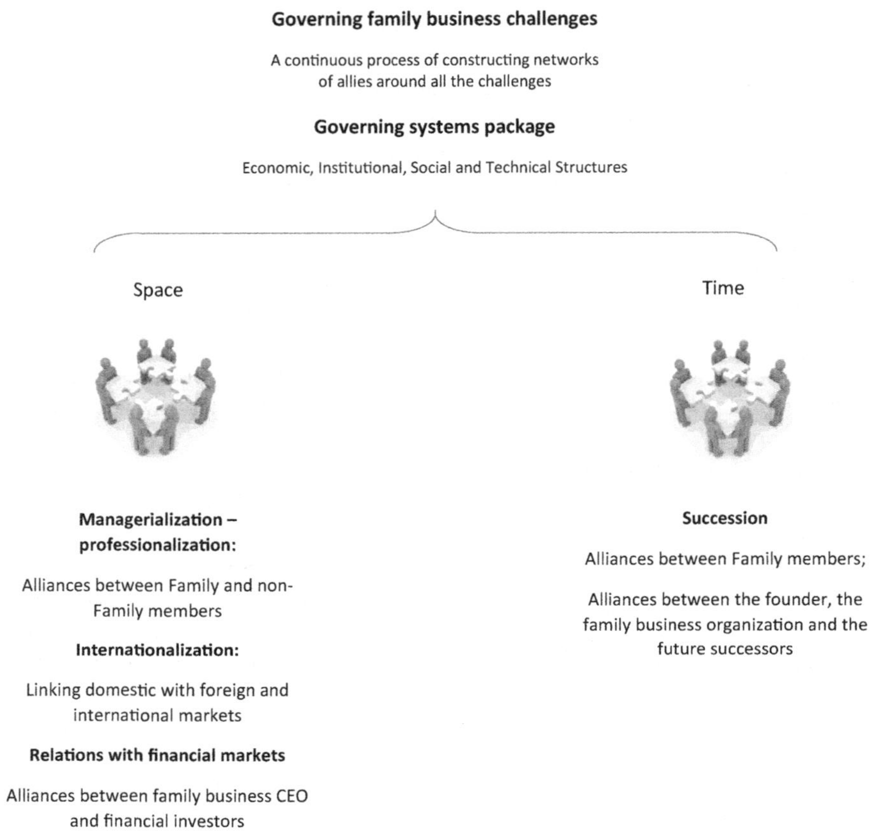

Fig. 2 Conceptual framework

(Chua et al. 2009; Dekker et al. 2013) and evaluation systems based on personal performance (Reid and Adams 2001; De Kok et al. 2006; Dekker et al. 2013).

Problems related to the social structure are also considered in internationalization studies which deal with cultural differences between domestic and foreign or international markets. The social structure is also considered discussing how family members are characterized by a risk aversion toward the investment in foreign markets (Sharma et al. 1997; Hall et al. 2001). Combining the social and the institutional structures is the way followed in choosing appropriate governance mechanisms with the purpose of governing the complexity of different and coexisting subsystems (i.e., the family and the business) (Calabrò et al. 2009), during the internationalization path. Studies have highlighted how, on the one hand, governance structures impact on a successful internationalization path (Zahra 2003); on the other hand, other studies have noticed that undertaking successful internationalization paths represents a fundamental instrument for business dimensional and organizational growth (Claver et al. 2007).

Studies on relations between family business and financial markets are mostly focused on the institutional structure, since it deals with the choice of governance mechanisms aimed to prevent family CEO from privileging the family's interests, against the financial investors. The choice of the theoretical lens to use in dealing with such a challenge is mostly influenced by value and behavioral assumptions, namely by the social structure underlying the theories. Therefore, while agency theory is informed on hedonistic assumptions, suggesting that managers act with the aim to defend family's interests (Anderson et al. 2012), the stewardship theory underlines the managers' emotional involvement which should ensure investors the pursuit of both the family and market risk preferences (Miller and Le Breton-Miller 2006; Miller et al. 2008). The role played by the social structure underlying the two theoretical lenses mainly used in this topic of family business research is very relevant, since it is able to direct the theoretical hypotheses toward two opposite directions: Agency theory suggests empowering board monitoring with the function of restricting managers' discretion; stewardship theory leaves more freedom to family managers, who are supposed to act in the long-term interest of the business.

Succession studies have mostly defined succession as a process where the critical point is the transfer of leadership between the incumbent and the successor. Issues related to the social structure are so discussed considering the effect of the so-called generational shadow on the organizational conflict that disturbs a succession process (Davis and Harveston 1999). Other succession studies have highlighted the linkage between the economic and the social structures. The studies by Giovannoni and Maraghini (2013), Giovannnoni et al. (2011), and Bracci and Maran (2012) discuss performance measures and management accounting and control practice changes emphasizing their role in transferring leadership, integrating values, and building trust. The economic and technical structures can be linked drawing on Giovannoni et al. (2011), who highlight how management accounting practices facilitate the transfer of the founder's knowledge of the business across generations and to the family and non-family professional managers.

Assuming the governance systems package as an instrument to deal with all the challenges, we see theories on governance to differ in the assumptions on actors' motivation and behavior, namely in the assumptions related to the social structure. These behavioral assumptions are formalized in the agency and stewardship theories, and we have discussed them about the relations between family firms and financial markets. Since governance studies are mostly informed by agency and stewardship theories as well, we extend to them the same arguments discussed earlier. We see that agency and stewardship theories differ in how they view the role of the social structure, and how the social structure has to be combined with the institutional and economic structures. While agency theory assumes a self-interested attitude of the actors, stewardship theory supposes that the management is trustworthy and able to act in the interest of all business members (Donaldson and Davis 1991).

Another difference among theories on governance refers to the stakeholders recognized to be relevant. This relevance is justified in terms of power and performance. This aspect can be examined viewing governance as a package of the social, institutional, and economic structures. Indeed, agency theory focuses on the conflict of interest between the "principal" (the ownership) and the "agent" (the management). In transaction cost theories, the family has a privileged position, since the management of the business by a single person, who represents the authority, reduces the organization costs. The theories of partnership consider as primary stakeholders those who confer risk capital and those who work in the business (Aoki 1984).

Another important difference among theories refers to the nature of the relationship among the actors involved in the family firm. This difference distinguishes centered and a-centered relations. According to this point, theories on governance are divided into hierarchical theories, the theories of partnership, and pluralist theories (Montemerlo 2000). The latter seem to be consistent with the view underlying the present chapter.

References

Airoldi G, Forestieri G (1998) Corporate governance. Etas, Milano. ISBN: 9788845308987

Ancona DG, Goodman PS, Lawrence BS, Tushman ML (2001) Time: A new research lens. Acad Manag Rev 26:645–663. https://doi.org/10.5465/amr.2001.5393903

Anderson RC, Duru A, Reeb DM (2012) Investment policy in family controlled firms. J Bank Finan 36(6):1744–1758. https://doi.org/10.1016/j.jbankfin.2012.01.018

Aoki M (1984) The cooperative game theory of the firm. Oxford University Press, Oxford

Bell J, McNaughton R, Young S (2001) Born-again global firms: an extension to the born global phenomenon. J Int Manag 7(3):173–189. https://doi.org/10.4337/9781848449534.00013

Bigliardi B, Dormio AI (2009) Successful generational change in family business. Measur Bus Excellence 13(2):44–50. https://doi.org/10.1108/13683040910961207

Bracci E, Maran L (2012) The role and use of management accounting systems (MAS) in family firms: a case study. Piccola Impresa/Small Bus 3:129–153. https://doi.org/10.14596/pisb.35

Braun M, Sharma A (2007) Should the CEO also be Chair of the Board? an empirical examination of family-controlled public firms. Fam Bus Rev 20(2):111–126. https://doi.org/10.1111/j.1741-6248.2007.00090.x

Brunetti G, Corbetta G (1998) Ruolo e funzionamento dei Consigli di Amministrazione nelle imprese di medie e grandi dimensioni proprietà familiare. In: Airoldi G, Forestieri G (eds) Corporate governance. Etas, Milano, pp 199–211. ISBN: 9788845308987

Bruni G (2002) La strategia del valore tra conflittualità ed equilibrio di interessi. Rivista Italiana di Ragioneria e di Economia Aziendale, 1–2:17–40

Busco C, Riccaboni A, Scapens RW (2006) Trust for accounting and accounting for trust. Manag Account Res 17:11–41. https://doi.org/10.1016/j.mar.2005.08.001

Cadbury A (1992) Report of the committee on the financial aspects of corporate governance. Gee & Co Ltd, December

Calabrò A, Mussolino D (2013) How do boards of directors contribute to family SME export intensity? The role of formal and informal governance mechanisms. J Manag Governance 17:363–403. https://doi.org/10.1007/s10997-011-9180-7

Calabrò A, Mussolino D, Huse M (2009) The role of board of directors in the internationalisation of small and medium sized family firms. Int J Globalisation Small Bus 3(4):393–411. https://doi.org/10.1504/IJGSB.2009.032259

Calabrò A, Torchia M, Pukall T, Mussolino D (2013) The influence of ownership structure and board strategic involvement on international sales: the moderating effect of family involvement. Int Bus Rev 22:509–523. https://doi.org/10.1016/j.ibusrev.2012.07.002

Cater JJ III, Justis RT (2009) The development of successors from followers to leaders in small family firms: an exploratory study. Fam Bus Rev 22:109–124. 10.1177/0894486508327822

Cattaneo C, Bassani G (2015) Sistemi di controllo formali nelle PMI familiari: una presenza possibile? Small Bus 1:31–52. https://doi.org/10.14596/pisb.176

Charkham J (1994) Keeping good company. A study of corporate governance in five countries. Oxford University Press, New York

Chittoor R, Das R (2007) Professionalization of management and succession performance: a vital linkage. Fam Bus Rev 20:65–79. https://doi.org/10.1111/j.1741-6248.2007.00084.x

Chrisman JJ, Chua JH, Steier L (2005) Sources and consequences of distinctive familiness: an introduction. Entrepreneurship Theory Pract 29(5):237–247. https://doi.org/10.1111/j.1540-6520.2005.00080.x

Chua JH, Chrisman JJ, Sharma P (2003) Succession ad non succession concerns of family firms and agency relationships with nonfamily managers. Fam Bus Rev 16(2):89–107. https://doi.org/10.1111/j.1741-6248.2003.00089.x

Chua JH, Chrisman JJ, Bergiel EB (2009) An agency theoretic analysis of the professionalized family firm. Entrepreneurship Theory Pract 33:355–372. https://doi.org/10.1111/j.1540-6520.2009.00294.x

Chua JH, Chrisman JJ, Sharma P (1999) Defining the family business by behavior. Entrepreneurship Theory Pract 23(4):19–39. https://doi.org/10.1177/104225879902300402

Churchill NC, Hatten KJ (1987) Non-market-based transfers of wealth and power: a research framework for family businesses. Am J Small Bus 11(3):51–64. https://doi.org/10.1177/104225878701100305

Claver E, Rienda L, Quer D (2008) Family firms' risk perception: empirical evidence on the internationalization process. J Small Bus Enterp Dev 15(3):457–471. https://doi.org/10.1108/2F14626000810892283

Claver E, Rienda L, Quer D (2007) The internationalisation process in family firms: choice of market entry strategies. J Gen Manag 33(1):1–14. https://doi.org/10.1177/030630700703300101

Coase RH (1937) The nature of the firm. Economica 4(16):386–405

Coda V (1997) Trasparenza informativa e correttezza gestionale: contenuti e condizioni di contesto. Cedam, Scritti di Economia aziendale in memoria di Raffaele D'Oriano, primo tomo, Padova

Corbetta GE, Montemerlo D (1999) Ownership, governance and management issues in small and medium-size family businesses: a comparison of Italy and the United States. Fam Bus Rev 12(4):361–374. https://doi.org/10.1111/2Fj.1741-6248.1999.00361.x

Corbetta G, Salvato C (2004) The board of directors in family firms: one size fits all? Fam Bus Rev 17(2):119–134. https://doi.org/10.1111/2Fj.1741-6248.2004.00008.x

Corbetta G, Tomaselli S (1996) Boards of directors in Italian family businesses. Fam Bus Rev IX(4):403–421. https://doi.org/10.1111/j.1741-6248.1996.00403.x

Daily C, Dalton D, Cannella A (2003) Corporate governance: decades of dialogue and data. Acad Manage Rev 28(3):371–382

Daspit JJ, Holt DT, Chrisman JJ, Long RG (2016) Examining family firm succession from a social exchange perspective: a multiphase multistakeholder review. Fam Bus Rev 29(1):44–64. https://doi.org/10.1177/0894486515599688

Davis JH, Schoorman FD, Donaldson L (1997) Toward a stewardship theory of management. Acad Manag Rev 22(1):20–47. http://www.jstor.org/stable/259223

Davis PS, Harveston PD (1999) In the founder's shadow: conflict in family firm. Fam Bus Rev 12(4):311–323. https://doi.org/10.1111/j.1741-6248.1999.00311.x

De Kok JMP, Uhlaner LM, Thurik AR (2006) Professional HRM practices in family owned-managed enterprises. J Small Bus Manag 44(3):441–460. https://doi.org/10.1111/j.1540-627X.2006.00181.x

De Massis A, Chua JH, Chrisman JJ (2008) Factors preventing intra-family succession. Fam Bus Rev 21(2):183–199. https://doi.org/10.1111/j.1741-6248.2008.00118.x

Dekker J, Lybaert N, Steijvers T, Depaire B (2015) The effect of family business professionalization as a multidimensional construct on firm performance. J Small Bus Manag 53(2):516–538. https://doi.org/10.1111/jsbm.12082

Dekker J, Lybaert N, Steijvers T, Depaire B, Mercken R (2013) Family firm types based on the professionalization construct: exploratory research. Fam Bus Rev 26(1):81–99. https://doi.org/10.1177/0894486512445614

Donaldson L, Davis JH (1991) Stewardship theory or agency theory; CEO governance and shareholders returns. Aust J Manag 16(1):49–64. https://doi.org/10.1177/031289629101600103

Dyer WG Jr (1989) Integrating professional management into a family owned business. Fam Bus Rev 2:221–235. https://doi.org/10.1111/j.1741-6248.1989.00221.x

Eddleston K, Kellermanns FW (2007) Destructive and productive family relationships: a stewardship theory perspective. J Bus Ventur 22(4):545–565. https://doi.org/10.1016/j.jbusvent.2006.06.004

Eddleston K, Kellermanns FW, Sarathy R (2008) Resource configuration in family firms: linking resources, strategic planning and environmental dynamism to performance. J Manag Stud 45(1):26–50. https://ssrn.com/abstract=1497784

Ells R (1960) The meaning of modern business. Columbia University, New York

Ensley MD, Pearson AW (2005) An exploratory comparison of the behavioral dynamics of top management teams in family and non family new ventures: cohesion, conflict, potency, and consensus. Entrepreneurship Theory Pract 29(5):267–284. https://doi.org/10.1111/2Fj.1540-6520.2005.00082.x

Fama EF (1980) Agency problem and the theory of the firm. J Polit Econ 88(2):288–307

Fernandez ZMJ, Nieto (2005) Internationalization strategy of small and medium-sized family businesses: some influential factors. Fam Bus Rev 18(1):77–90. 10.1111/2Fj.1741-6248.2005.00031.x

Forestieri G (1998) La corporate governance negli schemi interpretativi della letteratura. In: Airoldi G, Forestieri G (eds) Corporate governance. Analisi e prospettive del caso italiano. Etas, Milano, pp 3. ISBN: 9788845308987

Freeman RE (1984) Strategic management. A stakeholder approach. Pitman, Boston

Gallo MA, Pont CG (1996) Important factors in family business inter-nationalization. Fam Bus Rev 9(1):45–60. https://doi.org/10.1111/j.1741-6248.1996.00045.x

Gallo MA, Sveen J (1991) Internationalizing the family business: facilitating and restraining factors. Fam Bus Rev 4(2):181–190. https://doi.org/10.1111/j.1741-6248.1991.00181.x

Gedajlovic E, Lubatkin MH, Schulze WS (2004) Crossing the threshold from founder management to professional management: a governance perspective. J Manag Stud 41(5):899–912. https://doi.org/10.1111/j.1467-6486.2004.00459.x

Gillan SL, Starks LT (1998) A survey of shareholder activism: motivation and empirical evidence. Contemp Finan Dig 2(3):10–34. https://doi.org/10.2139/ssrn.663523

Giovannoni E, Maraghini MP (2013) The challenger of integrated performance measurement systems. Integrating mechanisms for integrated measures. Account Audit Account 26(6):978–1008. 10.1108/AAAJ-04-2013-1312

Giovannoni E, Maraghini MP, Riccaboni A (2011) Transmitting knowledge across generations: the role of management accounting practices. Fam Bus Rev 20(10):1–25. https://doi.org/10.1177/0894486511406722

Gnan L, Montemerlo D (2008) Le PMI familiari tra tradizione e novità. I risultati di una ricerca. EGEA, Milano

Goodman PS, Lawrence BS, Ancona DG, Tushman ML (2001) Introduction. Acad Manag Rev 26:507–511

Graves C, Thomas J (2006) Internationalization of Australian family businesses: a managerial capabilities perspective. Fam Bus Rev 19(3):207–224. https://doi.org/10.1111/2Fj.1741-6248.2006.00066.x

Graves C, Thomas J (2008) Determinants of the internationalization pathways of family firms: an examination of family influence. Fam Bus Rev 21(2). 10.1111/j.1741-6248.2008.00119.x

Hall A, Melin L, Nordqvist M (2001) Entrepreneurship as radical change in family business: exploring the role of cultural patterns. Fam Bus Rev 14:193–208. https://doi.org/10.1111/2Fj.1741-6248.2001.00193.x
Hall A, Nordqvist M (2008) Professional management in family businesses: toward an extended understanding. Fam Bus Rev 21:51–69. https://doi.org/10.1111/j.1741-6248.2007.00109.x
Harris LC, Ogbonna E (2007) Ownership and control in closely-held family-owned firms: an exploration of strategic and operational control. Br J Manag 18(5):5–26. https://doi.org/10.1111/j.1467-8551.2005.00471.x
Harvey M, Evans R (1995) Life after succession in the family business: is it really the end of problems? Fam Bus Rev 8(1):3–16. https://doi.org/10.1111/j.1741-6248.1995.00003.x
Hiebl MRW, Mayrleitner B (2017) Professionalization of management ac-counting in family firms: the impact of family members. Rev Manag Sci, 1-32. 10.1007/s11846-017-0274-8
Huse M (2006) Boards, governance and value creation. The human side of corporate governance. Cambridge University Press, Cambridge
Janjuha-Jivraj S, Woods A (2002) Successional issues within Asian family firms: learning from the Kenyan experience. Int Small Bus J 20(1):77–94. https://doi.org/10.1177/0266242602201006
Jensen M, Meckling WH (1976) Theory of the firm: managerial behavior, agency costs and ownership structure. J Finan Econ 3(4):305–360. https://doi.org/10.1007/978-94-009-9257-3_8
Justesen L, Mouritsen J (2011) Effects of actor-network theory in accounting research. Account Audit Account J 24(2):161–193. https://doi.org/10.1108/09513571111100672
Kelleci R, Lambrechts F, Voordeckers W, Huybrechts J (2019) CEO personality: a different perspective on the nonfamily versus family CEO debate. Fam Bus Rev 32(1):31–57. https://doi.org/10.1177/0894486518811222
Kelly LM, Athanassiou N, Crittenden WF (2000) Founder centrality and strategic behavior in family-owned firm. Entrepreneurship Theory Pract 25(2):27–42. https://doi.org/10.1177/104225870002500202
Lam W (2011) Dancing to two tunes: multi-entity roles in the family business succession process. Int Small Bus J 29(5):508–533. https://doi.org/10.1177/0266242610376357
Le Breton-Miller I, Miller D, Steier LP (2004) Toward an integrative model of effective FOB succession. Entrepreneurship Theory Pract 28(4):305–328. https://doi.org/10.1111/j.1540-6520.2004.00047.x
Lee KS, Lim GH, Lim WS (2003) Family business succession: appropriation risk and choice of successor. Acad Manag Rev 28(4):657–666. https://doi.org/10.5465/AMR.2003.10899446
Leotta A, Ruggeri D (2012) Changes in performance measurement and evaluation systems as institutional processes: the case of an Italian teaching hospital. In: Davila A, Epstain MJ, Manzoni J-F (eds) Performance measurement and management control: global issues—studies in managerial and financial accounting, vol 25. Emerald Group Publishing Ltd.
Leotta A, Rizza C, Ruggeri D (2017) Management accounting and leadership construction in family firms. Qual Res Account Manag 14(2):189–207. https://doi.org/10.1108/QRAM-09-2015-0079
Malinen P (2001) Like father, like son? Small family business succession problems in Finland. Enterp Innovation Manag Stud 2(3):195–204. https://doi.org/10.1080/14632440110105053
Malmi T, Brown DA (2008) Management control systems as a package—opportunities, challenges and research directions. Manag Account Res 19:287–300. https://doi.org/10.1016/j.mar.2008.09.003
Melin L, Nordqvist M (2000) Corporate governance processes in family firms. The role of influential actors and the strategic Arena. ICSB World Conference Proceedings
Miller D, Le Breton-Miller L (2006) Family governance and firm performance: agency, stewardship, and capabilities. Fam Bus Rev 19(1):73–87. https://doi.org/10.1111/j.1741-6248.2006.00063.x
Miller D, Le Breton-Miller L, Scholnick B (2008) Stewardship vs. stagnation: an empirical comparison of small family and non-family businesses. J Manag Stud 45(1):51–78. 10.1111/j.1467-6486.2007.00718.x

Miller D, Steier L, Le Breton-Miller I (2003) Lost in time: intergenerational succession, change and failure in family business. J Bus Ventur 18:513–531. https://doi.org/10.1016/S0883-9026(03)00058-2
Monks R, Minow N (2004) Corporate governance. Blackwell Publishing, Oxford
Montemerlo D (2000) Il governo delle imprese familiari. Egea, Milano
Montemerlo D (2009) Continuità generazionale e accordi familiari. Egea, Milano
Morris MH (1996) Factors influencing family business succession. Int J Entrepreneurial Behav Res 2(3):68–81. ISSN: 1355-2554
Motwani J, Levenburg NM, Schwarz TV, Blankson C (2006) Succession planning in SMEs: an empirical analysis. Int Small Bus J 24(5):471–495. https://doi.org/10.1177/0266242606067270
Moya MF (2010) A family-owned publishing multinational: the Salvat company (1869–1988). Bus Hist 52(3):453–470. https://doi.org/10.1080/00076791003721969
Mustakallio M, Autio E, Zahra SA (2002) Relational and contractual governance in family firms: effects on strategic decision making. Fam Bus Rev 15(3):205–222. https://doi.org/10.1111/j.1741-6248.2002.00205.x
Naldi N, Nordqvist M, Sjöberg K, Wiklund J (2007) Entrepreneurial orientation, risk taking, and performance in family firms. Fam Bus Rev 20(1):33–47. https://doi.org/10.1111/j.1741-6248.2007.00082.x
OECD (1999) OECD principles on corporate governance
Pugliese A (2008) Percorsi evolutivi della corporate governance. Il ruolo del consiglio di amministrazione dall'agency theory ad una prospettiva di contingency. Cedam, Padova
Quattrone P, Hopper T (2001) What does organizational change mean? Speculations on a taken for granted category. Manag Account Res 12(4):403–435. https://doi.org/10.1006/mare.2001.0176
Ray S, Mondal A, Ramachandran K (2017) How does family involvement affect a firm's internationalization? An investigation of Indian family firms. Glob Strateg J 8:73–105. https://doi.org/10.1002/gsj.1196
Reid RS, Adams JS (2001) Human resource management—a survey of practices within family and non-family firms. J Eur Ind Training 25(6/7):310–320. ISSN: 0309-0590
Rhodes RAW (1996) The new governance: governing without government. Polit Stud 44(4):652–667
Rocco TS, Plakhotnik MS (2009) Literature reviews, conceptual frameworks, and theoretical frameworks: terms, functions, and distinctions. Hum Resour Dev Rev 8(1):120–130. https://doi.org/10.1177/1534484309332617
Royer S, Simons R, Boyd B, Rafferty A (2008) Promoting family: a contingency model of family business succession. Fam Bus Rev 21(1):15–30. https://doi.org/10.1111/j.1741-6248.2007.00108.x
Rue LW, Ibrahim NA (1996) The status of planning in smaller family owned businesses. Fam Bus Rev 9:29–43. https://doi.org/10.1111/j.1741-6248.1996.00029.x
Sacristán Navarro M, Gómez Ansón S (2009) Do families shape corporate governance structures? J Manag Organ 15(3):327–345. https://doi.org/10.1017/S1833367200002650
Salvato C, Corbetta G (2013) Transitional leadership of advisors as a facilitator of successors' leadership construction. Fam Bus Rev 26(3):235–255. https://doi.org/10.1177/0894486513490796
Scholes L, Wright M, Westhead P, Bruining H (2010) Strategic changes in family firms post management buyout: ownership and governance issues. Int Small Bus J 28(5):505–521. https://doi.org/10.1177/0266242610370390
Schulze WS, Lubatkin MH, Dino RM, Bucholtz AK (2001) Agency relationships in family firms: theory and evidence. Organ Sci 12(2):99–116
Schulze WS, Lubatkin MH, Dino RM (2003) Towards a theory of agency and altruism in family firms. J Bus Ventur 18(4):473–490
Sharma P, Chrisman JJ, Chua JH (1997) Strategic management of the family business: past research and future challenges. Fam Bus Rev 10(1):1–35. https://doi.org/10.1111/j.1741-6248.1997.00001.x

Sharma P, Chrisman JJ, Pablo AL, Chua JH (2001) Determinants of initial satisfaction with the succession process in family firms: a conceptual model. Entrepreneurship Theory Pract 25(3):17–35. https://doi.org/10.1177/104225870102500302

Sharma P, Irving PG (2005) Four bases of family business successor commitment: antecedents and consequences. Entrepreneurship Theory Pract 29(1):13–33. https://doi.org/10.1111/j.1540-6520.2005.00067.x

Sharma P, Chrisman JJ, Chua JH (2003) Predictors of satisfaction with the succession process in family firms. J Bus Ventur 18(5):667–687. https://doi.org/10.1016/S0883-9026(03)00015-6

Sharma P, Salvato C, Reay T (2014) Temporal dimensions of family enterprise research. Fam Bus Rev 27(1):10–19. https://doi.org/10.1177/0894486513516058

Shepherd DA, Zacharakis A (2000) Structuring family business succession: an analysis of the future leader's decision making. Entrepreneurship Theory Pract 24(4):25–40. https://doi.org/10.1177/104225870002400402

Shleifer A, Vishny RW (1997) A survey of corporate governance. J Finan 52(2):737–783. https://doi.org/10.1111/j.1540-6261.1997.tb04820.x

Sinha A, Pandey J, Varkkey B (2017) Professionalizing religious family-owned organizations: an examination of human resource challenges. S Asian J Manag 24(2):8–24. https://www.questia.com/library/journal/1P4-1938166369/professionalizing-religious-family-owned-organizations

Songini L (2006) The professionalization of family firms: theory and practice. In: Poutziouris PZ, Smyrnios KX, Klein SB (eds) Handbook of family business research. Edward Elgar Publishing, UK, pp 269–297

Songini L, Vola P (2015) The role of professionalization and managerialization in family business succession. Manag Control 35:9–43. https://doi.org/10.3280/MACO2015-001002

Stavrou ET (1999) Succession in family businesses: exploring the effects of demographic factors on offspring intentions to join and take over the business. J Small Bus Manag 37(3):43–61.https://search.proquest.com/openview/cc11893aebea59648214e14b11d529d3/1?pq-origsite=gscholar&cbl=49244

Stewart A, Hitt MA (2012) Why can't a family business be more like a nonfamily business? Modes of professionalization in family firms. Fam Bus Rev 25(1):58–86. https://doi.org/10.1177/0894486511421665

Tatoglu E, Kula V, Glaister KW (2008) Succession planning in family–owned businesses: evidence from Turkey. Int Small Bus J 26(2):155–180. https://doi.org/10.1177/0266242607086572

Tricker B (1998) On ownership and control. Corp Gov Int Rev 6(2):75–77. https://doi.org/10.1111/1467-8683.00085

Van der Meer-Kooistra J, Scapens RW (2008) The governance of lateral relations between and within organisations. Manag Account Res 19:365–384. https://doi.org/10.1016/j.mar.2008.08.001

Ward JL (1988) The special role of strategic planning for family businesses. Fam Bus Rev 1(2):105–117. https://doi.org/10.1111/j.1741-6248.1988.00105.x

Ward JL (1991) Creating effective boards for private enterprises. Jossey Bass, San Francisco, CA

Ward JL (2004) Perpetuating the family business: 50 lessons learned from long-lasting, successful families in business. Palgrave Macmillan, UK

Ward J, Dolan C (1998) Defining and describing family business owner-ship configurations. Fam Bus Rev 11(4):305–310. https://doi.org/10.1111/j.1741-6248.1998.00305.x

Westhead P (2003) Succession decision-making outcomes reported by private family companies. Int Small Bus J 21(4):369–402. https://doi.org/10.1177/02662426030214001

Williamson OE (1979) Transaction-cost economics: the governance of contractual relations. J Law Econ 22(2):233–261

Yildirim-Öktem Ö, Üsdiken B (2010) Contingencies versus external pressure: professionalization in boards of firms affiliated to family business groups in late-industrializing countries. Br J Manag 21(1):115–130. https://doi.org/10.1111/j.1467-8551.2009.00663.x

Zahra SA (2003) International expansion of U.S. manufacturing family businesses: the effect of ownership and involvement. J Bus Ventur 18:495–512. https://doi.org/10.1016/S0883-9026(03)00057-0

Zahra SA (2005) Entrepreneurial risk taking in family firms. Fam Bus Rev 18(1):23–40. https://doi.org/10.1111/2Fj.1741-6248.2005.00028.x

Zellweger TM, Sieger P (2012) Entrepreneurial orientation in longlived family firms. Small Bus Econ 38:67–84. https://doi.org/10.1007/s11187-010-9267-6

Zhang J, Ma H (2009) Adoption of professional management in Chinese family business: a multi-level analysis of impetuses and impediments. Asia Pac J Manag 26:119–139. https://doi.org/10.1007/s10490-008-9099-y

Zingales L (1998) Corporate governance. The New Palgrave dictionary of economics and the law. Macmillan Reference, pp 497–503

Field and Empirical Evidence on Governing Family Business Challenges from Italian Family Firms

Learning Financial Language to Face Ongoing Challenges. The Case of Greenlife

Antonio Leotta, Carmela Rizza, and Daniela Ruggeri

Abstract The present chapter aims to better understand the interdependence between a family firm's challenges, by illustrating the case of Greenlife, a family firm characterised by a professionalisation process which started by hiring an external manager as general director of the company. Their managerial knowledge and the previous experience of the general director led to the introduction of management control tools with the help of an external advisor team who facilitated the use of the financial language among family and non-family members.

Keywords Family business · Professionalisation · Managerialisation · Succession · Financial language · Financial statement analysis

1 Introduction

In the various stages of its life cycle, the family firm faces challenges such as succession, professionalisation, managerialisation, the decision to enter foreign markets and so on. All of these challenges affect the family firm's survival, and its success can be the result of convergences and alliances between the family and non-family actors who are involved in managing the firm.

The different paths of professionalisation, managerialisation and succession (Giovannoni et al. 2011) can be followed simultaneously. When family members or non-family members professionalise (Dyer 1989), some may take part in the succession process, and there may be changes in the way of controlling the family firm, introducing control tools that can support the management of the firm and its

A. Leotta (✉) · C. Rizza · D. Ruggeri
Department of Economics and Business, University of Catania, Catania, Italy
e-mail: antonio.leotta@unict.it

C. Rizza
e-mail: c.rizza@unict.it

D. Ruggeri
e-mail: d.ruggeri@unict.it

A. Leotta (ed.), *Management Controlling and Governance of Family Businesses*, Contributions to Management Science,
https://doi.org/10.1007/978-3-030-47741-7_8

decision-making processes (Harris and Ogbonna 2007; Songini and Vola 2015). This can lead to a managerialisation process. Similarly, when family and/or non-family members succeed to the senior generation, the succession process could convert to professionalisation and/or managerialisation processes, involving family insiders and outsiders.

All these changes can be seen as interrelated processes that interfere with multiple phases of a family firm's life cycle, continually re-establishing the governance package (Bassani et al. 2016).

To deal with challenges such as succession, professionalisation and managerialisation require managing relationships between actors who are distributed in time and space, seeing them as lateral relationships that "are characterized by interdependence, complexity and continuous change" (van der Meer-Kooistra and Scapens 2008, p. 366). All actors involved in each of these challenges are interdependent, acting in organisational context that can be characterised by different degrees of complexity due to the challenge that the firm is facing: the difference between the leadership aptitudes, values and previous experiences of both successor and incumbent characterises the succession complexity; the difference between the technical backgrounds of family members and non-family professional managers defines the professionalisation complexity; the specific skills and knowledge required by the accounting control tools introduced in the family firm can increase the complexity of adopting them (Bassani et al. 2016); and the leadership style and the way of conducting business shape complexity in the decision-making process related to the internationalisation of a family firm.

Following these arguments, the present chapter aims to better understand the interdependence between a family firm's challenges, by illustrating the case of Greenlife,[1] a family firm characterised by a professionalisation process which started by hiring an external manager as general director of the company. Their managerial knowledge and the previous experience of the general director led to the introduction of management control tools with the help of an external advisor team who facilitated the use of the financial language among family and non-family members. The new managerial control tool, financial statement analysis, suggested new growth opportunities for the family firm, such as the potential of entering new markets and improving their investment decisions.

The Greenlife case study shows only some of the challenges that a family firm may face during its life cycle, but in doing so it shows the interdependence between the professionalisation and the managerialisation processes and other future challenges for the company. Evidence from the case study contributes to supporting the family firm literature on professionalisation and managerialisation, offering some reasons for reflection on interdependence, complexity and continuous change, which characterise the relationships among family and non-family actors.

The remainder of the chapter is structured as follows. Section 2 describes the methodology adopted, the data collection process and the company profile. Section 3

[1] The names of companies and interviewees have been changed to ensure the confidentiality of the informants.

talks about the case study, dealing with the professionalisation process (3.1), the managerialisation process (3.2) and the other challenges that characterised the family firm in the period under observation (3.3). Finally, conclusions are offered in Sect. 4.

2 Company Profile and Research Methodology

Greenlife is an Italian company which produces standardised extracts obtained from typical Mediterranean fruits and plants and uses them for nutraceuticals and cosmeceuticals. It is located in the south of Italy and was founded in 1997 by a university professor who wanted to make a business by applying his pharmaceutical knowledge to potential market needs.

The business idea was to take advantage of the resources in the areas surrounding the Etna volcano in order to produce nutraceuticals and cosmeceuticals. Greenlife's mission is to discover innovative active substances with the aim of improving the health and well-being of people worldwide.

The founder, who has a background in pharmaceutical know-how, discovered that it was possible to extract antioxidant agents from "Arancia Rossa", the Sicilian red orange fruits, and also from the leaves of olive trees, globe artichokes and prickly pear, which have nutritional benefits. Believing that the food supplements were very useful in improving the quality of human life, the founder visited many small villages in order to learn about possible uses in the medical field from older people.

At first, the productive centre was located in a small plant, but the company grew over the years (it now has a plant of 1200 square metres), and now exports its products to other countries.

In recent decades, the founder increased the company's cooperation with universities and scientific communities, believing that scientific support is a critical success factor in the nutraceuticals market. The nutraceuticals market was attractive due to low barriers to market entry, and Greenlife entered the market by applying its knowledge to its products and improving them through research projects by the family firm with the support of the local scientific community.

Since Greenlife was smaller than its competitors (10 million euros of revenue and 40 employers), the company's strategy consisted of diversifying its products in order to reduce product risk. This diversification strategy led the company to launch products into the market that were characterised by specific local components which attracted foreign clients. In the last decade, the company was able to export to many European countries and also to the Asian and Brazilian markets. To be a competitor in foreign markets increased the risks of foreign exchange, and so the founder discovered more about their potential clients and the characteristics of foreign markets by hiring local sellers.

Greenlife is a family firm that had not initially adopted a managerial approach: its development depended on the founder's insight. In recent years, Greenlife has promoted the development of worker teams who share and pursue common goals related to research and development projects, making them feel a fundamental part of the family firm. The founder has more recently delegated responsibilities to managers on the basis of their competences, increasing the trust that managers and employees have in the family. Organisational complexity increased due to hiring employees in the administrative, research and development areas. During the research period, Greenlife was owned by the founder's family and two non-family, minority shareholders. The two founder's children were involved in the business, exploiting their knowledge of the pharmaceutical field. They assumed an active role in managing the company. The daughter was the research and development manager, coordinating R&D projects and the related research teams, and the son was the sales manager in the company. They were both designated as possible future successors, which is why they were actively involved in the Greenlife organisation.

Both the founder and his children wanted to modernise the company by making substantial changes in terms of improving the production process, making investments in new machines and hiring new managers and employees with specific knowledge and skills. Accordingly, some years ago, the owners hired an external advisor, with managerial skills, to fulfil the role of general director. At that time, the company had no managerial control system and simply used financial accounting as a means of financial control.

After analysing the company and its specificities, the new general director suggested adopting some changes in management in order to support the firm's growth. The team research, composed of three university researchers, played an important role in this process by signing a partnership with the company. The aim of this cooperation was to introduce new managerial control systems.

A discussion of the case evidence will contribute to our understanding of how a family firm grows as it faces different challenges, such as international growth, preparation for succession, professionalisation, which started with the recruitment of an external advisor as a general director, and the managerialisation process, characterised by the introduction of managerial control tools.

Interventionist research was undertaken by means of a case study from inside the organisation. This case study is revelatory as will be used to analyse how a family firm can grow when facing different challenges (Yin 2009).

Since many of the processes are cognitive and hidden from direct observation, a three-person research team became part of the changes that involved the family firm in the observed period. That team, "not having complete control over the design of the experiment, [sought] to determine the experimental situation through observation, [acted] on that situation in concert with the host organization, [observed] process and outcome, and [analysed] findings in view of the relevant literature" (Jonsson and Lukka 2007, p. 374). In this sense, the researchers were active in trying to understand the meanings and actions of the actors who had a role in the family firm, and it also meant they were able to communicate and act together with organisational actors.

The interventionist approach used to conduct the case study affected the family firm by making a deliberate attempt to improve practices in the field. It also offered new insights to researchers by providing practical evidence of theoretical significance (Ahrens and Chapman 2006; Argyris et al. 1985; Albano 2012; Lyly-Yrjänäinen et al. 2017).

The research team organised the data sourcing process, defining data sources and data collection timing. The research covered the period from 2015 to 2019. The data collecting period lasted for a long time, during which the research team was able to gather data through direct interactions with all organisational actors. The main data was collected during the first year (2018), when the research team had their first meeting with the financial manager and one member of the administrative staff. The results of the meeting prompted the research team to conduct a preliminary analysis aimed at identifying the structural characteristics of the market and the technical and organisational aspects which characterised the company. The latter required an understanding of the production process through physical observations of the different phases at the production plant, and through meetings with the administrative staff, the employees involved in the production process and one of the founder's children.

After this first stage, the research team focused on the financial statement analysis, elaborating appropriate economic and financial performance indicators aimed at highlighting the determinants of financial and income flows, investment coverage and the cost-effectiveness of the main geographical areas of the business.

The main data sources were documentary data and interviews. The documentary data described Greenlife's profile and organisation, such as the documents accessed on Greenlife's website, official financial documents, internal reports and product description documents.

The process of interviewing involved the founder, the general director, the sales manager (the founder's son), members of board of directors, who were family and non-family members, one member of the administrative staff and one member of the production staff. Each was interviewed following a semi-structured questionnaire, which helped researchers to lead discussion on: defining the founder's needs; understanding the professionalisation process, and how to introduce managerial techniques into the family firm; identifying the information gaps in the decision processes; and describing the main challenges facing family and non-family members before and after the financial statement analysis.

All interviews were tape-recorded. A draft report was written and sent to the contact manager (the general director) to be approved. Upon approval, some extracts from conversations were reported in the text of the present chapter, while others were reported in the chapter indirectly, as narratives about interactions.

3 A Family firm's Challenges and Their Interdependence: The Case of Greenlife

This section describes the Greenlife case study, showing the events that occurred in the period under observation, chronologically. The growing phase of the family firm was characterised by two critical events: the hiring of the external advisor as general director of the company and the involvement of the external advisor team, composed of three university researchers, who helped the general director to introduce financial statement analysis into the company. The two critical events configure two important challenges that a family firm faces during its life cycle: the professionalisation and managerialisation processes.

The two challenges are interdependent, and so the description of each will be affected by the other process.

The involvement of family and non-family actors in both processes led them to identify new possibilities for the company to increase their financial performance and to discover new growing paths for the future.

3.1 Starting the Professionalisation Process Through a Non-family General Director

Greenlife's past success basically depended on the role of the founder, who was personally responsible for managing the critical activities of the company. This business model was characterised by flexibility and an ability to react quickly and adapt to a competitive and changing environment, as well as centralised decision-making processes and specialist and tacit knowledge that is essentially technological in nature (Jennings and Beaver 1997; Garengo et al. 2005).

The first phase of business development was characterised by international growth: Greenlife entered USA markets, exporting its nutraceutical products, which were appreciated by US customers. The growing trend in US demand allowed Greenlife to increase its reputation in the competitive US environment and to develop a strategic partnership, thus stabilising US commercial channels. This growth in production and sales volume meant that the entrepreneur lost control of the business, as he was unable to coordinate the structural constraints of the production plants with the growing demand, which, relying on his insights and experience, he found difficult to predict. He thus realised the need for professional experience and knowledge.

The Greenlife professionalisation process started when professionals gained legitimacy and authority thanks to their experience and skills. The entrance of a non-family manager, the general director, gave the company the opportunity to increase the technical knowledge that was lacking within the family.

In order to increase the company's profitability and longevity, the general director's first goal was to gradually build a middle management team of experts who could support the development of the company managerial view.

Professionalisation in the Greenlife company could thus be interpreted as a multidimensional process in which the mechanisms of decentralisation of authority and responsibility and other aspects related to the presence of both family and non-family professionals could be recognised (Gnan and Songini 2003; Stewart and Hitt 2012; Dekker et al. 2015).

The involvement of the general director in the family business management required the formal training and education of all organisational actors in order to develop a professional view of the business (Giovannoni et al. 2011; Culasso et al. 2016).

As emphasised in the literature, the professionalisation of a family firm requires the adoption of a professional approach by management that could also imply the managerialisation of the business when formal managerial mechanisms are introduced. This makes the difference and the interrelations between professionalisation and managerialisation processes clear: the first indicates the presence of non-family members in a family business with specific experience and professional skills, whereas managerialisation refers to the introduction of managerial systems and formal approaches.

The hiring of the general director was just the first step of the professionalisation process of the Greenlife company. He first attempted to establish a clearer governance structure (Flamholtz and Randle 2007; Songini 2006; Suáre and Santana-Martin 2004) in order to better define roles and delegate responsibilities (Chua et al. 2009). Simultaneously, he promoted formal financial control mechanisms (Chua et al. 2009; Giovannoni et al. 2011) that could better support the growing phase of the company. Therefore, the professionalisation process was introduced as a multidimensional concept.

When the founder decided to involve an external professional, he was conscious that a change was needed to improve the quality of management in the firm, as he stated: "*I was strongly convinced that it was not enough for the company to acquire new employers, money and new resources... a change was required in the way of doing business...I was convinced that it was the time to delegate to professionals in order to undertake new pathways...A consciousness of the company's competitive advantage and the extremely positive results reached in the past were not enough...I was convinced that we needed more!*" The owner can thus be considered a co-author of the change as well. As we learnt from the Greenlife general director, the owner recognised the importance of introducing a professional way of doing business.

Until the general director's involvement in 2016, the founder's business instinct was the main driver of the development of the company in increasing the volume and number of products it offered to the market, however, the growth phase made more difficult for the founder to follow everything personally. He stated, "*It was too much for one person and I was convinced that it was necessary to involve additional competences able to manage the growing phase*".

The founder's consciousness of the company's lack of managerial and professional competence led him to look for these competences by recruiting a manager with a strong background. In the founder's view, this is the way to support company growth.

The general director's first action to facilitate growth was to introduce a middle management team assigned to specific responsibilities and roles. These young managers were also enrolled in professional training focused on soft skills such as problem-solving and leadership strategies, in order to inspire their professional vision of the business. This organisational change meant that each function had specialised competences and roles.

This shows that the driving factors of managerial systems in this case were business size and growth (Giovannoni et al. 2011; Speckbacher and Wentgest 2012), which the founder was unable to achieve on his own. The founder's awareness of the lack of professional skills and capabilities was the engine that drove the company to change their way of doing the business, modifying the existing points of view and spreading a new common language that facilitated communication among actors with different backgrounds, experiences and knowledge.

The involvement of the general director allowed the firm to acquire information, thus allowing the possibility of sharing common mental models that could drive organisational actions.

3.2 Starting the Managerialisation Process Through the Introduction of Managerial Control Tools

Six months after his involvement in the company, the general director proposed engaging some external advisors to manage the introduction of managerial control tools to support the decision-making processes of the company. This proposal started the process of managerialisation (Schulze et al. 2001; Songini et al. 2013). The general director's proposal to involve university researchers as external advisors aimed to acquire specific knowledge about managerial control tools not yet used at the company. During an interview, the general director argued: "*When I started working at Greenlife, I spent some time trying to understand the company's dynamics, the role assumed by the family members and which organisational function could be improved through my past experiences in other companies... what I had clear in my mind was that the owners did not know the strengths and weaknesses of the company ...basically that was due to the absence of specific accounting tools that should have made the managers more conscious about the company's financial performances*".

University researchers offered the family firm a set of competences that were not present within the company's personnel. The external advisor team had to familiarise themselves with the company's issues, investigating how the specificities of the family firm could fit with the managerial principles that family and non-family members needed to learn.

In order to understand the company's needs and how the management control tools should support the family managers in making strategic and operational decisions, the external advisor team organised a meeting with company managers. While discussing the market and the product complexity that characterised Greenlife, the external advisor team and the company managers identified the following needs:

- to identify the drivers of financial flows in terms of inflows and outflows, and verify their synchronisation;
- to verify and analyse investment coverages, given their relevance to research and development projects, as recognised by the company managers;
- to verify the adequacy of product prices in relation to the level of unit costs;
- to identify cost and responsibility centres;

- to monitor the cost variability of raw materials such as plants and foods, which had a production volume that was strongly affected by weather conditions;
- to assess and monitor operational risk due to the dynamics of both supply and end markets, which meant the business turnover fluctuated;
- to gain greater control over product lines, which could help commercial decisions in terms of opportunities to enter the markets of specific geographical areas or maintain the current market position.

The meeting with the general director and a member of the administrative staff was important in order to understand the specificities of both the company and the market in which it operates.

After collecting the information required to study the company context, the external advisor team and the general director decided that financial statement analysis would be the first tool introduced into the company. It would be the first step to understanding strengths and weakness related to economic and financial issues.

The financial statement analysis conducted by the external advisor team covered a three-year period (2015–2017). The result of this analysis was discussed with the general director and later with the board of directors, composed of family and non-family members.

The financial statement analysis made the company outcomes comprehensible to owners who did not have any managerial skills. Some critical issues were underlined by the external advisor team. First of all, the structural costs were inappropriate comparing to revenues. In 2015 the company was characterised by a high level of revenue that decreased in the following year. In 2015, the staff members worked hard in order to satisfy the demand from customers, but the structure of the company was not adequate to maintain that level of production, and in 2016, the revenue decreased again.

The general director pointed out: "*I immediately realised that the big revenue difference between 2015 and 2016 was an unusual situation: although the revenue had grown in 2015, the same could not be said for the structural costs. It was evident that the company structure was too light to maintain that level of revenue*". The external advisor team argued that these economic results had two consequences: first, the incongruence between revenue and cost levels determined an increase in taxes in 2015; second, the increased level of revenue could generate stakeholders' misunderstandings about the Greenlife's economic condition. Given the increased level of revenues, the structural costs should thus have been coherent, and it meant that more investments had been made to support the company's growth. Indeed, in the following years, the top management made structural investments in new machinery, in order to improve the production process and sustain the high levels of revenue.

Another critical issue that was highlighted by the external advisor team was related to the working capital management.

The working capital had grown in the observed period, basically due to the trade policy adopted by Greenlife and the increasing amount of inventory. The founder's son (sales manager) argued: "*I agree with you…the levels of inventories depend on the specificities of the market in which the company works… our company is definitely affected by the seasonal trends of plants and fruits, which are the raw materials of our products... For this reason, we prefer stocking more raw materials than the quantity that we really need ... so that we still have them even if it is not the right time of the year...It is very difficult to make a detailed program about the volume of the products to produce: the inventory policy is finally unpredictable*". The founder recognised how critical the level of inventory was, and said: "*we need to improve the trade policy of our company...the use of a high working capital is definitely not appropriate*". The financial statement analysis thus gave the owners important information in order to correct distortions in inventory numbers.

The results of the analysis conducted by the external advisor team made evident another important point related to the company's solvency. Greenlife was characterised by a low debt ratio, even though the firm realised that they could obtain cheaper funding from financial institutions. This analysis revealed that the company did not use their leverage to cover investments.

The accounting data that the external advisor team provided during the meeting with the board of directors led family and non-family members to follow a managerial logic, facilitating important changes in managing financial resources. Before the external manager entered the company, liquidity was wrongly used to cover the medium-long-term debts. The external advisor team suggested a better use of financial leverage, as discussed by the general director during the meeting: "*when I started my work at Greenlife I noted how the decisions on investments and their coverage were made without thinking about the financial leverage...it was better to rely on the company's own money than on loans... when I know very well that it is better to borrow when the return is greater than the cost of money*".

The external advisor team also noted that the use of the financial sources was not appropriate: short-term sources were used for long-term projects. During the various meetings that the external advisor team had with the board of directors, family and non-family members learnt the importance of covering structural investments using long-term sources.

The case highlighted the role of the external advisors in explaining how the suggested managerial control tool could be used. In doing so, the external advisors attempted to simplify the main financial concepts they were introducing, in order to promote understanding among all organisational actors. The general director stated, "*The first meeting was hard! Even if the external advisors attempted to simplify the discussion, everyone was dubious! There were some people (the founder, his daughter, his son, the production manager, and the other stockholder) who ignored the financial language; they were not used to interpreting the intrinsic meanings of financial statement numbers, so many misunderstandings occurred! In order to avoid that, the main concept of the financial statement analysis was illustrated...We were in a lesson! Everyone was involved.... People who knew the financial language were sometimes hesitant (the accountant, the office worker), because a new way of reading the financial statement was proposed...*".

The professionalisation and managerialisation processes were helping to spread a new language among all the organisational actors, allowing the company to better sustain the decision-making processes.

Initially, professionalisation launched a shift in current reality concerning the use of professional tools and the dissemination of managerial culture within the organisation, and also promoting the managerialisation process. Given that the owners and their staff did not have an economics background, they had to learn these new concepts over time in order to engage in the decision-making processes in which they were involved.

This shows that the interactions and communications between the organisational actors, enacting professionalisation and managerialisation, enhanced the sharing of information, helping all the actors to interpret how a business should be handled and the pathways that should be pursued in the future. Meetings in which professionals and non-professionals were involved allowed, through interactions, an understanding of the main facts characterising the business. Additionally, these interactions offered the opportunity to extensively evaluate the company's results, identifying weaknesses and strengths using a new language. The latter allowed all organisational actors to be more conscious of their roles and responsibilities. The founder's son argued: *"Changes arose since the moment the general director was hired and when external advisors gave us a new perspective of managing the company…each person was involved in the decision-making process… roles and responsibilities were clarified for each person…we were carrying on collaborating, but in a different way!"*.

The professionalisation and managerialisation processes in the Greenlife company are still ongoing and have been able to activate some learning processes that involved all organisational actors. In this context, professionals have the role of promoting profound change in an organisational culture, pursuing the spread of managerial culture, promoting the implementation of managerial practices able to support professional decisions, and mitigating problems related to delegation (Songini and Vola 2015).

3.3 *The Spread of Financial Language and the New Challenges of Greenlife*

Case evidence has highlighted the usefulness of financial statement analysis in order to convey an important message to the owners of family firms: to pay attention to business profitability on one hand, and to investments growth and financial solvency, on the other.

The managerialisation process which characterised Greenlife departed from the dominant view of professional management (Cabrera-Suárez et al. 2018), extending it as "an in-depth enough understanding of the owner family's dominant goals and meanings of being in business (…)" (Hall and Nordqvist 2008, p. 63). Hiring an external manager as the general director and involving an external advisor team in introducing the financial statement analysis required these non-family people to learn family values in order to find a means of integration between the family view and the managerial way of doing business.

The financial statement analysis conducted by the external advisor team was aimed to identify the critical issues that the family firm should have solved and to enable the owners to grasp growth opportunities.

Being conscious of the peculiarities of Greenlife's costs led the company to evaluate opportunities to make new investments using their financial leverage in order to decide whether to use their own money or to ask for a loan. In recent years, the company purchased new machinery via long-term loans, and also thanks to the fact that the company had a very good credit rating (average rate of 1.5%).

Following a suggestion from the external advisors to make more investments, the owners of the company decided to open a branch in New Jersey (USA). This decision was the result of a previous analysis of the US market. The sales manager and his team, some years ago, decided to launch Greenlife products onto the US market. The sales manager hired local sales people in order to build a light commercial network which aimed to stipulate commercial contracts with American companies. It was clear to the sales manager that American customers preferred to know the company from which they bought products, and for this reason preferred local companies to foreign ones. The need for the company to internationalise its products led the owner to make more investments in the US market, creating a stable organisation in that country. A greenfield strategy was realised.

The professionalisation and the managerialisation processes also made it possible to undertake a way of growth based on family's values. The family values in Greenlife were integrated with professional experiences that characterised the founder and his children's backgrounds.

Although the founder's children played an active role in managing the company, a succession process had not begun yet because the founder was still in charge of the leadership. The founder and his children recognised the importance of the role of outsiders, such as the external advisor who will become the general director of the company, during a future intra-family succession (Salvato and Corbetta 2013). Hiring the general director in that growth phase of the company meant to gain long-standing experience with the general director who could support the establishment of the new generation.

Case evidence also showed that establishing financial language among all organisational actors supported a greater consciousness of how business results were reached. Using financial statement analysis, they learned what processes and activities caused specific financial results, and who was responsible for these results.

Professionalisation and managerialisation prompted the dissemination of a managerial culture within the organisation, allowing all organisational actors to recognise the importance of managerial tools through the financial statement analyses. Financial statement analyses revealed such important issues. The founder and his staff began to discuss how to solve these issues with the support of the professionals. Interactions between organisational actors were supported by the financial statement analyses, which worked as a medium of the new language, and gradually became more common among the organisational actors involved in the decision-making processes of the company.

Organisational learning was not immediate, and required interactions and communication between individuals in order to enhance the process of creating new knowledge and updating the organisation's shared mental models. Meetings in which financial statement analysis was discussed supported the organisational members in evaluating the weaknesses and strengths of the company. The financial language allowed people to become more conscious of their current financial results and able to discuss risks and opportunities for the company.

As shown in the case study, the different paths of professionalisation, managerialisation, internationalisation and succession preparation occurred almost simultaneously. When the general director professionalised the company, he proposed the introduction of managerial control tools that could support the decision-making processes regarding entry to international markets and organised the potential successors.

4 Conclusions

The case evidence is coherent with the theoretical arguments discussed in the first part of this volume. Indeed, the evidence reveals how the main challenges that Greenlife dealt with were interrelated processes that developed over time and involved different family and non-family actors. The evidence reported in the previous paragraphs will be developed further by following the chronological description outlined in the Gantt chart in Fig. 1. This indicates how Greenlife's processes of internationalisation, succession preparation, professionalisation and managerialisation were interrelated, and how their success depended on relationships, which were lateral in nature, among actors distributed in time and space.

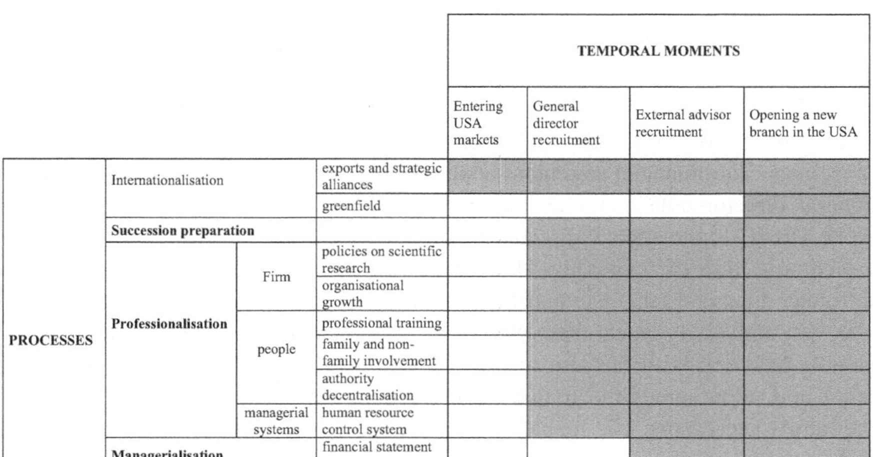

Fig. 1 Gantt chart of Greenlife's development processes

The need to professionalise Greenlife management was perceived by the founder during the growing phase of the business, while the firm was entering the US market. A sense of uncertainty was experienced by the entrepreneur, who was losing control and was unable to decide whether to develop the productive capacity and other structural dimensions in line according to the market demand. This is why the founder determined to hire his external advisor as general director of the company. The professionalisation process started when this decision was realised. The general director had full power and decided to revise the governance structure of the company, designing a clearer distribution of roles and responsibilities, promoting professional trainings for company's executives and middle managers, decentralising authority and decision-making processes and so strengthening the ties between family and non-family members. Of the professionalisation aspects discussed in Chapter "Professionalization and Managerialization in Family Firms: A Still Open Issue" of the present volume, firm and people were the two main aspects where Greenlife, through its new general director, invested in. Firm policies, centred on the founder's value of scientific research, were coherent with the company organisational development, while Greenlife's people were oriented towards professional training, family and non-family involvement, and authority decentralisation. The spread of managerial culture, which motivated the general director, had an impact on the design and implementation of a specific managerial system: a new human resource control system.

Professional training and managerial training were encouraged by the general director as a response to the founder's concerns about the future of the business and, therefore, about the roles that the founder's son and daughter were supposed to play in Greenlife business. Professionalising Greenlife was intended by the founder, in agreement with the new general director, as a long-term strategy for preparing Greenlife succession. In such a strategy, professionalisation and the subsequent introduction of managerial techniques were intended as a knowledge transfer in favour of the founder's daughter and son.

The revenues were increasing but the company structure was not adequate to sustain the production growth. With this idea in mind, the general director perceived the lack of a common language which should have allowed the new responsibility centres to coordinate with each other and to converge towards common objectives. The financial statement analysis was the managerial technique that the general director considered necessary to make the new governance structure at work. However, the general director did not have the competences to introduce such a technique into the company. He wanted to find out someone who was able to introduce financial language and teach it to family and non-family members. That was why university researchers were hired as new external advisors, new professionals recruited with the aim to provide Greenlife with a new managerial technique and, at the same time, to teach managerial principles and financial concepts to the family successors. The managerialisation process of Greenlife started when the three external advisors were recruited: they were in charge to teach family and non-family members the financial language necessary to develop financial and management control systems in Greenlife. In this sense, financial statement analysis was a managerial technique introduced as a response to the emerging needs of the new human resource control system developed by the general director, and as a response to the founder's need for succession preparation. The main impact of the financial statement analysis was mostly perceived in Greenlife organisational culture. During the meeting discussing the results of the financial statement analysis, the general director acted as a mediator between professional and family values. He managed the contamination of the family values with the financial culture and, at the same time, he helped the external advisors interpret the financial results in terms of future possibilities coherent with the family vision of the business. The financial statement analysis was repeated in the two years following its introduction. So, discussing financial results in light of Greenlife's development strategy became an organisational practice that informed Greenlife decision-making process, making it more transparent and rational, since decisions were based on what was financially feasible and not. This practice reinforced organisational communication among Greenlife's top and middle managers, and between Greenlife's family and non-family members.

The professionalisation of Greenlife, started with the recruitment of the new general director, favoured the introduction of a new managerial technique, such as the financial statement analysis, thanks to the awareness of the general director about the necessity of a common language within the organisation, and to the ability of the general director to mediate among family, non-family and professionals. The roles the general director played were coherent with his mission: preparing family members for the future succession. The introduction of financial statement analysis as a new organisational practice was a way to managerialise Greenlife. At the same time, the introduction of such a practice added a new component to Greenlife professionalisation process, which was coherent with the developing human resource control system, enriching the Greenlife's managerial culture with new financial concepts.

Speaking financial language allowed Greenlife's family and non-family members to see the financial impact of their development strategy, disclosing new opportunities that, otherwise, would have been lost by the business. That was the case for the decision to open a new Greenlife branch in the USA (New Jersey) with the aim of sustaining the growing trend of US demand for Greenlife's products. The internationalisation of Greenlife received important support thanks to the new financial language and, consequently, to the new managerial view which had been developing in Greenlife. This second wave of the Greenlife internationalisation strategy was different from the first, as it was made conscious by the use of the financial language which assisted in the strategic choice of the new investment. The realised international growth of the business was also accompanied by an increased organisational complexity which saw family members occupying important positions in Greenlife governance.

References

Ahrens T, Chapman CS (2006) Doing qualitative field research in management accounting: positioning data to contribute to theory. Acc Organ Soc 31:819–841. https://doi.org/10.1016/j.aos.2006.03.007

Albano R (2012) La ricerca-intervento. TAO Digital Library, Bologna

Argyris C, Putnam R, McLain SD (1985) Action science. Jossey-Bass, San Francisco, CA

Bassani G, Cattaneo C, Cristiano E, Leotta A (2016) Governing family business. A research map. In: Marchi L, Lombardi R, Anselmi L (a cura di), Il governo aziendale tra tradizione e innovazione, Franco Angeli, Milano

Cabrera-Suárez MK, García-Almeida DJ, De Saá-Pérez P (2018) A dynamic network model of the successor's knowledge construction from the resource- and knowledge based view of the family firm. Fam Bus Rev 31(2): 178–197. https://doi.org/10.1177/0894486518776867

Chua JH, Chrisman JJ, Bergiel EB (2009) An agency theoretic analysis of the professionalized family firm. Entrep Theory Pract 33:355–372. https://doi.org/10.1111/j.1540-6520.2009.00294.x

Culasso F, Giacosa E, Manzi LM, Truant E (2016) Professionalization in family firms versus non family businesses in Italy. Impresa Progetto 3:1–21

Dekker J, Lybaert N, Steijvers T, Depaire B (2015) The effect of family business professionalization as a multidimensional construct on firm performance. J Small Bus Manage 53(2):516–538. https://doi.org/10.1111/jsbm.12082

Dyer WG Jr (1989) Integrating professional management into a family owned business. Fam Bus Rev 2:221–235. https://doi.org/10.1111/j.1741-6248.1989.00221.x

Flamholtz E, Randle Y (2007) Growing pains: transitioning from an entrepreneurship to a expertly managed firm. Jossey-Bass, San Francisco, CA

Garengo P, Biazzo S, Bititci US (2005) Performance measurement systems in SMEs: A review for a research agenda. Int J Manag Rev 7(1):25–47. https://doi.org/10.1111/j.1468-2370.2005.00105.x

Giovannoni E, Maraghini MP, Riccaboni A (2011) Transmitting knowledge across generations: the role of management accounting practices. Fam Bus Rev 24(2):126–215. https://doi.org/10.1177/0894486511406722

Gnan L, Songini L (2003) The professionalization of family firms: the role of agency cost control mechanisms. Working paper no. 104/03 SDA Bocconi

Hall A, Nordqvist M (2008) Professional management in family businesses: Toward an extended understanding. Fam Bus Rev 21(1):51–69. https://doi.org/10.1111/j.1741-6248.2007.00109.x

Harris LC, Ogbonna E (2007) Ownership and control in closely-held family-owned firms: an exploration of strategic and operational control. Br J Manag 18(5):5–26. https://doi.org/10.1111/j.1467-8551.2005.00471.x

Jennings P, Beaver G (1997) The performance and competitive advantage of small firms: a management perspective. Int Small Bus J 15(2):34–58. https://doi.org/10.1177/0266242697152004

Jonsson S, Lukka K (2007) There and back again: doing interventionist research in management accounting. In: Chapman CS, Hopwood AG, Shields MD (eds) Handbook of management accounting research, pp 377–398

Lyly-Yrjänäinen J, Suomala P, Laine T, Mitchell F (2017) Interventionist management accounting research: theory contributions with societal impact. Routledge

Salvato C, Corbetta G (2013) Transitional leadership of advisors as a facilitator of successors' leadership construction. Fam Bus Rev 26(3):235–255. https://doi.org/10.1177/0894486513490796

Schulze WS, Lubatkin MH, Dino RN, Buchholtz AK (2001) Agency relationships in family firms: theory and evidence. Organ Sci 12(2):99–116. https://doi.org/10.1287/orsc.12.2.99.10114

Songini L (2006) The professionalization of family firms: theory and practice. Handbook of research on family business. Edward Elgar, Cheltenham

Songini L, Vola P (2015) The role of professionalization and managerialization in family business succession. Manag Control 1:9–43. https://doi.org/10.3280/MACO2015-001002
Songini L, Gnan L, Malmi T (2013) The role and impact of accounting in family business. J Fam Bus Strat 4(2):71–83. https://doi.org/10.1016/j.jfbs.2013.04.002
Speckbacher G, Wentges P (2012) The impact of family control on the use of performance measures in strategic target setting and incentive compensation: a research note. Manag Account Res 23(1):34–46. https://doi.org/10.1016/j.mar.2011.06.002
Stewart A, Hitt MA (2012) Why can't a family business be more like a nonfamily business? Modes of professionalization in family firms. Fam Bus Rev 25(1):58–86. https://doi.org/10.1177/0894486511421665
Suáre KC, Santana-Martín DJ (2004) Governance in Spanish family business. Int J Entrep Behav Res 10(1–2):141–163. https://doi.org/10.1108/13552550410521425
Meer-Kooistra J, Scapens RW (2008) The governance of lateral relations between and within organizations. Manag Acc Res 19: 365–384. https://doi.org/10.1016/j.mar.2008.08.001
Yin RK (2009) Case study research: design and methods, 4th edn. Sage, Thousand Oaks, CA

Professionalization and Managerialization: Original Levers from Molino Nicoli Spa

Gaia Bassani, Cristiana Cattaneo, Francesca M. Cesaroni, and Annalisa Sentuti

Abstract The chapter analyzes the case of a family business that is experiencing a fifth generational transition and that started some time ago some parallel paths of professionalization and managerialization. These processes are managed by external consultants and non-family professionals, above all the Managing Director. The interpretation of empirics is aimed at understanding the main levers (or aspects) that the company uses during the professionalization and managerialization processes. First, the injection of high professional skills/abilities. Second, the willingness of the family members to professionalize and to introduce of governance mechanisms. Third, internal coaching to develop new methods and practices of work. Fourth, the construction of a family–non-family partnership for strategic purposes. Fifth, the introduction of routines for managers. Sixth, the introduction of management control systems and an enterprise resource planning system to support the decision making in the short and long term. Seventh, the introduction of the management accounting function.

Keywords Professionalization · Managerialization · Management control system · Professional · Succession · Family business

---

G. Bassani (✉) · C. Cattaneo
Department of Management, Economics and Quantitative Methods, University of Bergamo, Bergamo, Italy
e-mail: gaia.bassani@unibg.it

C. Cattaneo
e-mail: cristiana.cattaneo@unibg.it

F. M. Cesaroni · A. Sentuti
Department of Economics, Society, Politics, University of Urbino Carlo Bo, Urbino, Italy
e-mail: francesca.cesaroni@uniurb.it

A. Sentuti
e-mail: annalisa.sentuti@uniurb.it

A. Leotta (ed.), *Management Controlling and Governance of Family Businesses*, Contributions to Management Science,
https://doi.org/10.1007/978-3-030-47741-7_9

1 Introduction

What levers characterize a professionalization and managerialization process? We refer to these processes according to the definition provided in Chapter "Professionalization and Managerialization in Family Firms: A Still Open Issue". In order to get a deeper insight into the topic, this chapter proposes an interesting case history. Some triggers emerge from the case.

We did not intend to come up with generalized conclusions but sought to get an original empirical insight into the professionalization and managerialization processes related to the development and growth of a family business. We tried to be clear about the research question at the outset, while recognizing that this question can only be tentative at this stage of enquiry (Eisenhardt 1989).

Data was collected and analyzed using a qualitative research method. This method is appropriate since we want to know how professionalization and managerialization come into place in a family context. Data consists of descriptions and accounts provided by participants in the research site and is collected two times over a period of five years.

The case study was started in 2014 and concerned the introduction of the enterprise resource planning (ERP) system and governance mechanisms. This family business was an appropriate site for the study since it was in the middle of a reorganization toward succession of the fifth generation of entrepreneurs. Furthermore, accessibility was good because the incumbent's son-in-law was working on his degree dissertation with two of the researchers.

Data was collected from October 2014 till March 2015. One of the two degree supervisors had intense discussions with the student who was working in the Molino Nicoli spa[1] as a purchase employee. In that moment, two external groups of consultants were on the case. A first group of consultants was supporting the incumbent over the succession process and the second group of consultants was introducing the ERP system. The student/incumbent's son-in-law was working with the ERP consultants to improve his knowledge of, and abilities with, the system. He was the person chosen by the incumbent and the successors to develop the ERP following the introductive project with the consultant. He was active during the entire introduction process and fully worked in the business. He noted all the technical aspects of the implementation, but of extreme importance, he noticed the cultural aspects of the business, including plenty of enthusiasm, effort, and resistance. Furthermore, he lived the introduction of some governance systems through his wife, who is the incumbent's daughter. In the first entry into the case, the researchers had only informal discussions with the student; however, the frequent interactions provided a rich description of the situation.

The second entry into the case was in September 2019 when the two researchers interviewed the non-family Managing Director and the graduate student. The interview lasted 1 h and 40 min and was recorded and completely transcribed. The two

[1]All the names mentioned are real. The company and the interviewees give their consent to use names and data.

researchers noted the emerging levers/aspects in a notebook during the interview. They discussed these aspects when the interview was finished and they sent their notes and interpretation to the other two external (off-the-case) researchers. Internal and external documents rounded off the analysis. The reading of theoretical works and discussions with colleagues is produced the chapter in its present form.

According to the main conclusions depicted in Chapter "Professionalization and Managerialization in Family Firms: A Still Open Issue", professionalization and managerialization in the Molino Nicoli spa are tightly related phenomena. In the case study, family and non-family professionals and an external member of the board of directors (i.e., professionals) stimulated the introduction of formal management control systems (i.e., managerialization) that, in turn, stimulated the professionalization of the company, transforming it from an entrepreneurial to a managerial firm.

The rest of the chapter is outlined as follows: The second section is dedicated to an overview of the family business and its main stages of development. Section three lists the original levers/aspects of professionalization and managerialization, and section four describes the emerging framework in which each lever/aspect has been related to the four dimensions of professionalization described in the literature review (i.e., People, Firm, Culture, and Systems; Chapter "Professionalization and Managerialization in Family Firms: A Still Open Issue".

2 Who is Molino Nicoli Spa?

The context of the study is hereinafter described. Molino Nicoli spa is a company of five generations of millers. Founded in 1869, the relationship that binds the company to the agricultural world has, over the course of these long years, been increasingly strengthened. The maize processing company covers the market for yellow flours, breakfast cereals, and other products destined for human consumption.

2.1 The Main Historical Paths

Over the first 100 years, the Molino Nicoli spa could be considered an artisan mill. The industrial boost starts in the 1970s. Some peculiar paths can be identified (Fig. 1).

1970–1980s: In these years, Molino Nicoli launches the sale of cornmeal branded Nicoli in the Mass Market Retailer channels; sales boost both on the domestic and foreign markets.

1982: The company starts the cultivation of precious qualities of corn (vitreous variety); collecting corn in panicles allows the product to be preserved, avoiding artificial drying which alters its organoleptic properties. In the same year, the company becomes a joint stock company.

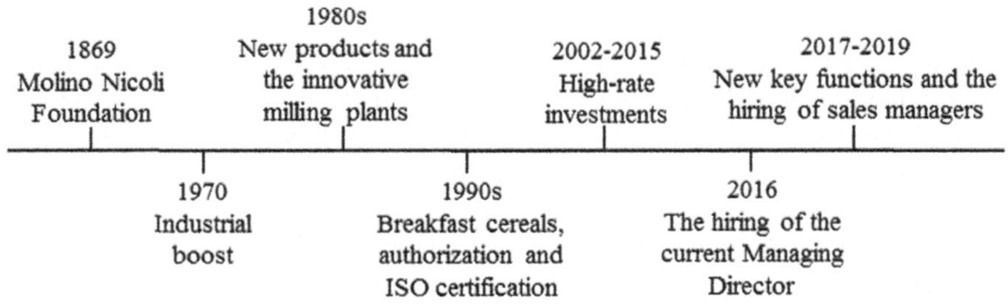

Fig. 1 Timeline

1988: Innovative milling plants are activated that allow the processing of "wet" rather than dry corn.

1992: The production and sale of breakfast cereals begin.

1994: The company obtains the certification for organic production.

1995: The company obtains the ministerial authorization necessary to vitaminize cereals for breakfast.

1997: The company obtains the ISO 9002 quality system certification.

2000: The company obtains the GMOs-free product certification and the traditional steam cooking certification for the production of corn flakes.

2002–2015: High-rate investments are made in buildings, automated production lines, the dryer automation system plant, and packaging systems. With these investments, Molino Nicoli maintains high-level quality standards.

2016: An outside Managing Director is hired and the previous family Managing Director becomes the President of the board.

2017: A new building for allergen-free production opens.

2017–2018: established key organizational functions: Planning, Production, Purchasing, R&D.

Mid 2018–beginning of 2019: Two sales managers are hired, one for the Italian market and the other for the international market.

2019: Efforts to enter the USA and Canadian gluten-free markets are made.

2.2 *The Firm Organization*

The recent and constant growth of products and market share favors the hiring of new employees in different areas. Until 2016, the Managing Director was the incumbent (the current President). A multitude of factors (i.e., the growing complexity in the markets and products and the path of business development) sparks off a management crisis throughout the firm. The Managing Director is no longer able to manage all the business processes himself. The company needs to spread empowerment and responsibility over the management team and needs to acquire business and strategy

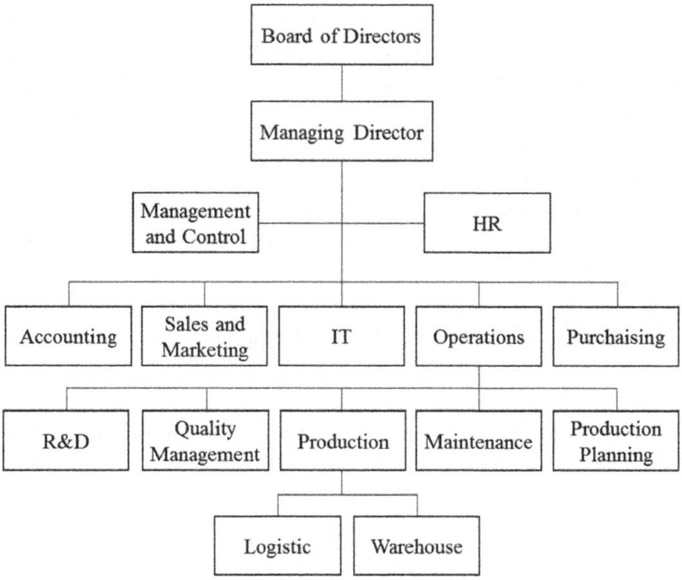

Fig. 2 Organizational chart

expertise. In September 2016, the current Managing Director is hired. He has worked for almost 30 years in an important family multinational in the food sector.

The new Managing Director promotes a reorganization of activities and relations among the different organizational areas. From 2016, the number of employees doubled, a reorganization was crucial. The present 150 employees are engaged in the following areas, mainly in the operations function (Fig. 2).

The operations function is the main area of the business. The Operations Director (Stefano Nicoli) is the core person of the business development. He is the President's son, he has passion, new ideas, and he is very experienced in the business. Stefano manages the core industrial functions, such as Research and Development, Quality Management, Maintenance, Production, and Production Planning. Production includes the milling department, the storage silos, the gluten-free area, and the center for drying and storage of maize. The milling and silo storage departments for cereals and flour are the historical core business. Until the 1990s, these departments produced both final products for mass market retailers and semi-finished products (flour) for the food and livestock industries. Today, the department mainly carries out the products of the Nicoli industrial supply chain. The gluten-free area is crucial for the recent development of the company. It was established as soon as the company received ministerial authorization. The drying and storage maize area is reserved for the company transformational process. This is mentioned as "Warehouse" in Fig. 2. Logistics is coordinated by the Production Manager with the supervision of the Operations Director.

Another crucial area is reserved to Purchasing. The main objective of this area is to ensure a continuous balance between high quality and the right price. The supply chain is based on established relationships that are regulated by informal norms (trust and yearly acquaintance) and formal contracts. The Sales and Marketing area and the Research and Development area are deeply involved with the Purchasing activities. Both of these areas mark an important change in the last years in terms of employees involved, international relationships boost, and more structured activities aligned with strategic purposes. The Sales and Marketing area is directly managed by the Managing Director who has recently hired two professional managers with long experience in sales in the Italian and international markets. Marketing activities are run by the daughter-in-law of the President who has a degree in languages and a past experience in the travel business.

Since 2014, the Management and Control function has been established. It is managed by the son-in-law of the President and it provided useful information for the Managing Director as well as the Board of Directors. The Accounting function, IT, and the Human Resources function complete the organizational skeleton.

2.3 The Markets and Products

The good results achieved by the company over the years are based on precise strategic choices pursued with determination and tenacity. Among the most significant, we can first mention the closure of the production of semi-finished products for the industry and the establishment of the controlled supply chain.

Until the early 1990s, the company's turnover was divided into semi-finished products for industry (food or livestock) and finished food products. The former were generic articles, for which customization was not possible, to be sold in a market characterized by high competition on the demand side. In this market, important volumes could be developed but with limited unit profit margins. Otherwise, food products lent themselves to different customizations, both in content and format, and could be identified by their own brand, or by a private label. In addition to allowing greater unit margins, this sector presented interesting development prospects as well as particular niches which could be profitably entered. Starting in the second half of the 1990s, the company chose to forgo sales in the sector characterized by low margins and strong competition, focusing only on the food sector while maintaining overall sales volumes.

In pursuing the goal of the highest quality of its articles, and with the conviction that a food product can be of quality only if high quality raw materials are also used, the company has activated a rigorous control over the entire supply chain (certification UNI EN ISO 22005: 2008). The supply chain begins with the stipulation of cultivation contracts with the farmers and the subsequent control of all the cultivation operations from sowing to harvest. It continues with the drying of maize, their storage, and their subsequent milling in plants exclusively dedicated to the Nicoli production chain. The company, a unique case in Europe, has the possibility to carry out all of the processing activities of the cereal in-house, from harvesting to the packaged food product. All processing cycles can, therefore, be customized according to the company's specific needs.

The company very clearly knows that it cannot compete with the quantitative levels of the multinationals and that it cannot be a leader in the sector. It has, therefore, turned its attention and its strategic efforts to particular market segments to make the most of its competitive levers and gain its competitive advantage.

In the yellow flour sector, the so-called traditional one, the company now holds a leading position, recognized above all by virtue of the genuineness of the product. In fact, maize cultivations avoid the use of herbicides. The processing methods, although using modern machinery, refer to "old-fashioned" systems with particular methods of drying the wheat-turkish that are aimed at guaranteeing better yields and maintaining intact the nutritive principles. Packaging solutions are carefully designed to stimulate the interest of consumers who are more attentive to genuineness and naturalness.

In the breakfast cereals sector, the company is entering a constantly growing market, mainly due to the transformation of the eating habits of Italians that have become closer to Anglo-Saxon ones. Molino Nicoli immediately understood the potential of these products, and by focusing on differentiation and quality, it established itself in the market (not only in Italy), becoming a reference producer.

For both sectors, development was also possible thanks to all the services connected to sales and logistics that the company is able to provide. High quality is the main objective and the main stimulus for continuous improvement of the company. It is the result of detailed procedures that invest all the processing phases from procurement to production and final packaging. A brief description is hereinafter provided.

The supply is acquired through a careful selection of the maize varieties produced by the farms connected with the Nicoli mill through cultivation and collaboration contracts. In recent years, this link has become closer and has led the company to enter into agreements directly with the farmers. This fact ensures the full control of the supply chain and guarantees a complete traceability of raw materials. The laboratory of analysis that is the core of the research and development function evaluates all the incoming raw materials and guarantees compliance with the agreed procedures.

Production takes place through the use of automated systems with high technological content that allow the probing of every phase of the process, during which the raw material is not subjected to thermal stress; the finished product thus retains all the nutritional characteristics. The company made great investments in technology 4.0 and implemented production lines with highly innovative machinery.

Finally, the packaging phase covers a fundamental aspect in the preservation of the product, and Molino Nicoli spa has reached a level of maximum reliability. By using vacuum packaging lines, it is possible to maintain the quality of the products for long periods of time.

A common feature of the market segments of the company can certainly be found in the category of foods that can be qualified as healthy or light products for people who by necessity or by choice are oriented toward a healthy and balanced diet. The

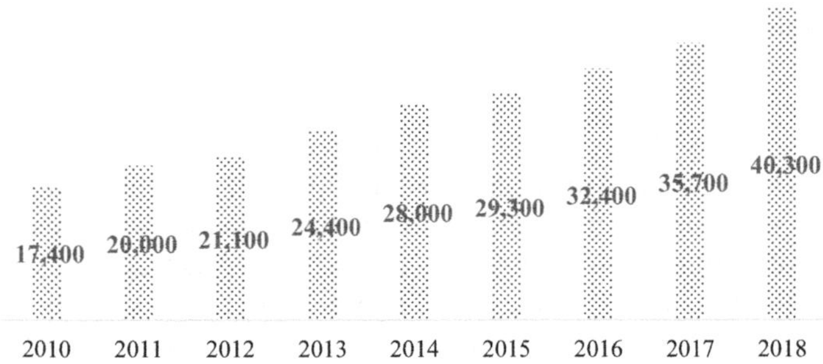

Fig. 3 Turnover (KEuro) 2010–2018

company's product range therefore includes biologic foods and foods that are no-salt, fat-free, gluten-free or have the addition of supplements such as iron or vitamins.

The company sells to the B2B market the 90% of its products with private label and the 10% with own labels. The challenge that the company is pursuing is to increase the percentage of own brand sales, even by using additional distribution channels. Pharmacies and specialized stores represent a channel for the Italian market with a product portfolio registered and approved by the Ministry of Health for reimbursement. Also, retailers are more and more interested in products oriented to wellness and health (e.g., without allergens and free from).

The effects of product innovations and organizational changes are clear in terms of performance. Figure 3 shows the Molino Nicoli turnover trend from 2010 to 2018. The data confirms the growth in volume and value generated by the company. About fifty percent of the turnover is made by sales from outside Italy. In terms of margins, the company shows an increase in the last three years. In 2016, the percentage of earnings before interest, taxes, depreciation, and amortization over turnover was 14%, while it is 21% in 2018. And the President continuously invests in the company, especially in terms of production plants, facilities, and equipment.

2.4 The Corporate Governance

The corporate structure of Molino Nicoli spa is entirely under the control of the Nicoli family (80% Mr. Giovanni Nicoli and 10% each child, Stefano and Francesca). The father and his children are also personally involved in the management of the company. In fact, until 2016, Giovanni held the position of Managing Director and is now the President, while his son Stefano has the role of Operations Director and his daughter Francesca manages the Purchasing area. Recently, Stefano has been appointed Vice President. The three family members sit on the Boards of Directors, together with the present Managing Director and an external professional.

In this process of growth and change, Molino Nicoli is also facing a succession process. It is a process that has lasted for some years and that is bringing the new generation, Stefano and Francesca, to the head of the company. The succession path has been accompanied by expert consultants who have supported the definition of the business with respect to the family perimeter.

3 The Levers of Professionalization and Managerialization

With respect to our case study, the determinant levers of professionalization and managerialization and the relation between these two processes can be understood only by examining how extensively involved the levers were in the structuring of family and non-family actors' working activities and practices. The levers are described according to previous studies.

3.1 Injection Of High Professional Skills/Abilities

During the latest years, non-family, high-skilled persons have been introduced into Molino Nicoli spa. In 2015, the President decided to welcome a highly trusted and experienced professional, a non-family consultant, who now sits on the Board of Directors. The non-family consultant had a long career in Barilla working as HR Director and as a Division Director. During that period, he had the opportunity to know the current Managing Director of Molino Nicoli very well. When the President expressed the desire to introduce a non-family manager with high skills and the potential to grow the company, he suggested the current Managing Director.

The Managing Director is 58 years old with 35 years of experience, 27 years with Barilla, during which time the company encountered many disruptive phases. Barilla is a family company, too. Barilla encouraged him to develop his professional knowledge; he also developed the awareness to be part of a family business. "*This implies that the family is inside the company and the company is a sort of heritage to be transferred to the next generations*" (Managing Director 2019). Barilla transmitted concrete daily messages, creating within Barilla a strong sense of belonging that accompanied the managerial experiences of all the managers. In Molino Nicoli, too, the family has an essential role, perhaps even more than in Barilla.

In the last two years, the Managing Director and the Operations Director established key business functions and they hired two sales managers with long experience in sales and markets similar to Molino Nicoli's. The professional background and the direct knowledge of the national and international players are two strategic aspects for a commercial expansion of the business.

3.2 Family Members' Willingness and the Introduction of Governance Mechanisms

The President has long been aware of the need to make a change in the company in accordance with the recent complex scenarios and the daily challenges. The President refers principally to professionalization, managerialization, and succession processes. Although the President is a very energetic person and is a workaholic, he is invested in the succession process. He promoted support from specialized family business consultants to create a successful succession plan. A book was created with clearly described governance rules and the President's roles were also clearly defined. During this process, "*the awareness was born that it then became the willingness to abandon a hierarchical structure and to adopt a functional organization structure based on the principle of empowerment*" (Managing Director 2019).

The family members' willingness to regard every business process as one that could shape the future of the firm has increased in the last years. In 2017, Molino Nicoli introduced the Board of Directors. In 2018, a new collegial control board was created, the Executive Committee, composed of the three owners (i.e., the President and the two children) and the Managing Director. The four members of the Executive Committee also sit on the Board of Directors, along with the external consultant. While the long-term strategies and investments are discussed during the Board of Directors meetings, budgets, ex-post performance, and short-term projects compose the agenda for the Executive Committee.

3.3 Internal Coaching to Develop New Methods and Practices of Work

The Managing Director in close agreement with the Operations Director introduces a learning by doing approach involving highly experienced workers. "*It is not possible to ask people who have worked for many years in the same way to change*" (Management Accountant 2019). The Operations Director, after a careful analysis of the production processes, identified ways to save time and effort. This analysis occurred simultaneously with the introduction of automated production lines integrated with the ERP system. This system collects a lot of information regarding the use of machinery, waste, production hours, downtime, use of resources, etc. He then instructed the Management Accountant and the IT employee to work alongside the workers for some periods of time in their daily work.

The Management Accountant has made the workers, mainly in the production area, aware of the importance of a timely and complete collection of information regarding the production process. The automated process also lightened the daily activities of workers.

3.4 *Construction of a Family–Non-family Partnership for Strategic Purposes*

The Managing Director writes a draft of strategic memorandum and initiates a strategic dialogue with the family Operations Director. This dialogue is embodied in an in-depth analysis of each point of the memorandum for a validation of the contents. Strategic objectives are discussed in terms of market, products, resources, and actions. The creation of a win–win relationship between the family highly-operationally skilled top manager and the non-family highly-strategically skilled Managing Director is essential to provide a balanced (family and business) strategic intent.

The design of this partnership has not been easy. The company is not used to formalize a strategic path and the investments were mainly based on innovative insights without adopting a proactive attitude to the strategy.

Stefano and Francesca have had no work experience other than in the family business. There is, therefore, the need to create a path of training on the job. "*The Managing Director also plays the role of internal coach; thus, the new generation can acquire the necessary skills to manage the company in competitive and international markets*" (Management Accountant 2019). The coaching is daily and constant and is intensified when necessary to discuss strategic issues and solve complex problems. The way in which the Managing Director manages these relationships is a sort of partnership and he filters out family issues. This relationship not only dampens the tensions and rivalries between family and non-family members but also between the family members.

3.5 *Introduction of Organizational Routines*

An intranet system is introduced where everyone can share documents and projects. This shared space becomes essential to promote an alignment between family and non-family managers and among all workers engaged in multiple business areas.

In addition, the Managing Director introduces a cross-functional weekly meeting. The family Operations Director, the family Purchasing Director, the family Marketing Manager, the non-family Managing Director, and the other non-family managers participate at this meeting. The agenda of the meeting is decided by the Managing Director and the President is not involved. "*This weekly routine favored the interaction between the functions and the use of shared tools and documents*" (Managing Director 2019).

Audit reports containing sales, purchase, and production information are fundamental for the discussion during the weekly meetings. The creation of moments of formal sharing has favored the spread of structured and routinized reports that the managers of the different areas present to highlight the most significant trends and challenges to find a shared solution.

Every Friday afternoon, there is a commercial meeting at which the development of numerous projects is discussed. Recently, the projects have been included in a tool that is constantly updated and shared in the intranet system.

3.6 Introduction of Management Control Systems and an ERP to Support the Decision Making in the Short and Long Term

In mid-2014, Stefano and Francesca were aware of the need to introduce a more formal decision-making process in order to create a clear distinction between strategic and operational decisions and short- and medium-to-long-term investments. With this aim, they introduced management accounting and control systems to manage multiple information and provide summaries of data as well as the opportunity to delve into the details.

For this reason, in 2015, Molino Nicoli spa introduced the ERP. Six months earlier, the design of the system started with the mapping of existing business processes and the identification of needed customizations. The introduction of the ERP system was carried out in two steps. First, by implementing those components that would allow replacement of the previous management system. Second, by implementing the new applications for the management of production, quality, and maintenance of the plants. These activities were previously performed using the Access query.

Data migration from the old management system lasted one year and did not encounter particular resistance. The implementation of new applications, in contrast, necessitated more time, as it required a review of the procedures and daily activities of the staff, especially from the production workers, who saw no immediate benefits from the new system.

"*With the complete automation of production, a series of business processes were replaced with computerized automatic detection procedures. Before these processes were at the discretion of the line workers who compiled a series of information on paper forms*" (Management Accountant 2015).

System production planning and programming has been introduced, allowing the automatic generation of Purchasing orders through an algorithm that calculates the amount of raw materials needed to produce the planned quantities based on sales orders, stocks, and reorder points of inventory. The radio frequency has been installed to register the movement of goods in the raw material and finished product warehouses. The presence of radio frequency allows for the traceability of the raw material batches used for the production of each specific sales order. This alignment generates immediate and transparent information on the traceability of goods and on the fulfillment of the quality standards.

During the shipping activity, the radio frequency proves to be really indispensable since a series of automatic controls, such as the expiration date, help the warehouse worker to ship a lot of orders on time. Also, when suppliers deliver the raw materials, the radio frequency activity starts the quality control procedures before the goods proceed to the production process.

In order to be able to use the bar-code readers, it was essential to ask the suppliers to conform their labels to the Indicod standard, and then the company did the same with the finished products. The company has equipped all the production departments with personal computers and printers to generate labels with the same information for each batch produced. For each printed label, the system automatically carries out a warehouse accounting registration to prove that the goods in stock are available for the next shipments.

Line staff working in the production and logistic areas receives orders directly from the ERP system and no longer by paper documents. The automation of the process avoids the human error of code transcriptions from personal computers to paper and vice versa.

The automation of the process and the link with the ERP system has allowed the structuring of a cost management system with cost centers and bills of materials. In fact, a bill of materials and a particular processing cycle are linked to each item to be produced. While the bill of materials allows the determination for each unit produced of the cost per recipe, the processing cycle identifies those direct labor and energy costs necessary to produce one unit of product. The sum of the bill of materials and processing cycle costs determines the production cost of each product unit. Programming the hourly production standards of the production and packaging lines, the ERP system generates a report with efficiency parameters for each plant and work shift.

When a new purchase is inserted into the ERP system, through the presence of bills of materials, the total costs are automatically updated. This allows the Management Accountant to continuously monitor the real marginality of each product and batch sold. The presence of the new Managing Director has given new impetus to the data cleaning and to the systematic use of the new system. Furthermore, the Managing Director introduces the quarterly income statement with a clear situation by customer, product, and company, and the forecasting and budget systems.

The budget is managed up to the earnings before interest and taxes with details by customer and product. The first budget was introduced in 2014 from a non-family sales manager, a person with many years of experience in the food and large-scale retail sector. Before the Managing Director, the budget was a system useful to manage sales quantities and turnover. The ex-ante quantities were ex-post checked for a constant alignment of production and Purchasing quantities. Nowadays, this system has evolved as all the business areas and, in particular, the Purchasing, Production, and Sales and Marketing areas prepare their own budget in terms of quantities and values. The master budget is approved and formalized by the Board of Directors and is then constantly monitored by the Management Accountant and the Managing Director. Any revisions are discussed by the Board of Directors.

"*The design and the implementation of the management control systems alone are not enough to guarantee the success of the project. Thus, we must add well-defined and clear procedures that regulate the operations of the various function managers.*

Today we can say that the managing and control path is fully running" (Managing Director 2019).

3.7 Introduction of a Management Accounting and Control Function

The introduction of the ERP system has made it necessary to identify a person to be dedicated to the implementation and use of the information that the system produces. Francesca's husband was chosen to develop the ERP and the management control systems mentioned above. He has worked in the company since 2006 as an accounting employee. He has previous experience in the same role in three different companies. The external consultants, the non-family member of the Board of Directors, and the Managing Director support directly the new Management Accountant along the entire processes. The Management Accountant directly produces the quarterly income statement and the forecast and coordinates the drafting of the budget. The management accounting function is very important as it allows the production of data and reports for the Managing Director and the members of the Board of Directors for an informed decision making.

On a personal level, the Management Accountant is particularly appreciated in the company for his ability to smooth out tense situations by favoring a positive atmosphere between the family and non-family members. "*He is a figure of balance in the company and also in the Nicoli's family. Roberto (the Management Accountant) is that person that I'd take with me*" (Managing Director 2019).

4 The Emerging Framework

This section aims to frame the levers that have emerged from the empirics into the theoretical evidence provided by the academic studies. The case supports the multi-dimensional concept of professionalization. In fact, Molino Nicoli experience goes beyond Culasso et al.'s (2018) definition of professionalization. Here, professional managers are involved in the business but family managers also become professionals (Dyer 1989) or work hard to increase their professional skills. This is the case with the two siblings, Stefano and Francesca, and for the Management Accountant (Francesca's husband) and the Marketing Manager (Stefano's wife). The non-family professionals, and the Managing Director in particular, are orchestrating this training and professional process.

Moreover, the case shows that professionalization is thoroughly linked with managerialization. The family members introduce the ERP system and then the Managing Director introduces organizational routines and implements and develops new management control systems. Although the management accounting and control function were introduced in 2015, now it reaches a formalization. The ERP and the management control system outputs are managed directly by the Management Accountant, and detailed information supports the strategic and daily decision-making processes.

Finally, the cultural competence of the non-family professionals and of the Management Accountant emerges. In some cases, both family and non-family members were even unaware of the importance of values and close relations in favor of connotations of objectivity, universality, and rationality, which are attributes traditionally subscribed to professional management. This is not the case of Molino Nicoli. The Managing Director acquires the Molino Nicoli identity gradually by developing an ability to view the situation from the perspective of the family members. He recognized that working closely with the family members to understand their perspectives would enable a smooth cooperation in their everyday organizational life. His cultural competence (Hall and Nordqvist 2008) is evident and is likely to work more effectively than formal competence.[2]

According to the framework presented in Chapter "Professionalization and Managerialization in Family Firms: A Still Open Issue", we associate the empirical levers to the four dimensions of people, firm, culture, and systems that pave the way for the professionalization and managerialization processes. In particular, as regards the people dimension, we consider the injection of high professional skills/abilities, the family members' willingness, the introduction of governance mechanisms, and, finally, the construction of a family–non-family partnership for strategic purposes.

In the firm dimension, we consider the introduction of organizational routines and the management accounting function. In the cultural dimension, we consider the internal coaching, and in the systems dimension, the introduction of the ERP and management accounting and control systems.

Figure 4 depicts the emerging levers of the case study according to the framework presented in Chapter "Professionalization and Managerialization in Family Firms: A Still Open Issue".

The **injection of high professional skills or abilities** is a core element in the professionalization process (e.g., Steward and Hitt 2012). The abilities and skills of the Managing Director are encoded in the personality traits depicted by Kelleci et al. (2019). The authors describe non-family CEOs as persons who prefer control and an independent decision making. They promote a trusting relationship and they appear more relaxed than family CEOs. Then they acknowledge the importance of detailed information and data for acting. In our case, the high skills and experience of the Managing Director are amplified by the cultural competence he demonstrated in these three years.

As argued by Hiebl and Mayrleitner (2017), abilities have the same importance as does **family's willingness** to professionalize. Both are necessary conditions. Chrisman et al. (2015, p. 311) defined willingness as the "disposition of the family

[2]By formal competence, we mean someone with formal management education, no close bonds, industry experience, and the ability to take a universal, non-contextual, and objective impersonal and non-emotional approach to the job.

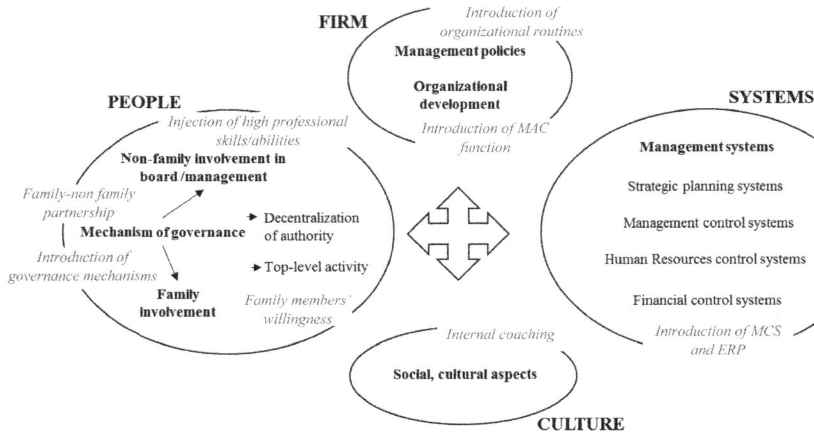

Fig. 4 Emerging levers according to the framework presented in Chapter "Professionalization and Managerialization in Family Firms: A Still Open Issue"

owners to engage in idiosyncratic behavior based on the goals, intentions, and motivations that drive the owners to influence the firm's behavior in directions diverging from those of non-family firms or the institutional norms among family firms." Professionalization is definitely an idiosyncratic situation. Succession is another peculiar situation, and some authors (De Massis et al. 2008; Le Breton-Miller et al. 2004; Richards et al. 2019) contextualize the concept of ability and willingness in that circumstance. Molino Nicoli should be considered as an empirical example of family willingness to professionalize and succeed. The President encourages Francesca and Stefano to prepare the way for the growth of the business. In particular, he welcomes a friend of his (a consultant) as a member of the Board of Directors, he accepts the opportunity to hire a high-skilled non-family Managing Director, he supports the introduction of the ERP system, and, finally, he encourages the development of an ad hoc succession program managed by external consultants. All these are key elements of a manifest willingness to professionalize and succeed.

The next lever considered is the **introduction of governance mechanisms**. Many authors consider the Board of Directors as one of the most important governance mechanisms (Mustakallio et al. 2002; Zhang and Ma 2009). Formal strategic planning (Dekker et al. 2013) is another mechanism and, finally, the introduction of an Executive Committee, which is more related to the succession planning process.

While non-family professionals are important sources for professionalization of family businesses, some authors (Dekker et al. 2013; Hall and Nordqvist 2008; Stewart and Hitt 2012) advance doubts regarding whether the help of non-family experts is required for family businesses to professionalize. The case of Molino Nicoli dissolves doubts in this sense. But the point of the authors goes beyond the abilities of non-family professionals to professionalize. In fact, another key point is the presence of a relaxed relationship between family and non-family managers. This point is relevant for the governance of the business.

Usually, when family managers run the business and non-family managers join at a certain point, the need to create a new balance emerges. This relationship is not so well investigated in the extant literature, but the case study gives clear evidence about this relationship. There is a strong intention of the Managing Director to accomplish a proactive relationship with family managers, in particular with the Operations Director, Stefano. They are working together to develop a strategic plan for the business. **The Managing Director would construct a family–non-family partnership to manage the firm through new markets and products**. According to these goals, Stefano's high technical skills and family values are essential. The Managing Director knows markets very well and has a long experience in running complex businesses and situations. This partnership is useful for a contamination of abilities and experiences. And in this situation, the Managing Director has the opportunity to coach Stefano and the other family managers. The daily activities and interactions are really important for this strategic purpose.

Moreover, the Managing Director introduces some **organizational routines** that are relevant to promote new working methods and an internal cooperation among the different areas. This signifies that companies design organizational routines to introduce, assimilate, and adapt knowledge. Routines can be considered as team forms of learning that the company uses for its objectives. Family business studies indirectly mention organizational routines, talking about social capital evolution and transmission or knowledge absorption in general. This aspect is crucial to professionalize and managerialize a business, but it is underdeveloped in the academic literature.

The **establishment of the management accounting function** can also be considered a sort of organizational routine. Just a few studies mention management accounting in terms of the function (Barbera and Hasso 2013; Giovannoni et al. 2011). Apparently, no scholars analyze management accounting in terms of persons in charge of this function (i.e., the management accountant).

When we talk about **culture of a family business**, we mean the result of values and norms of a founder that are rooted in the family and its history (Fletcher et al. 2012; Zahra et al. 2004). These values and norms manifest themselves in a rather stable way of thinking. Through socialization and particular mechanisms, these values and norms are transmitted over generations and shape a relatively stable family culture that, over time, is likely to also characterize the business. In this context, the intuition to develop an internal coaching is worthy of mention. This method is perceived as not invasive and more effective because the subjects are both engaged in the same cultural context. Shams and Lane (2011) described the practice of coaching in a family business as a delicate crafting to ensure that each part of the family is being given appropriate attention. In particular, the coaching should necessarily consider family values, ethics, traditions, interpersonal relations, emotions, communication patterns, and leadership styles. The internal coaching developed in Molino Nicoli intrinsically encompasses these cultural features.

Finally, the **introduction of the ERP** and the management accounting and control systems characterized the case study. Previous studies have described the introduction (e.g., Chua et al. 2009; Craig and Moores 2005, 2010; Rue and Ibrahim 1996) and the use (e.g., El Masri et al. 2017; Filbeck and Lee 2004; Speckbacher and Wentges

2012; Upton et al. 2001) of different management accounting and control systems that provide benefits for incumbents and new generations (Giovannoni et al. 2011; Mazzola et al. 2008). All these systems provide very useful information for managing the business and the strategies accordingly.

5 Conclusion

The case study described in this chapter allows an exploration of the relevant aspects of the professionalization and managerialization processes of a family business. This stimulates a greater understanding of the two concepts as a unique process and of the profound relationships between people, firm, culture, and system dimensions of professionalization. In general, this also contributes to develop two aspects. First, it helps to understand how the development processes of management accounting and control systems are interrelated with the presence of a willing family member and to particular abilities of family and non-family professionals. Second, it stimulates the adoption of a qualitative approach in investigating phenomena related to family businesses.

Finally, the levers identified in the case study suggest three streams for further research. First, the construction of a family–non-family partnership for developing a shared decision making and to implement a formal strategic process. Second, the design and introduction of organizational routines; and third, the exploration of the establishment of the management accounting function. This case represents an original context for professionalization and managerialization processes that occurred during a succession transition. Further investigations are recommended in this context as well, providing a longitudinal analysis of the levers that emerged and all the relevant aspects that affected the growth of the business.

References

Barbera F, Hasso T (2013) Do we need to use an accountant? The sales growth and survival benefits to family SMEs. Family Bus Rev 26(3):271–292. https://doi.org/10.1177/0894486513487198

Chrisman JJ, Chua JH, de Massis A, Frattini F, Wright M (2015) The ability and willingness paradox in family firm innovation. J Prod Innov Manag 32(3):310–318. https://doi.org/10.1111/jpim.12207

Chua JH, Chrisman JJ, Bergiel EB (2009) An agency theoretic analysis of the professionalized family firm. Entrepreneurship Theory Pract 33:355–372. https://doi.org/10.1111/j.1540-6520.2009.00294.x

Craig J, Moores K (2005) Balanced Scorecard to drive the strategic planning of family firms. Family Bus Rev 18(2):105–122. https://doi.org/10.1111/j.1741-6248.2005.00035.x

Craig J, Moores K (2010) Strategically aligning family and business systems using the Balanced Scorecard. J Family Bus Strategy 1:78–87. https://doi.org/10.1016/j.jfbs.2010.04.003

Culasso F, Giacosa E, Manzi LM, Dana L (2018) Professionalization in family businesses. How to strenghten strategy implementation and control, favouring succession. Manag Control 1:45–71. https://doi.org/10.3280/MACO2018-001003

De Massis A, Chua JH, Chrisman JJ (2008) Factors preventing intra-family succession. Family Bus Rev 21(2):183–199. https://doi.org/10.1111/j.1741-6248.2008.00118.x

Dekker JC, Lybaert N, Steijvers T, Depaire B, Mercken R (2013) Family firm types based on the professionalization construct: exploratory research. Family Bus Rev 26(1):81–99. https://doi.org/10.1177/0894486512445614

Dyer WG Jr (1989) Integrating professional management into a family owned business. Family Bus Rev 2:221–235. https://doi.org/10.1111/j.1741-6248.1989.00221.x

Eisenhardt KM (1989) Building theories from case study research. Acad Manag Rev 14(4):532–550

El Masri T, Tekathen M, Magnan M, Boulianne E (2017) Calibrating management control technologies and the dual identity of family firms. Qual Res Acc Manag 14(2):157–188. https://doi.org/10.1108/QRAM-05-2016-0038

Filbeck G, Lee S (2004) Financial management techniques in family businesses. Family Bus Rev 13(3):201–216. https://doi.org/10.1111/j.1741-6248.2000.00201.x

Fletcher D, Melin L, Gimeno A (2012) Culture and values in family business—a review and suggestions for future research. J Family Bus Strategy 3:127–131

Giovannoni E, Maraghini MP, Riccaboni A (2011) Transmitting knowledge across generations: the role of management accounting practices. Family Bus Rev 24(2):126–150. https://doi.org/10.1177/0894486511406722

Hall A, Nordqvist M (2008) Professional management in family businesses: toward an extended understanding. Family Business Review 21(1):51–69. https://doi.org/10.1111/j.1741-6248.2007.00109.x

Hiebl MRW, Mayrleitner B (2017) Professionalization of management accounting in family firms: the impact of family members. Rev Manag Sci 1–32. https://doi.org/10.1007/s11846-017-0274-8

Kelleci R, Lambrechts F, Voordeckers W, Huybrechts J (2019) CEO personality: a different perspective on the nonfamily versus family CEO debate. Family Bus Rev 32(1):31–57. https://doi.org/10.1177/0894486518811222

Le Breton-Miller I, Miller D, Steier LP (2004) Toward an integrative model of effective FOB succession. Entrepreneurship Theory Pract 28(4):305–328. https://doi.org/10.1111/j.1540-6520.2004.00047.x

Mazzola P, Marchisio G, Astrachan J (2008) Strategic planning in family business: a powerful development tool for the next generation. Family Bus Rev 21(3):239–258. https://doi.org/10.1177/08944865080210030106

Mustakallio M, Autio E, Zahra SA (2002) Relational and contractual governance in family firms: effects on strategic decision making. Family Bus Rev 15(3):205–222. https://doi.org/10.1111/j.1741-6248.2002.00205.x

Richards M, Kammerlander N, Zellweger TM (2019) Listening to the heart or the head? Exploring the "willingness vs. ability" succession dilemma. Family Bus Rev. ISSN 0894-4865

Rue LW, Ibrahim NA (1996) The status of planning in smaller family owned businesses. Family Bus Rev 9(1):29–43. https://doi.org/10.1111/j.1741-6248.1996.00029.x

Shams M (2011) Key issues in family business coaching. In: Shams M, Lane DA (eds) Coaching in the family owned business. A path to growth. Karnac books Ltd., London

Speckbacher G, Wentges P (2012) The impact of family control on the use of performance measures in strategic target setting and incentive compensation: a research note. Manag Acc Res 23(1):34–46. https://doi.org/10.1016/j.mar.2011.06.002

Stewart A, Hitt MA (2012) Why can't a family business be more like a nonfamily business? Modes of professionalization in family firms. Family Bus Rev 25(1):58–86. https://doi.org/10.1177/0894486511421665

Upton N, Teal EJ, Felan JT (2001) Strategic and business planning practices of fast growing family firms. J Small Bus Manage 39(1):60–72. https://doi.org/10.1111/0447-2778.00006

Zahra SA, Hayton JC, Salvato C (2004) Entrepreneurship in family vs. non-family firms: a resource-based analysis of the effect of organizational culture. Entrepreneurship Theory Pract 28(4):363–381

Zhang J, Ma H (2009) Adoption of professional management in Chinese family business: a multi-level analysis of impetuses and impediments. Asia Pacific J Manag 26:119–139. https://doi.org/10.1007/s10490-008-9099-y

Beyond the Founder. Which Conditions Can Favor or Hinder the Professionalization of Family Firms?

Annalisa Sentuti, Francesca M. Cesaroni, Gaia Bassani, and Cristiana Cattaneo

Abstract This chapter analyzes the experience of two family businesses that carried out a succession process and undertook a process of professionalization with opposite results. In one case, the founder gave great impetus to the professionalization process, to favor business development and growth. The successor replicated the same approach and emphasized the involvement of external professionals and the implementation of management control systems, to ensure the longevity and the viability of the family firm. In the other case, the founder was always reluctant toward professionalization and, as a result, centralized decision making and control. The successor tried to promote the professionalization of the firm, but she was not able to achieve this goal, leading the company into decline after the founder's exit. The comparison between the two case studies allowed us to highlight some factors that led to a positive or negative outcome of the process of professionalization.

Keywords Family business · Succession · Professionalization · Management control system · Professional

A. Sentuti (✉) · F. M. Cesaroni
Department of Economics, Society, Politics, University of Urbino Carlo Bo, Urbino, Italy
e-mail: annalisa.sentuti@uniurb.it

F. M. Cesaroni
e-mail: francesca.cesaroni@uniurb.it

G. Bassani · C. Cattaneo
Department of Management, Economics and Quantitative Methods, University of Bergamo, Bergamo, Italy
e-mail: gaia.bassani@unibg.it

C. Cattaneo
e-mail: cristiana.cattaneo@unibg.it

A. Leotta (ed.), *Management Controlling and Governance of Family Businesses*, Contributions to Management Science,
https://doi.org/10.1007/978-3-030-47741-7_10

1 Introduction

Maintaining the control of the company in the hands of the family, and involving external managers in government and management, can play a key role in ensuring family firms' longevity and growth. However, this implies the ability of family owners to delegate key functions to non-family managers and introduce management control systems to support the control and evolution of their business.

Is it a difficult process to accomplish? Sometimes, it is. While some successful cases highlight the potential of professionalization, other cases demonstrate the difficulty that family businesses has in delegating decision-making power to non-family members and their resistance to introduce management control systems.

This chapter aims to analyze the conflicting experiences of two Italian family businesses: Teseo S.p.A. and Volta S.p.A.,[1] both currently led by the second generation (the founder's daughter in both cases). They have carried out a professionalization process with opposite results: positive in the first case and negative in the second.

In Teseo S.p.A., the founder implemented a profound and extensive professionalization process, which favored business growth and its transition from an entrepreneurial to a managerial firm. The successor was able to keep a high emphasis on the involvement of external professionals and the implementation of management control systems to ensure the longevity and viability of the family firm. Conversely, in Volta S.p.A., the founder was firmly reluctant to professionalize the company, and he centralized decision making and control in his own hands. The succession process immediately stimulated the professionalization of the business. However, despite the best premises for an effective path of growth and development, the professionalization process failed, and the company's viability worsened, with negative consequences for the business's growth and its financial performance.

The comparison between these two different experiences has enabled us to reflect on some factors that can lead, or not, to a successful professionalization process. Specifically, findings show problems that may arise during this process and permit the identification of some guidelines that may be helpful for family businesses in making informed choices and reaching positive outcomes.

The rest of the chapter is organized as follows. The next section illustrates the methodology adopted for this research. Section three is dedicated to the family businesses analyzed: an overview of each case is offered, and their most important stages of development are described. Last section presents a discussion of the results and the main conclusions drawn from the two case studies.

[1]The names of companies and interviewees have been changed to ensure the confidentiality of the informants.

2 Methodology

We have adopted a qualitative in-depth case study method to present and discuss a multiple case study (Eisenhardt and Graebner 2007; Miles et al. 2014). Recently, family business scholars have called for qualitative studies aiming at deepening the complex dynamics between family and business during particular events and circumstances (Litz 1997; Nordqvist et al. 2009; De Massis and Kotlar 2014).

Based on a purposeful case selection (Patton 1990), two of the authors selected the analyzed cases thanks to their personal networks, to be sure that the chosen cases were consistent with the research goals.

A multitude of data was collected. In-depth, face-to-face, semi-structured interviews with successors were the primary source of data. Given the complexity of the Volta S.p.A. case, data was triangulated with several interviews with the successor and other interviews with the incumbent and other family and business members (mother, sister, general director, financial manager, and administrative assistant). The successor, general director, and administrative assistant were interviewed several times over the years. In total, 14 interviews were carried out from 2005 to 2019. With regard to Teseo S.p.A., two interviews with successors were carried out in 2018 and 2019. In both cases, the interviews lasted from 45 min to 3 h and were recorded and transcribed verbatim. Secondary sources (e.g., business documents, company websites, and field notes collected during the interviews) provided further information about the businesses and their family contexts.

Collected data and information were synthesized into a case study summary and collectively analyzed by the authors (Miles et al. 2014). Emerging findings were discussed, and a comparison between the two cases was developed.

The two cases are presented in the next section, along with excerpts from the interviews, to highlight connections between professionalization and succession and understand how they affected businesses' longevity.

3 The Two Case Studies

3.1 Teseo S.p.A.

A family business with the desire to grow

Teseo was founded in 1972 (Fig. 1) when Ugo Gazzola decided to listen to a suggestion from a friend, a pasta producer. New regulatory provisions had recently banned the sale of bulk food, and the obligation to sell only packaged foods had opened up new business opportunities. Gazzola did not miss the chance and, with other minority shareholders, put together the capital needed to open a company that produced flexible plastic packaging for the food industry.

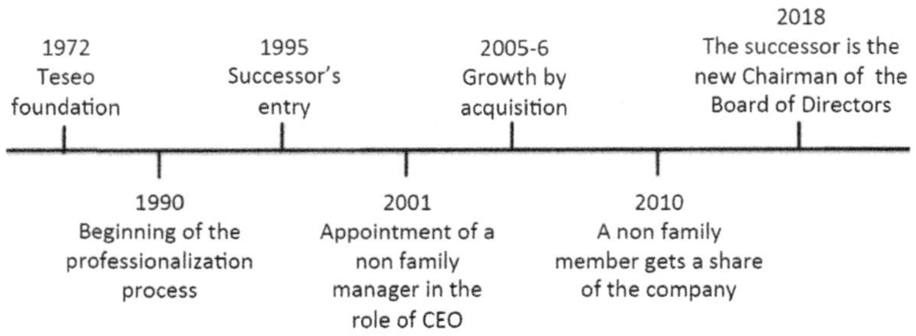

Fig. 1 Teseo timeline

However, he never led or managed the company. From the beginning, Alessandra–Ugo's firstborn daughter and, at the time, the only adult was the company's main shareholder, while Ugo continued to work as a civil servant. Alessandra turned out to be very adept at doing business and immediately revealed excellent management and leadership skills, as well as intuition, sensitivity, and strategic vision.

Unfortunately, Alessandra Gazzola had an administrative background, and this represented a significant drawback, as the company operated in a sector where technology played a crucial role. Precisely, for this reason, after a short period, she decided to involve her brother Riccardo in the business. He is an ingenious mechanic, so Alessandra started a successful collaboration with him, thanks to their ability to divide tasks and the complementarity of their skills and competences.

However, the business was struggling to take off, especially since it had to compete with some big players in the packaging sector. Then, Alessandra Gazzola had a timely intuition to ally herself with one of the leading companies, to which she sold 50% of Teseo, while Alessandra and Riccardo shared the other 50%. This operation allowed Teseo to make a considerable qualitative leap. The alliance allowed Teseo to buy raw materials at much more competitive prices. But above all, this operation allowed the company to acquire valuable know-how and technical skills—especially in the characteristic area of molding. These skills were indispensable to make processes more efficient, raise the company's technological level, and make it more competitive.

At the beginning of the Nineties, Alessandra Gazzola bought back the shares previously sold and she and her brother remained the only owners. In the same period, the company started a process of steady expansion and development. This process was possible thanks to another one of Alessandra's inspired ideas. In fact, she decided to involve managers, engineers, and other professionals, who were appointed to important managerial roles. They were often very young and did not have previous experience. Nevertheless, they were hired because they presented new competencies and skills that were needed to simulate the company's growth. In the 1995 also Serena Andrisani—the only daughter of Alessandra Gazzola—joined the company, immediately after graduating in Economics, and began her gradual career path in the company.

The decision to strengthen its managerial structure represented a decisive step and a key turning point for the company's success. Alessandra Gazzola proved to be very aware of her knowledge and limits of competence. So, even if, in the following years, she continued to be the fundamental point of reference for the company and to play an irreplaceable role as company's leader, she realized the need to "*fill an empty box with value*". She very honestly admitted: "*We have come this far, but this is our maximum limit. And how can we move forward if we don't find someone to take us there?*". This is why she decided to hire engineers and technical experts to fill roles that required highly qualified and specialized skills, that neither she nor her brother was equipped with.

The success they achieved up to that point allowed Alessandra Gazzola to undertake a new phase of growth through acquisitions. In 2005, Teseo took over a company specialized in flexography. The acquisition proved to be strategic because it allowed Teseo to significantly expand its product range and diversify its customer portfolio, being able to respond to the needs of smaller buyers who required smaller quantities. Less than a year later, Teseo took the opportunity to take over a second company, specialized in the application of cold solder. This acquisition allowed Teseo to include relevant multinational companies—such as Mars and Nestlè—in its client portfolio, and to better satisfy their needs for productive backup and risk assessment.

The role of the family and the willingness to take a step back

Following these acquisitions, Teseo Group was born. Today, it has 700 employees and a robust management structure. The latter is the result of a choice made several years ago by Alessandra Gazzola. She has always firmly believed that investing in specialized know-how and professionalizing the company is the best recipe to ensure its longevity over time, even if this means limiting space for the family.

In fact, the family does not have management roles, as the latter are wholly entrusted to external managers. In 2001, one of the company's long-time managers was appointed CEO. Over the years, he has gained the full trust of the family, so much so that in 2010, he received a share of the company—he is the only non-family shareholder—as a sign of gratitude for his great commitment and dedication to the company. Alessandra Gazzola and her daughter, along with another external director, also participate in the board of directors. Several managers have also been hired—Industrial Manager, Business Development and R&D Manager, HR Manager, Administration, and Finance Manager, etc.—in addition to several experts in staff positions—Management Accounting System, IT system, etc.

The creation of this structure was not an easy choice. Alessandra Gazzola, like most entrepreneurs, used to devote herself to the company completely—especially in the early years—and she was also personally involved in the technical and production issues. For this reason, her daughter recalls: "*My mother worked really hard. She used to spend her days in the production department, and if anyone had a stomach ache, she knew it*". Thus, it was not easy for her to delegate and rely on external experts. If she succeeded, it was thanks to her great foresight, her will to always put the company's survival ahead of any other personal or family goal, and her awareness that this result could only be obtained if the family was willing to take a step back for the good of the company.

An important role in this delegation process was played by the introduction of a management control system. It was an indispensable tool that allowed Alessandra Gazzola to control the company trends and also supervise the aspects that were no longer directly under her control.

The succession process: a step toward the future

Serena Andrisani started her career within the society in Human Resources and, some time later, moved to sales and customer service, and finally to Marketing.

Her first few years of experience allowed Serena Andrisani to immediately get in touch with what they used to consider the heart of the company, that is, its human side. Although technology has always been of great importance to Teseo, its actual asset is intangible, and it is made of people. That is why Serena often repeats that even the most sophisticated machinery "*without people cannot make a difference*".

In this regard, Serena has a great advantage because the years she spent in the company enabled her to become very familiar with all the employees. Furthermore, Serena has been blessed with great empathy and innate relational skills, and these qualities have allowed her to gain the trust and esteem of the company's staff. In this way, it was easy for her to free herself from the image of the little girl who played with plastic cuttings next to her mother and to be accepted and appreciated as the company's new leader.

At the end of a 15-year-learning process, in 2018, Serena Andrisani took over the role of President of the Board of Directors, replacing her mother, who continued to participate as a simple director. The existence of a robust managerial structure undoubtedly facilitated the succession process, which occurred without trauma for the company. The definitive passage of the baton did not change the leadership style and the relationship between the family and the company. This result was possible thanks to a governance structure that allowed the company to be free from the dependence on a single person.

In the new role of President of the Board, Serena Andrisani continued to minimize the family's interference in corporate management and decisions and confined herself to the role of supervisor of the main corporate strategy decisions. She states: "*It was a very clear and firm choice. My mother and I decided to keep the company and the family separate. It is more important for us that the company grows and flourishes. It doesn't matter if it's not my mom and I who run it*".

The only aspect of corporate life that Serena Andrisani did not want to abandon was human resources. For Serena, an essential part of her role is the direct relationship with employees. This relationship has developed over the years and has been fueled by her ability to become familiar with all the employees, to understand their needs and perceive their moods and feelings.

According to Serena Andrisani, this is also the true added value of being a family business: "*We are a great team but guided like a family*". And being able to preserve this spirit, despite three plants and 700 people currently employed, is a challenge that Serena and her mother intend to continue to win, as they have done until now.

Thanks to this spirit, Alessandra and Serena have succeeded in creating a particularly virtuous combination of family presence and involvement of external managers.

The latter guarantee professional management of the company, while the family represents an irreplaceable element of identity, expression of values, and principles that have always characterized the life of the Group.

Serena Andrisani is well aware that: "*Professionalization has been key to improve the business and introduce not only new technologies but also new organizational structures and new processes … we have changed a lot!*".

The Group has been able to grow, introduce important technological innovations, enter new markets, and improve its financial and competitive performance. These results are the consequence of a will pursued with tenacity since the early stages of the company's life: equipping it with qualified skills, choosing managers and directors not only within the family but also within turning outwards to achieve the best combination between business needs and professional skills available.

This recipe was first introduced by Alessandra Gazzola and then shared and replicated by her daughter Serena. Both are firmly convinced that this is the best solution to guarantee the continuity of the company over time.

3.2 *Volta S.p.A.*

From the business creation to the succession process

Volta S.p.A. is a small business that was founded 40 years ago by Giorgio Saltieri. It operates in the machinery industry and creates innovative building systems for the construction market. As often happens in many small businesses, in the early stages, the founder was directly involved in every activity—engineering, production, and sales—with the help of a few key collaborators. From the beginning, the building systems were distributed, through sales agents, worldwide. Central and South America, Africa and Asia, and developing countries with a high growth trend in the construction market, were the main markets of the firm. For several years, the main point of reference for the entire business and its stakeholders was the founder. The whole company revolved around his experience, ideas, skills, entrepreneurial spirit, and commitment.

The turning point arrived when his daughter—Emma—decided to join the business and follow in her father's footsteps. It was 1998; Giorgio was 58 years old and Emma 28. The idea of selling the company—previously considered by the founder—was rapidly replaced by the desire to move forward. With this in mind, the father and daughter worked together to make the company grow and prosper. They also shared some initiatives to ensure a smooth and effective succession process. Before joining the business, Emma had got a degree in economics and business management and worked as an accountant for three years. Since she was a child, she had desired to work in the family business and was very committed to the preparation required to enter the family business and have a career from within. Her strong interest in the firm stemmed from her deep bond with her father and her great admiration for him, her model: "*When my father started the business I was a kid, so I was growing up alongside this business. I was always with my dad. (…) Since I was very young, my idea was 'I want to work with Dad.' And I made all my choices based on the idea of working in our family firm*".

Two other family members were involved in the business: Anna, the founder's wife, and Sofia, the second-born daughter. Anna was the head of the administrative office, but her primary role was that of "*peacemaker*" between incumbent and successor "*just in case*" they needed. Sofia had got a Law degree and was in charge of the business's legal affairs. With her sister and her father, she shared the ownership of the business, while her mother was not a shareholder.

The process of professionalization and managerialization

In her early years, in the family business, Emma's effort was mainly devoted to acquiring a broad knowledge of the company, its products, and markets. After this training period, she began working alongside her father, with growing power and responsibility. In particular, she followed first-hand several business areas (e.g., human resources, management control) and supported her father in foreign trade. At the same time, she promoted a significant professionalization process, with a dual purpose. Firstly, fostering business growth: "*Our main goal is to grow. During the last few years, we have started to advance toward the United States and the Italian market. We are developing different strategies and a new organizational structure, hiring new professionals in different areas*". Secondly, the involvement of external professionals was necessary to expand the professional skills available in the company. Emma had administrative and financial skills, and it was, therefore, necessary to equip the company with other technical and engineering skills necessary to be successful in the construction sector. Emma admitted: "*My main difficulty is that I don't know the product so well. My father considers the product an extension of himself, but for me, it's just a product. I need time to acquire the same capabilities. He has them by nature, while I have to get them by experience. Thus, we decided to hire two engineers in the production area*".

In the same period, Emma fostered the introduction of a certified quality system—in line with the UNI EN ISO 9001 regulation—and a managerial control system. According to Emma, the latter was necessary because "*my father managed the company in a 'rough' way, while I think that when a business grows it needs tools to know its financial flows, to make a budget […] especially for our company, which has no steady financial flows because we produce to order. Thus, we implemented a management system to improve the organization of some business areas and to control our activities*".

Emma's entrance gave a big push to the professionalization of the company and transformed it from a founder-centered organization to a more formalized company, with clearer roles, differentiated functions, the sharing of responsibilities, delegation processes, the involvement of non-family managers, and the introduction of managerial systems. Thanks to all these initiatives, Emma gained her collaborators' consensus, and her leadership role began to be legitimized.

Emma and her father also decided to hire a long-time consultant who had worked with the firm for more than thirty years and knew both the business and the family well. The founder and all family members trusted him. Two important tasks were delegated to him: on the one hand, supporting the administrative and financial areas; on the other hand, favoring communication between incumbent and successor and between family members, keeping the attention on the business and its issues, avoiding interference and overlaps between business and family. Following his suggestions, weekly formal meetings were organized, and the family members, with the supervision of their consultant, were encouraged to plan strategies and discuss problems and solutions.

Thanks to these changes, in the following years, the company grew and expanded its markets worldwide. Other marketing managers were hired to develop sales abroad, and, among them, Emma's husband was also hired. In addition, the succession process was proceeding successfully. Both the founder and his daughter were very satisfied. She said: "*I'm tied to this company with a love relationship that my father has transmitted to me since I was a child. I didn't created the business but with my Dad's help and support, I'm changing the business, and every day I see the result of what I did and what I'm doing*".

Some years later, Emma had a baby, so she decided to hire a general director and a financial manager to ensure the control and management of the company during her maternity leave. In the following years, the company continued to grow, other employees were hired, and turnover increased further. Meanwhile, the succession process came to an end, and in 2013, the founder definitively left the business, and Emma became the new CEO.

From an entrepreneurial to a managerial firm: a missed opportunity

Against all the odds, the professionalization process unexpectedly underwent a sharp decline (Fig. 2 synthesizes the Volta's experience throughout the timeline of the major events occurred).

The general manager provided some explanations. He showed great disappointment because—in his words—"*I'm a general director only on paper... I joined the company during Emma's pregnancy, and I thought she wanted to have fewer commitments in the business and needed a general director. Never more wrong! She never left her job. I have never been involved in the sales managers meetings, nor the board of directors. The board of directors includes only the founder, Emma, and her mother*". He also complained that Emma continuously boycotted his proposals to introduce

Fig. 2 Volta timeline

more advanced managerial control systems: "*I prepared the MBO [Management By Objectives] with a reward system tied to achievements for 3 consecutive years. For three years, it remained on Emma's desk till the end of the year when she said 'By now the year is over…'. Then, the following year she started again: 'Do we want to do the MBO?' She knew how much it meant to me, especially because I came from a company based on this approach. She asked me to set it up every year, but we never implemented it*".

In 2014, the general director left the business. He admitted: "*My job as general director is totally inadequate. You can have your business card, you can have the title, they can say: 'You are the general manager'… But, here, I don't have the possibility to work with a managerial approach. The family makes all strategic and operational decisions. They won. They surely won. I was not able to apply my methods, my way of working*".

At the same time, other professionals also declared their uneasiness in the family business. For example, the financial director felt the presence of Emma's mother as an obstacle to the introduction of managerial systems: "*Mrs. Anna plays two roles, paradoxically, very different from each other. One is formal: she does a series of operations, such as bank transfers. She personally makes transfers, one by one. It's crazy! There are web tools that would allow us to go much faster and simplify our accounting procedures! Nevertheless, she wants to maintain her control of this activity. The second role is overseeing the financial area, monitoring how resources are used. She is the controller of the owner family and the 'family financial eye' for every day operations. She writes each revenue and expense day by day. She is the family eye of company's finances. Unfortunately, her presence not only slows down daily activities but also hinders any possibility to improve our work*".

Also, in the foreign sales area, several professionals perceived the cumbersome "shadow" of the family over the business. His colleagues did not consider Emma's husband an effective sales manager. He achieved very poor results, but his career was very quick, and this demotivated other sales managers, who decided to leave the business.

After the general manager's exit, the situation further deteriorated, and the organizational climate sharply declined. Sometime later, even the financial director decided to leave the company. Even though the professionalization process had started with the best conditions, it ultimately proved to be a failure. As a result, the growth of the firm also stopped, and its longevity was seriously jeopardized.

4 Discussion and Conclusions

The comparison between the two case studies shows important differences in the approach adopted by the two companies in carrying out the professionalization process. Great differences also exist in the role of the professionalization process in influencing the success and longevity of businesses. Specifically, our analysis reveals that differences stem mainly from the following: (1) differences in the relationship between family and business; (2) peculiar goals attributed to the professionalization process in each case.

With regard to the first issue, in the Teseo S.p.A., the family owners have always been aware that they should stay in the background to leave room to and not overshadow external professionals, who were considered the actual business assets. Even though the management is completely composed of non-family members, and the CEO is an external professional, the family owners have never felt like they have lost control of the business or become less important. Conversely, they decided to involve also the CEO in the family business ownership to motivate him and interact with him not just on the basis of a labor contract but also based on a stronger tie. "*First the business, then the family*" is the leitmotif passed down from the founder to successor. Being a family business in Teseo has always meant managing the firm as a family, to ensure a familiar organizational climate and devote attention to human resources. The family is the spirit of the enterprise, an invisible presence in the whole organization, and not an operational presence in the company. This approach has favored the attraction and retention of highly skilled professionals and has ensured the longevity and viability of the family firm.

In the Volta case, the family never let go of the control of the company. Even though the successor seemed interested in professionalizing the business, she and the other family members continued to steer the firm in a very "familistic" way. Even after hiring several managers and a general director, and after the introduction of formal managerial tools and systems, informal management and control approaches prevailed. No delegation of decision-making processes, the strong presence of the family in business operations, difficulty in separating the family from the business logics (e.g., promotion based on family ties instead of skills and achievements) hindered the professionalization process, also compromising the viability and longevity of the business. Thus, in the first case, professionalization has been in the DNA of the family business since it was founded, a key value of the family owners. Conversely, in the second case, professionalization was a missed opportunity because the family was not able to reduce its power and control.

Regarding the second issue, existing studies mostly state that growing the business across generations and improving its viability and performance over time are the main purposes of professionalization within family businesses (Dyer 1989; Daily and Dollinger 1992; Corbetta 1995; Chittoor and Das 2007; Songini and Vola 2015). However, the case studies presented in this chapter reveal that professionalization may be directed toward different purposes.

Supporting business viability and flourishing was surely the main goal pursued in the Teseo case. On the contrary, in Volta case, the choice to professionalize seems to have been dictated by the successor's personal reasons. In the beginning, the professionalization process was carried out with a positive impact on the company's performance and its growth process. Nevertheless, after the father's exit, a reversal of the situation occurred. Emma showed a loss of interest in the involvement of non-family professionals, as well as in the adoption of formalized management and control systems. She clearly began to oppose delegating decision-making power: non-family managers (above all, the general director) were not allowed to enhance their professional knowledge and skills, as they were excluded from key decision-making processes and limited in their autonomy.

In general, the real successor's reasons and behavior were characterized by great ambiguity. Emma explicitly stated her willingness to professionalize the company, to equip it with more advanced managerial tools, and make it grow. However, the successor's behavior was inconsistent and completely at odds with these goals. Her main goal was probably to legitimize herself as a business leader and show everyone she was the one who had made the business grow and transform it from an entrepreneurial business to a managerial company. However, Emma (and her family) was not ready to limit her influence and presence within the business. Moreover, when she felt overshadowed by the general manager, she decided to boycott the professionalization process. This reason can also explain her desire to firmly keep the control of sensitive information, not to share it with "outsiders", i.e., with non-family members (especially the general director and the financial director). The control of the information allowed the successor to keep the decision-making power centered on her, without jeopardizing her leadership role. The risk to be avoided was essentially the possibility that the general director would shadow her leadership role, compromising her need for legitimacy, in the eyes of her father, other family members, and the rest of the company.

From a theoretical standpoint, the analysis presented in this paper contributes to enrich knowledge about factors and conditions that can affect the effectiveness and the success of professionalization processes in family businesses. In particular, our case adds new elements to the conclusions of Hall and Norqdvist (2008). These authors maintain that external managers need a particular competence—namely socio-cultural sensitivity—when they are involved in a family firm. That means that for professionalization processes in family firms to be successful, non-family managers should possess not only technical and specialized competencies but also cultural competencies. Non-family managers should be able to understand owner family's explicit and implicit values, rules, and main objectives. In the absence of these skills, it is very likely that the professionalization process will fail, even if non-family managers are highly qualified and prepared.

The analysis of the case studies presented in this chapter has also allowed us to draw some conclusions about possible relationships between professionalization and the succession process. From this point of view, the two cases show profound differences.

In the first case (Teseo S.p.A.), the professionalization process was promoted by the founder and began several years before the succession. The latter did not hinder or slow down the professionalization process. Indeed, the presence of a professional company somehow facilitated the succession process. In fact, the successor entered a context in which the "business first" logic was already clearly affirmed. Consequently, from her first entry into the family business, it was clear what her role in the organization, her power and responsibility, and what skills and competencies she had to possess to fulfill her role would be. Therefore, the successor's takeover at the helm of the family business was conditioned neither by the personal relationship between mother and daughter nor by the prevalence of personal and family goals.

On the contrary, the latter played a prominent role in the Volta case. In this company, the professionalization process did not precede the succession process but was instead promoted by the successor. This circumstance allows us to observe that when the professionalization process takes place in conjunction with succession, it is also necessary to consider the successor's attitude, to understand the reasons for the success or failure of the professionalization process. In the Volta case, the ambiguity of the successor's motivations behind the involvement of the general director was the main reason for the failure of the professionalization process. Despite the successor's explicit reasons, her implicit and hidden reasons—mainly due to her need for personal legitimacy/accreditation—were predominant. These reasons hindered the work of the general director and prevented the company's professionalization process, with negative consequences for its viability and growth.

The analysis presented in this paper also emphasizes the possibility of analysing the professionalization process of a family member, a theme neglected by literature due to the difficulty of finding empirical evidence. Our analysis presents all the conditions specified by Dyer (1989), namely the strong will of family members (especially Emma in the Volta case) to be able to work in the family business, the ability to learn the needed skills, the will to perpetuate and to ensure the continuity of family values through the direct control and management of the business, and the short-term need to change the strategic direction undertaken to meet the environmental challenges. Thus, a two-way professionalization concept emerges, as it concerns not only the inclusion of non-family managers but also the professional growth of family members.

In conclusion, future studies should promote a longitudinal vision to better understand the purposes of professionalization and succession processes in the medium and long term. Studying the professionalization process in family firms involved in a succession process can be a useful clue to the understanding of the evolutionary intersections of these two major challenges in the context of family businesses. In addition, further research could resume Dyer's conclusions (1989) and deepen the dynamics of professionalization among family members, non-family members, and professional managers, which would also help us to gain a deeper understanding of the professionalization paths of family managers.

References

Chittoor R, Das R (2007) Professionalization of management and succession performance—a vital linkage. Family Bus Rev 20(1):65–76. https://doi.org/10.1111/j.1741-6248.2007.00084.x

Corbetta G (1995) Patterns of development of family businesses in Italy. Family Bus Rev 8(4):255–265. https://doi.org/10.1111/j.1741-6248.1995.00255.x

De Massis A, Kotlar J (2014) The case study method in family business research: Guidelines for qualitative scholarship. J Family Bus Strategy 5(1):15–29. https://doi.org/10.1016/j.jfbs.2014.01.007

Daily CM, Dollinger MJ (1992) An empirical examination of ownership structure in family and professionally managed firms. Family Bus Rev 5(2):117–136. https://doi.org/10.1111/j.1741-6248.1992.00117.x

Dyer WG Jr (1989) Integrating professional management into a family owned business. Family Bus Rev 2(3):221–235. https://doi.org/10.1111/j.1741-6248.1989.00221.x

Eisenhardt KM, Graebner ME (2007) Theory building from cases: opportunities and challenges. Acad Manag J 50(1):25–32. https://doi.org/10.5465/amj.2007.24160888

Hall A, Nordqvist M (2008) Professional management in family businesses: Toward an extended understanding. Family Bus Rev 21(1):51–69. https://doi.org/10.1111/j.1741-6248.2007.00109.x

Litz RA (1997) The family firm's exclusion from business school research: explaining the void; addressing the opportunity. Entrepreneurship Theory Pract 21(3):55–71. https://doi.org/10.1177/104225879702100304

Miles MB, Huberman AM, Saldana J (2014) Qualitative data analysis. A methods sourcebook, 3rd edn. Sage, London, UK

Nordqvist M, Hall A, Melin I (2009) Qualitative research on family businesses: the relevance and usefulness of the interpretive approach. J Manag Organ 15(3):294–308. https://doi.org/10.1017/S1833367200002637

Patton M (1990) Qualitative evaluation and research methods. Sage, Beverly Hills, CA

Songini L, Vola P (2015) The role of professionalization and managerialization in family business succession. Manag Control 1:9–43. https://doi.org/10.3280/MACO2015-001002

Internationalisation in Family Businesses. The Case of Mamagra

Elena Cristiano

Abstract The chapter makes an empirical verification of theories highlighted in the first part, through the study of a family business that, with the takeover of the new generation, has successfully pursued its international expansion. The analysis was conducted in two stages: an analysis of second data based on documents (e.g. financial statements, directors' reports, etc.) provided by the examined enterprise; semi-structured interviews to the controlling family's members. In order to study the internationalisation process, the degree of internationalisation, measured in terms of the correlation between foreign sales and total sales (foreign sales/total sales), and the different adopted forms of internationalisation (direct export, consortia among enterprises, technical-productive collaboration agreements and subcontracting agreements) have been evaluated.

Keywords Family business · Internationalisation · Strategic alliances · Delocalisation · International growth

1 Introduction

The international expansion of SMEs derives from the combined action of a number of internal and external factors, which are present in the phases of a business activity at various levels. Among the "internal" variables that may be considered as remarkable explanatory elements of the internationalisation processes, just recently the relationship between the ownership structure and the access to foreign markets has become particularly important. Entrepreneurial, managerial and financial resources are of great importance in the process of internationalisation of family businesses. The globalisation of markets and business practices represents the main factor that drives these companies to expand their operations towards international paths. In addition, internationalisation is an important dimensional and organisational growth opportunity, thus allowing for revitalising both the family system and the enterprise

E. Cristiano (✉)
Department of Business Economics and Law, University of Calabria, Rende, Italy
e-mail: elena.cristiano@unical.it

A. Leotta (ed.), *Management Controlling and Governance of Family Businesses*, Contributions to Management Science,
https://doi.org/10.1007/978-3-030-47741-7_11

system, through new job opportunities for the members of the controlling family and through the business sustainability for the future generations. Being a family business has many implications on their international behaviour, especially if it is taken into consideration the fact that, inside them, sometimes, divergent systems coexist. These systems evolve and change in the different stages of the life cycle. In fact, the presence of family members, with a different level of risk perception and risk appetite, may influence the decision to undertake international activities. This chapter aims at providing with a contribution to the study of this particular aspect, through an in-depth analysis on the internationalisation of the Italian small and medium-sized businesses, focusing specifically on the analysis of the influence that the family nature of the management and the human capital have on the international development. Basing on the theoretical formulations of the international entrepreneurship and stewardship theory, the main objective of this chapter is to determine whether, and to what extent, the generational involvement, the presence of altruism and trust affect the decision to internationalise the family business. This chapter also aims at providing some food for thought for the study on the internationalisation of family businesses.

The propensity to internationalisation of family businesses is often limited by the focusing on domestic markets (Gallo and Garcia Pont 1996), by the inadequate monitoring of the global market and by the lacking orderliness of evaluation of the international context (Okoroafo 1999). Such factors, besides the widespread strategic orientation (Coda 1988) based on the conservation and continuity and besides the primary objective of keeping the independence and the business control, would make family businesses less oriented to search for opportunities of expansion abroad. That would make the level of family businesses' internationalisation lower than other business contexts. Anyway, there are also other different analyses. Based on a study of 490 US manufacturers, Zahra (2003) observes that the family ownership of the business and its systems of governance, with the involvement of family members in the management, positively correlate with internationalisation.

The chapter makes an empirical verification of theories highlighted in the first part through the study of a family business that, with the takeover of the new generation, has successfully pursued its international expansion. The analysis was conducted with a view to the relationship between corporate governance, management control, with particular attention to the international entrepreneurship theory and the stewardship theory. The use of this latter, as the theoretical grounds for the study of the internationalisation of family businesses, contributes to a better clarification of some research questions that remain open. These questions include, for example, if and to what extent the decision to internationalise may be influenced by the generational involvement, the presence of altruism and trust among family members. The analysis was structured in two parts: an analysis of secondary data based on documents (e.g. financial statements, directors' reports, etc.) provided by the examined enterprise and semi-structured interviews to the controlling family's members and the study of the degree of internationalisation, measured in terms of the correlation between foreign sales and total sales (foreign sales/total sales), and the different forms of internationalisation adopted (direct export, consortia among enterprises, technical-manufacturing collaboration agreements and subcontracting agreements) have been evaluated.

2 Theoretical Foundations for the Study of the Empirical Case

In the new global economic scenario, the internationalisation process has to be adequately planned in order to allow the development of the distinctive resources, sources of new competitive advantages. For this purpose, it becomes fundamental to provide governance authorities with skills and resources appropriate for supporting the necessary processes of international development. The entrepreneur's personal characteristics, the system of social relationships in which he/she is in and, therefore, his/her ability to foresee the business development potentialities in an international perspective (Caroli and Lipparini 2002; Chandler and Hanks 1994; Collins 1991; Gallo et al. 1991; Philp 1998; Shane et al. 1993) often determine the set up of a SME abroad. The effect of such elements on the business strategy options is much higher if the business size is smaller. The complexity of the governance structures of SMEs in general (and of the family ones in particular) is determined by the institutional overlap of three systems, which obviously should represent different logics, that is, the family, the ownership and the business (Lansberg 1983). The level of involvement of the family in the ownership and/or in the management determines some situations of mutual conditioning of the three systems, thus influencing the level and the scope of the division of labour processes, the choice of the control mechanisms and of the performance measurement systems, the effectiveness of the official bodies (first among everything, the Board of Directors) (Demattè 1995; Gubitta 1999; Montemerlo 2010). The fusion among emotions, feelings and mechanisms of allocation of governance powers, which characterises the specificity and complexity of small and medium-sized family businesses' governance, conditions the capacity of the entrepreneur and of his/her family members to reconsider their own roles, in relation to the needs of the business development. Especially in the presence of greater competitive and strategy complexities, the entrepreneur is often inhibited by the symbiosis between family and business. The internationalisation processes are conditioned by the different level of risk and of strategic, organisational and management involvement in the international competitive context. Numerous scientific contributions prove that in family businesses such processes develop gradually and progressively in most cases, only after having taken all the opportunities offered by national markets (Calabrò and Mussolino 2011). Nevertheless, there are some cases of family businesses, the so-called *born global firms,* which are already internationalised at the beginning (Knight and Cavusgil 2004; Wright et al. 2007). The *international entrepreneurship theory* provides useful elements to understand the international behaviour of family businesses, especially as regards the role played by the main decision-makers (Andersson 2000). Family businesses are often characterised by the presence of a sole decision-maker (that is, the founder) (Westerberg et al. 1997), who often finds himself/herself to face two forces of opposite nature. On the one hand, he/she has to pursue the opportunities beyond the national boundaries (therefore, he/she has to expand the activity) and on the other hand, he/she has to keep the business (and the family's) total or majority control, thus following low-risk projects in the traditional/local market. Many scholars suggest that often the second force prevails over the first one, thus causing the poor propensity of many family businesses to expand their activities beyond the national boundaries (Okoroafo 1999; Fernández and Nieto 2005). Nevertheless, there are also some cases of family businesses which succeeded in reaching an equilibrium between the growth in foreign markets and the decision-making centralisation, or the internationalisation process of which is triggered by a particular *event* of a family business' life cycle, such as, for example, the generational passage and the subsequent involvement of the new generations in the business activity. The creation of new products/services, the achievement of new markets and the international sale transactions are some of the activities which may be carried out by the new generations (Sharma et al. 1997). Therefore, the presence of the second force and/or of the following generations may be beneficial to reach a new successful entrepreneurial impulse (Salvato 2004). The role of the main decision-makers, the dedication and experience, the changes in the ownership, the composition of the board of directors often represent the stimulating elements for a change in the strategy in such direction. Consequently, it is undeniable that the advent of new generations in a family business may positively influence the propensity towards international entrepreneurial activities (that is, the creation of new products/services, the achievement of new markets and the international sale transactions). In order to understand the international dynamics of family businesses, it is useful to examine the hypotheses underlying the *stewardship theory,* which make reference to compliant behaviours, in which the interests of the different stakeholders are aligned with the business ones (Corbetta and Salvato 2004; Eddleston and Kellemanns 2007; Eddleston et al.2008). With regard to the *theory of the firm,* such approach better adapts to the particular nature of *family firms* (Jensen and Meckling 1976; Fama 1980), if compared to the agency theory, the hypotheses of which suggest the opportunistic behaviour by the economic agents. In fact, in family businesses, there are different levels of *altruism* in line with the hypotheses of the *stewardship theory,* such as the long-term orientation, the presence of systems of values shared between the family and the business, the direct identification of the family with the business (Davis et al. 1997), the reciprocity relationship, the participatory decision-making process and the shared control in the business governance system (Eddleston and Kellemanns 2007). The different decision-makers, variously involved in the strategic direction of the family business, may act in the interest of the company (and be some stewards), thus fostering and supporting the strategy option of becoming international. Everything develops in a logic of sharing of the entrepreneurial risks related to such strategy option (James 1999) and in the presence of a direct and open communication system (McCollom 1988). Therefore, the role played by the family business' founder/owner is fundamental. He/she may behave in two different ways. If his/her interests are completely aligned with the specific needs of the business, it is not difficult to obtain the full support by the other family's members. On the contrary, if his/her interests are egoistical and opportunistic, some conflicting mechanisms are triggered: these mechanisms may damage both the family and the business (Schulze et al. 2001). Possible conflicts between the family's objectives (for instance, to safeguard the family control for the future generations) and the business-specific objectives (e.g. to develop in a global market), related to the decision to internationalise or not the activities, may be softened by the presence of altruism and trust that, moreover, also facilitates the propensity to the inherent risk related to the international activities (Zahra 2003). The mutual trust may be the result both of an emotional bond with another person (Lewis and Weigert 1985; Rempel et al. 1985; Drolet and Morris 2000), and of the awareness of the skills and reliability of the other party (Cook and Wall 1980; Butler 1991). In the case of family, the trust relationships existing between the founder/owner and the other subjects involved in the decision-making process (the family and non-family members) may be based on the recognised competence and/or on the moral integrity. In the *competence-based trust,* different members (the family and non-family ones) involved in the decision-making process related to the family business' internationalisation, develop an adequate level of trust on the founder/owner's skills, on the basis of the indications provided by him/her in relation to the ways through which internationalisation may be pursued (Dutton and Duncan 1987; Bantel and Jackson 1989). The development of a participatory decision-making process consolidates, in the other stakeholders involved in the process, the certainty as regards the correct implementation of the internationalisation strategy (Fryxell et al. 2002), thus letting the level of the risk perception reduce: a level which is connected to the decision to internationalise. The founder/owner, despite the involvement of many other subjects, is often the main decision-maker (Corbetta and Salvato 2004; Gedajlovic et al. 2004). The emotional bonds with the founder/owner may influence the decision to become international. The presence of trust should guarantee simpler decision-making processes and allow the whole organisation to rapidly adapt to the pressure of the external environment, thus ensuring a greater level of elasticity to know how to take the opportunities (with the related risks), which each time arise. Therefore, in family businesses, where this trust typology is developed, the different members (the family and non-family ones), involved in the decision-making process, are more willing to support the decisions made by the owner/founder, the choice of internationalisation of the family business included. In such case, the level of the risk perception connected to the decision to internationalise is reduced.

Generational involvement, altruism and trust existence in the decisions are, therefore, at the basis of the system of governance informal mechanisms which may, in a different way, influence the international growth of family businesses (Calabrò and Mussolino 2011).

3 The Internationalisation of Family Businesses. Empirical Evidence

Consistently with numerous qualitative studies (Eisenhardt 1989; Yin 2003), conducted by using the *case study analysis*, with the awareness of the limits that such applied methodology has and far from providing absolute generalisations, the following study aims at examining in-depth the knowledge on the topics, objects of investigation, and at contributing to providing with an empirical verification. In order to study the internationalisation process, some indicators have been created to measure the amount of investment, the links and the scope of the operations which define it. The degree of internationalisation (DOI), which expresses the business volume generated by the business beyond the national boundaries, may be measured in terms of the correlation between foreign sales and total sales, or *foreign sales/total sales (FSTS)*. Such indicator (FSTS) is the most widespread in literature (Zahra 2003; Fernandez and Nieto 2005; Gomez-Mejia et al. 2007; Calabrò et al. 2013; Calabrò and Mussolino 2013; Oesterle et al. 2013; Sciascia et al. 2013), both for the facility to find and elaborate information and for a matter of comparability among the results deriving from different studies. Other indicators concern the correlation between foreign assets and total assets, or foreign assets/total assets (FATA); the correlation between foreign employees and total employees, or (foreign employees/total employees (FETE); the correlation between foreign subsidiaries and total subsidiaries (foreign subsidiaries/total subsidiaries) (Hitt et al. 2006). The international business scope of the enterprise is measured through the number of countries (Zahra 2003; George et al. 2005; Naldi and Nordqvist 2008) or geographical macro-regions (Cerrato and Piva 2012) where the enterprise exports or sells its own products, and through the number of foreign branches (Sherman et al. 1998).

A precious pearl, nestled in the pleasant and sunny *Piana di Sibari* (the *Plain of Sibari*, in the province of *Cosenza*, Calabria), *"Mamagra"*[1] represents one of the most significant agricultural-and-food family businesses of Calabria. This business promotes the organic farming and the traditional products, it has the BIO SUISSE certification, it satisfies the IFOAM standards requirements and it meets the requirements provided for by the technical specifications of NOP relative to the USDA organic standards. Organic products, controlled by I.C.E.A. (Ethical and Environmental Certification Institute), comply with the rules provided for by the EEC Regulation no. 2092/91. All the production processes are rigorously inspected and recognised with a quality certification, since all productions have to be excellent. Spirit of the ancestors, expression of a millennial culture, custodian of the refined and genuine tastes of the present, Mamagra's businesses developed in a unique and precious territory. Sibari, the "heart" of Magna Graecia, is a mosaic of culture, art, tradition and innovation. Corigliano Calabro, the centre of the area of "*Sibaritide*" (an area which includes the Municipalities of Calopezzati, Cassano allo Ionio, Corigliano Calabro, Crosia, and Rossano), is a fertile and vital land. Starting from its etymological origin

[1]The names of companies and interviewees have been changed to ensure the confidentiality of the informants.

("*chorìon elàion*", the town of olive trees), it reveals its ancient vocation for the cultivation of the olive tree, a gift of nature. Since the beginning, the respect for the land and its fruits, the love for nature and good tastes have been important inputs, aimed at obtaining the best from a land which is so dedicated to the "beautiful" and "good" aspects, fostered by a mild and temperate climate which allows cultivations of any type. The will to protect the quality of the fruits that nature nobly offers led the business to practise a form of agriculture, which is careful about preserving the quality and genuineness of cultivations, thus offering healthy and traditional products on the market. Moreover, the business stands out for its will to constantly improve its products and to continuously optimise its know-how. It is an entrepreneurial organisation, which is well-structured commercially and industrially. It also follows some cooperating strategies with small local producers, who focus on cultivation. This choice allows the provision of high-quality raw material, which is aligned with the business production standards.

The business was set up in 1946, when the activity of the olive-press started. It was used for the animal-traction milling of its own olives and of the local farmers' ones. With the generational passage, there was the first technological change with the introduction of the "crusher hydraulic" press. In 1987, in the business, there was the introduction of the first heir with the creation of the partnership "Oleum Molendini S.a.s." (a limited partnership). The business activities of "Oleum Molendini S.a.s." are the following: the olive purchase and milling, as well as the bottling and packaging of oil; the production, the processing, the marketing of agricultural-and-food products, of Calabrian traditional products; the production and processing of vegetables preserved in oil, of dried and seasonal fruit, of jams, of fruit in syrup and of drinks in general. And finally, there is the marketing of its own products and not only, on its own and on behalf of a third party, with its own brand. Between 1991 and 1995 the generational passage was completed with the involvement of the other heirs. Currently, the business is managed skilfully and enthusiastically by three family Mamagra's members, one son and two daughters: Angelo, who is the person in charge of the organisational-commercial sector; Maria Grazia, who is the person in charge of the administrative-accounting sector; Anita, who is the person in charge of the commercial sector of fruit and vegetables. The changeover was gradual and the atmosphere has always been serene and collaborative, marked by the right equilibrium between the founders' sound traditional values and the heirs' technological and organisational innovation. The introduction of the son and daughters in the business implicated a productive revolution, especially in the sector of the oil production and in the product marketing. Over the years the partnership has uninterruptedly operated on the business functions, thus proceeding with important investments, which, nowadays, characterise it as one of the most representative businesses with regard to the oil production chain in the province of *Cosenza*. Over the years, besides the commitment in terms of financial resources, which have concerned the modernisation of the production processes, also other important promotion campaigns of the business brand have been launched. Nowadays, this brand is well known both in Italy and abroad. In 1992, the business started the activity of bottling and packaging of olive oil, which, currently, covers 70% of the marketed product (the remaining 30% of the product represents an "unpackaged product"). Over the years the business, besides processing the olives coming from the partners' family businesses, has acquired a very high number of customers, thus currently arriving at producing, about 6000 (six thousand) quintals of olive oil (virgin and extra virgin) in the whole oil campaign. Today, the business produces extra-virgin olive oil in three different lines: PDO, organic and conventional farming. Starting from the local market, the family business expanded the reference market, thus reaching the national and foreign market (Germany, Great Britain, Belgium, Switzerland, Austria, the USA, Japan, Canada, Brazil, Lithuania and Taiwan).

The internationalisation process was carefully planned and the decision was supported by the results obtained after the implementation of a management control, though still informal and based on both index construction and an adequate accounting of the costs resulting from a budget analysis. The company is managed by family members and non-family members are not allowed to participate in decision-making.

The company is fairly strong in long-term solidity and has a balanced condition of solvency. This financial situation let the family business to consider the decisions about internalisation in a more serene way.

In recent years, the company has applied production and marketing policies that have led to an increase in sales revenues, with actions aiming to double the turnover volume in the years to come. The choices were also made on the basis of studies on the olive industry, such as the ISMEA (2018) report that points out some peculiar aspects, i.e. the declining trend of production and the excessive variability of the same in recent years; consumption is always higher than production, meaning that Italy is not self-sufficient; import is always greater than export, so that the trade balance is structurally negative; import is needed to meet the domestic demand. The extreme fragmentation of Italian production can be also deducted from the number of olive mills, considering that in Spain their number oscillates between 1600 and 1700, but Spanish production is fairly above a million of tons. Of the approximately 4600 active olive mills, 20% are located in Apulia, 15% in Calabria and 12% in Sicily, followed by Tuscany with a 9% share. Comparing the weight of regional production, it is clear that Apulia has larger mills if compared with the rest of Italy. As for the share of cooperative mills with respect to national production, these are mainly located in Apulia and Tuscany, accounting only for 20% of the total. This large quantity of mills, although on the one hand, increases the systemic costs, on the other, it could stand as a guarantee of quality. Of all the quality oils recognised in the European Union, almost 40% are produced by Italian brands. The production of certified oil, however, does not exceed 2–3% of the total in quantitative terms. The share in terms of value reaches 6%. The certified Italian production of PDO/PGI olive oil in 2016 was still below the threshold of 10 thousand tons, a definitely scarce value with respect to its potential. Olive oil production is concentrated in the Mediterranean Basin, where Spain and Italy are the largest exporters in the world (60% and 20%, respectively). Italian production accounts on average for 15% of global production (compared to an average of 45% in Spain). On the import side, the market space is occupied by few large customers (Italy itself accounts for a third of the total, followed by the USA). The company wants to take advantage of the growth opportunities in the industry, such as its geographical location. In fact, the firm is located in one of the most gifted geographical areas for the cultivation of olive trees, both in terms of quantity and quality of the product. Production can be differentiated by cultivar, production methods, and origin, not to mention the landscape, the historical, cultural and anthropological value of the olive groves—all these factors play a role in the growing attention to quality. On the basis of these elements, given that the company is already well positioned and can benefit from the above-mentioned opportunities for achieving the intended goal, the family has planned to stipulate some agreements with one of the two major national producers of olive oil; to purchase, after its evaluation, some land to be used for the cultivation of olive trees and increase the production of the raw material; to expand the production and marketing of olive oil on the domestic market, increasing the share to be sold under its own trademark; to strengthen its presence on the international arena by means of agreements with major foreign producers. In this regard, for some years, the company entered in a consortium of producers located in different European countries, including Spain. Internationalisation is currently driven by exports. This kind of investment is characterised by a high degree of flexibility and a low degree of control, positioning itself in the lower right quarter of the matrix depicting the internationalisation methods, as in Fig. 1 reported in Chap. "The Growth of Family Businesses: The Path to Internationalization" of the present volume. In the case of the company under examination, there is a high degree of investment flexibility, so that resource allocation can be modified at any time without incurring in excessively high costs. The company has put in place collaborative relationships with its subsidiaries; hence, the investment is more similar to strategic alliances rather than exports. The analysed company (family-centred model), in the early stages of its internationalisation process, relied on direct export. However, as it became progressively familiar with the foreign country, it started to collaborate with local intermediaries (indirect export) to mitigate the risk of the investment. The possibility of opening sale branches (USA) and production branches abroad (Spain, Germany) is currently taken into consideration. The family leadership, in fact, believes that in some cases (Spain, for instance) the benefits deriving from the partnership with foreign entities are greater than the risks of losing control, which are indeed very low. Therefore, the presence of successors in the ownership is in line with the SEW perspective.

International expansion was made possible thanks by the ability of the new generation to change its strategic and managerial vision. The company, which for years gained benefit from its technical/production know-how and from the consequent, strong competitive advantage in the local area is given by its reputation, decided to make its excellence visible beyond the domestic boundaries. This strategic turning point was supported by the entire leadership and was made possible, in particular, by the dedication of two of the three heirs who are leading the company, with a substantial amount of time dedicated to looking for contacts and trade opportunities (marketing and sales) abroad. The beginning was a bit stereotypical, e.g. investing in industry fairs, travels and trade missions to present their offer. In addition to the above-mentioned devotion to the effort, some important drivers for success were discipline and commitment and, above all, the acquisition of knowledge and methods for a more rational approach to business. This effort was complemented by the change of the professional profile of the workforce through the building of a dedicated commercial team. A choice that proved to be fruitful was to hire foreign professionals residing in Italy. They belonged to nationalities and cultures close to those of the target countries, so that they were able to deal with their counterpart on the same grounds, other than being particularly competent from a technical or commercial point of view and willing to gain potential customers. The choice of foreign countries was made in some cases according to their attractiveness (e.g. USA, Japan, Canada, where, at the same price, the value of the domestic product is higher than the value of the corresponding competitor products); in other cases (e.g. Germany, Belgium, Great Britain and Switzerland), the criterion was that the potential price on the foreign market is potentially higher than the price on the domestic market and lower than the price of competing foreign products. The international development, in terms of marketing and sales, required also the adaptation of other functions such as design, production, certifications, logistics, custom operations and administration-accounting. The peculiarities due to national background, coupled with the different needs of new customers, have imposed a change in every single company operation, even the most elementary and less relevant ones, but above all, it required the adaptation to new standards by the existing workforce. The initial, albeit minimal, individual resistances were overcome by leveraging on the best interest and on the need to act for the common good, i.e. the continuity of the company. The combined effect of these changes sparked a real metamorphosis of the company that, while maintaining its family and SME perspective, has "shed its skin" to adapt to the international development and enabled further growth by triggering a virtuous circle of progressive enlargement of its sphere of action. The organisational change resulting from the strategic choice to cross the national borders became the driver for new market opportunities.

The conducted analysis shows that the business focused, at the beginning and for a long time period, on the national market (national sales/total sales), thus opening up towards foreign markets only over the last years. The degree of internationalisation, calculated by comparing foreign sales with total sales for every year, in fact, indicates a greater concentration on the national market. On the whole, in the examined five-year term, the relationship between foreign sales and total sales is equal to 21%. Nevertheless, consistently with the strategy elaborated by the leadership, in the analysed five-year term, an increasing incidence of such indicator may be observed, thus directing greater attention to foreign markets (Fig. 1).

In 2018 (the last examined year), compared with 2014 (the first examined year), for an increase of 5% in total sales, an increase of 82% in the relationship between foreign sales and total sales and a decrease of 6% in the relationship between national sales and total sales were observed.

The growth rate over the five-year period considered increased by 37%, with a higher incidence of foreign sales (61%) than that of national sales (32%). In particular, the FS/TS ratio increased by 67% and the NS/TS ratio by 36% (Fig. 2).

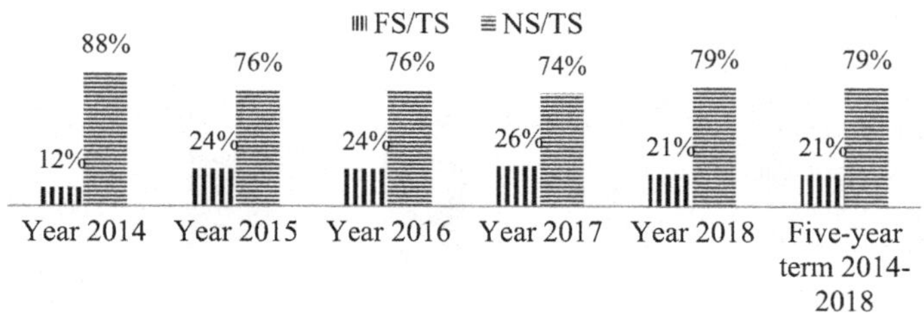

Fig. 1 Incidence of the percentage of foreign and national sales on the total of sales *Source* Processing on data of "Oleum Molendini S.a.s." Years 2014–2018

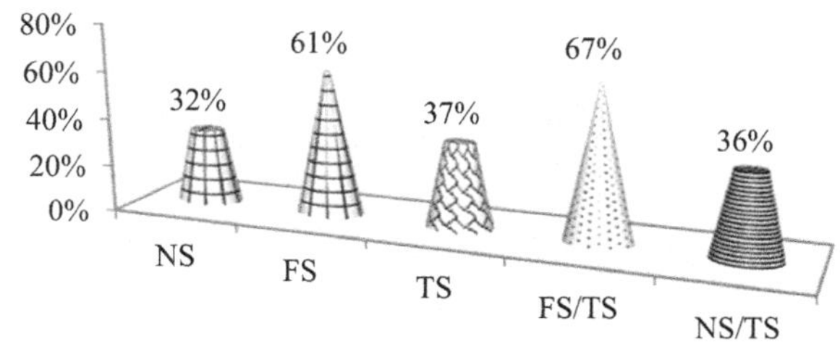

Fig. 2 Growth rate of the FSTS in the five-year term 2014–2018 *Source* Processing on data of "Oleum Molendini S.a.s." Years 2014–2018

Considering the foreign sales of the whole examined five-year term, the greater percentage of foreign sales (24%) was observed in 2018 (Fig. 3).

In 2005, the partnership "Oleum Molendini", a wholly family-owned business, created the cooperative enterprise "OP Bonum naturae", a limited liability consortium (a Consortium Ltd.). The ownership structure, in which the family business held a majority stake, opened up towards outside, thus involving a substantial number of other leader businesses in the sector of fresh fruit and vegetables, located in the areas of the *Alto Ionio Cosentino* and of the *Sibaritide*. Through well-known brands, today the group (Bonum naturae, Biosybaris, Acinapura Bio) aims at marketing fresh fruit and vegetables, organic products and high-quality integrated farming products all over the world. The products are certified and marketed through the national and foreign mass distribution channel (the Italian "GDO", *Grande Distribuzione*

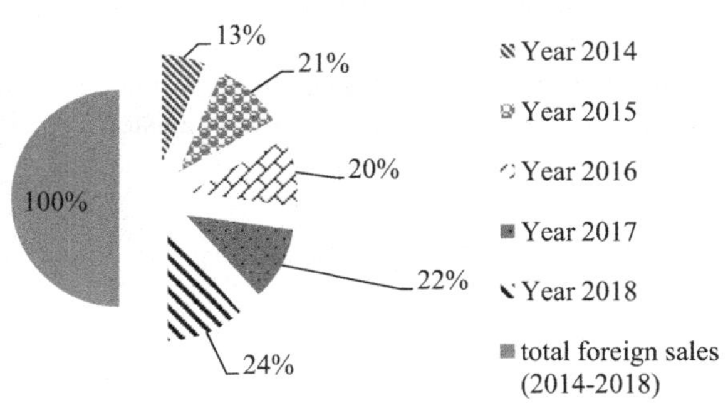

Fig. 3 Percentage of the foreign sales in the five-year term 2014–2018 *Source* Processing on data of "Oleum Molendini S.a.s." Years 2014–2018

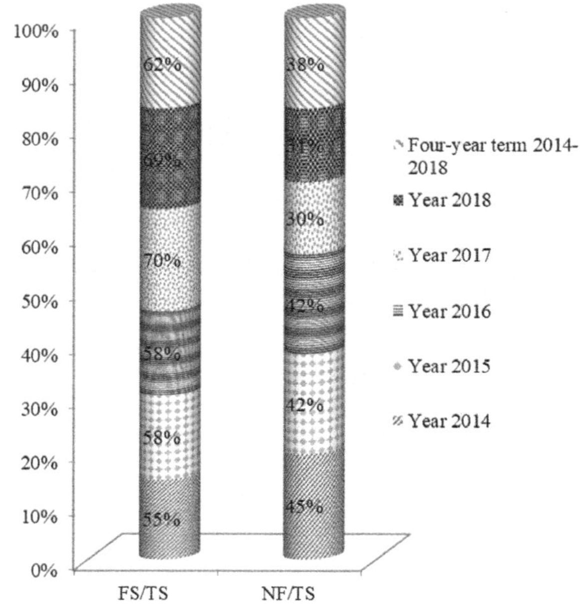

Fig. 4 Percentage of the foreign sales and the national sales on total sales in the five-year term 2014–2018 *Source* Processing on data of "Carpe NaturamBonum naturae" Years 2014–2018

Organizzata). Differently from "Oleum Molendini S.a.s.", initially and mainly the consortium turned to foreign markets, which were more open to the idea of the organic product, as shown in Fig. 4, it is shown by the greater incidence of foreign sales, compared with the national ones on the total amount of sales.

Starting from 2013, a greater opening towards the national market may be observed. In fact, though the percentage of sales abroad was still predominant, a growing trend of national sales, compared with total sales, was recorded, especially in the last examined year compared to the previous one. Such trend corresponded to a change in the strategy of the leadership which, once strengthened the position abroad, aimed at reinforcing its own presence on the national market, in which, over the last years, if compared to the past, a greater request for the organic products may be observed. On the whole, in the examined five-year term, the growth rate shows an increase in sales (36%), both foreign (40%) and national (29%), although with a still prevalent incidence of the former (FS/TS equal to 46%) on the latter (NS/TS equal to 34%) (Fig. 5).

Considering the foreign sales of the whole examined five-year term, the greater percentage of foreign sales (22%) was registered in 2018 (Fig. 6).

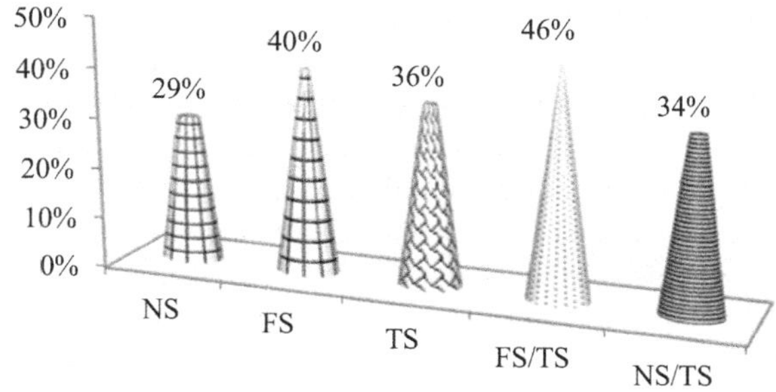

Fig. 5 Growth rate of the FSTS in the five-year term 2014–2018 *Source* Processing on data of "Bonum naturae" Years 2014–2018

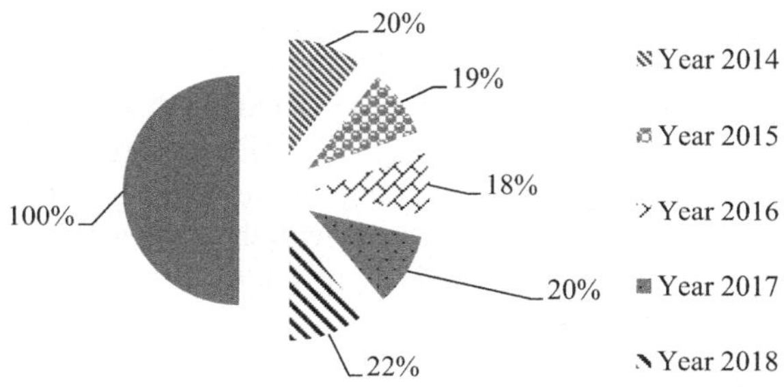

Fig. 6 Percentage of foreign sales in the five-year term 2014–2018 *Source* Processing on data of "Bonum naturae" Years 2014–2018

4 Concluding Comments

In the examined family business, over the decades, its members have acquired much experience with regard to the soil cultivation, the processing of fruit and vegetables and their preservation.

The company stands as an example of a family business capable of reaching an internal equilibrium and the right management of the family–business relationship. In fact, the company aims to create a peaceful and familiar environment, not only among the family members, but also within the company as a whole, by involving every employee in business matters. Our analysis suggests that the critical and sensitive aspects of this relationship, such as succession or recruitment of workforce, were carried out in a well-tempered way. The recruitment strategy was focused on the selection of professionals who had adequate and specific skills; the same members of the family are engaged in continuous learning and are constantly increasing their know-how. The union between family and company is considered a strong point and, other than being profitable for both, can be traced back to the main product of the company. Olive oil mirrors the history of the area and the traditions handed down by the family to the new generations, thus creating new development opportunities for the local community, as shown by the participation of the company in various producers' associations in the fruit and vegetable industry. The control and management/direction are reserved to family members only. Over the years, the new generation has proven to be willing to innovate and change, as demonstrated not only by the choice to internationalise, but also by the will to formalise the management control system, an operation that is often met by resistance in family businesses. The third generation has a deep respect for its father's work, whom the generation esteems (trusts) very much, especially for his strong integrity. The family culture deeply influences the family and the organisation as a whole. The new generation is characterised by the continuing vocational training, skills and orientation, incentivised by the predecessor, who also passed down to the new generation a participatory leadership style. Decisions are discussed and made collectively.

The work environment of the company is inspired by the principles of stewardship theory, where the interests of the various actors are aligned with those of the company and there are different dimensions of altruism, such as the long-term orientation. Other aspects are the presence of shared values between the family and the business; the direct identification of the family with the business; the reciprocity relationship; the participatory decision-making and the shared control in the corporate governance system. The decision-makers, involved in various ways in the strategic direction of the family business, are acting in the interest of the company by showing the will of sharing the risks connected with the strategic choices and with the presence of a direct and open communication system. These aspects were influential on the choice of expanding beyond national borders.

In the case of "Oleum Molendini S.a.s." the international activity has allowed to go beyond the critical aspects related to the saturation of the reference national market, whereas in the case of "Bonum naturae" the international activity has allowed for taking advantage of the greater maturity of foreign markets, if compared to the Italian ones, in terms of preferences and financial soundness.

Family businesses may find, in the opening up of their governance outside, a precious source of resources (also financial ones) and skills, necessary to become international successfully. Similarly, it would be desirable to involve the new generations, above all considering the fact that the generational passage is a very delicate situation in the business activity. The entrance of young successors into the business, as in the case analysed, not only promotes the field training of the same and encourages an appropriate succession planning, but it might foster the business expansion abroad. The success of a business is connected with the human capital quality of its employees, consequently, the possibility that the young successors actually represent an opportunity of growth and renewal might depend on their level and type of education, as well as on their real experience matured inside the business. The development of interpersonal dynamics based on altruism and trust increases the propensity to share the risks related to the decision to internationalise the business (and the family). In such a way, the main decision-makers of family businesses reach their awareness of what are the factors which may intervene in the decision-making dynamics relating to the internationalisation processes. The timing, the choice of the target markets and the ways of internationalisation may vary with relation to the particular phase of the life cycle in which the family business is, to the level of the generational involvement, to the founder's point of view and to other specific characteristics of governance.

The examined case confirms that internationalisation requires organisational changes and the overcoming of a variety of resistances through the adoption of a new mindset, even in family businesses. The internationalisation, firstly intended to be a new strategic direction for expanding into new markets (by geographical area and distribution channels), becomes a reason for the change, in microscopic and macroscopic terms, for the professional profile of people, their tasks and their responsibilities, entailing a different balance of forces in the organisational structure.

References

Andersson S (2000) The internationalization of the firm from an entrepreneurial perspective. Int Stud Manage Org 30(1):63–92. https://doi.org/10.1080/00208825.2000.11656783

Bantel KA, Jackson SE (1989) Top management and innovations in banking: does the composition of the top team make a difference? Strateg Manag J 10:107–124. DOI: 10.1002/smj.4250100709

Butler JK (1991) Toward understanding and measuring conditions of trust: evolution of a conditions of trust inventory. J Manag 17(3):643–663. DOI: 10.1177/014920639101700307

Calabrò A, et al (2013) The influence of ownership structure and board strategic involvement on international sales: the moderating effect of family involvement. Int Bus Rev 22:509–523

Calabrò A, Mussolino D (2011) How do boards of directors contribute to family SME export intensity? The role of formal and informal governance mechanisms. J Manag Govern On-line first. DOI: 10.1007/s10997–011–9180–7

Calabrò A, Mussolino D (2013) How do boards of directors contribute to family SME export intensity? The role of formal and informal governance mechanisms. J Manage Governance 17:363–403

Caroli MG, Lipparini, A. (2002). Le piccole e medie imprese italiane e i percorsi di crescita internazionale: il quadro di riferimento. In: Caroli MG, Lipparini A (a cura di), Piccole imprese oltre confine, Carocci, Roma.

Cerrato D, Piva M (2012) The internationalization of small and medium-sized enterprises: the effect of family management, human capital and foreign ownership. J Manage Governance 16:617–644

Chandler GN, Hanks SH (1994) Founder competence, the environment, and venture performance. Entrepreneurship Theory Pract 18(3). DOI: 10.1177/104225879401800306

Coda V (1988) L'orientamento strategico dell'impresa. Utet, Torino

Collins DJ (1991) A resource-based analysis of global competition: the case of the bearings industry strategic management. J Summer (numero monografico)

Cook J, Wall T (1980) New work attitude measures of trust, organizational commitment and personal need non-fulfilment. J Occup Psychol 53:39–52. https://doi.org/10.1111/j.2044-8325.1980.tb00005.x

Corbetta G, Salvato C (2004) The board of directors in family firms: one size fits all? Family Bus Rev 17(2):119–134. https://doi.org/10.1111/j.1741-6248.2004.00008.x

Davis JH et al (1997) Toward a stewardship theory of management. Acad Manag Rev 22(1):20–47. https://doi.org/10.2307/259223

Del Bravo F (edited by) (2018) AgrOsserva. La congiuntura agroalimentare. Rapporto annuale ISMEA

Demattè C (1995) Consigli d'amministrazione: organi inutili o essenziali centri regolari? Economia Manag 1

Drolet AL, Morris M W (2000) Rapport in conflict resolution: accounting for how face-to-face contact fosters mutual cooperation in mixed motive conflicts. J Exp Soc Psychol 36:26–50. DOI: 10.1006/jesp.1999.1395

Dutton JE, Duncan RB (1987) The creation of monument for change through the process of strategic issue diagnosis. Strateg Manag J 8:279–295. https://doi.org/10.1002/smj.4250080306
Eddleston K et al (2008) Resource configuration in family firms: linking resources. Strategic planning and environmental dynamism to performance. J Manag Stud 45(1):26–50. https://doi.org/10.1111/j.1467-6486.2007.00717.x
Eddleston K, Kellermanns FW (2007) Destructive and productive family relationships: a stewardship theory perspective. J Bus Ventur 22(4):545–565. DOI: 10.1016/j.jbusvent.2006.06.004
Eisenhardt K (1989) Building theories from case study research. Acad Manag Rev 14(4): 532–550. DOI: 10.2307/258557
Fama EF (1980) Agency problem and the theory of the firm. J Polit Econ 88(2):288–307
Fernandez Z, Nieto MJ (2005) Internationalization strategy of small and medium-sized family businesses: some influential factors. Family Bus Rev 18(1):77–90. https://doi.org/10.1111/1741-6248.2005.00031.x
Fryxell et al (2002) After the Ink Dries: the Interaction of Trust and Control in US-based International Joint ventures. J Manag Stud 39(6):865–886. DOI: 10.1111/1467-6486.00315
Gallo MA, Garcia Pont C (1996) Important factors in family business internationalization. Family Busi Rev 9(1): 45–60. DOI: 10.1111/j.1741-6248.1996.00045.x
Gallo MA, Sveen J (1991) Internationalizing the family business: facilitating and restraining factors. Family Bus Rev 4(2):181–190. DOI: 10.1111/j.1741-6248.1991.00181.x
Gedajlovic et al (2004) Crossing the threshold from founder management to professional management: a governance perspective. J Manage Stud 41(5): 899–912. DOI: 10.1111/j.1467-6486.2004.00459.x
George G, et al (2005) Ownership and the internationalization of small firms. J Manage 31(2):210–233
Gomez-Mejia, et al (2007) Diversification decisions in family-controlled firms. J Manage Stud 47(2):223–252
Gubitta P (1999) Consigli di valore. I modelli di corporate governance come risorsa, in Sviluppo & Organizzazione 175, settembre-ottobre.
Hitt M, et al (2006) International diversification: antecedents, outcomes, and moderators. J Manage 32(6):831–867
James HS (1999) Owner as manager, extended horizons and the family firm. Int J Econ Bus 6(1):41–55. 102. DOI: 10.1080/13571519984304.
Jensen M, Meckling WH (1976) Theory of the firm: managerial behavior, agency costs and ownership structure. J Financ Econ 3(4):305–360. DOI: 10.1016/0304-405X(76)90026-X
Knight GA, Cavusgil ST (2004) Innovation, organizational capabilities, and the Born-Global Firm. J Int Bus Stud 35(2):124–141
Lansberg I (1983) Managing human resources in family firms: the problem of institutional overlap. Org Dyn 12(1). DOI: 10.1016/0090–2616(83)90025–6.
Lewis JD, Weigert A (1985) Trust as a social reality. Soc Forces 63(4):967–985. DOI: 10.1093/sf/63.4.967
Mccollom ME (1988) Integration in the family firm: when the family system replaces controls and culture. Family Bus Rev 1(4):399–417. DOI: 10.1111/j.1741-6248.1988.00399.x
Montemerlo D (2010) Continuità generazionale e accordi familiari. Principi e regole per l'impresa, la proprietà e la famiglia, Egea, Milano
Naldi L, Norqvist M (2008) Family firms venturing into international markets: a resource dependence perspective, frontiers of entrepreneurship research, vol 28(14), Article 1
Oesterle, et al (2013) The influence of ownership structure on internationalization. Int Bus Rev 22:187–201
Okoroafo SC (1999) Internationalization of family businesses: evidence from northwest Ohio USA. Family Bus Rev 12(2):147–158. DOI: 10.1111/j.1741-6248.1999.00147.x
Philp NE (1998) The export propensity of the very small entreprise. Int Small Bus J 16. DOI: 10.1177/0266242698164005

Rempel JK, Holmes JG, Zanna MP (1985) Trust in close relationships. J Pers Soc Psychol 49(1):95–112

Salvato C (2004) Predictors of entrepreneurship in family firms. J Private Equity 7(3):68–76. https://doi.org/10.3905/jpe.2004.412339

Schulze WS, Lubatkin MH, Dino RN, Buchholtz AK (2001) Agency relationships in family firms: theory and evidence. Organ Sci 12(2):99–116

Sciascia S, et al (2013) Family involvement in the board of directors: effects on sales internationalization. J Small Bus Manage 51(1):83–99

Shane et al (1993) Do international and domestic entrepreneurs differ at start-up? In Birley S, Macmillan IC, Subramony S (eds) Entrepreneurship research: global perspectives, Norgh Holland, Ambsterdam

Sharma P et al (1997) Strategic management of the family business: past research and future challenges. Family Bus Rev 10(1):1–35. https://doi.org/10.1111/j.1741-6248.1997.00001.x

Sherman HD, Kashlak R J, Joshi MP (1998) The effect of the board and executive committee characteristics on the degree of internationalization. J Int Manage 4:311–335

Westerberg M et al (1997) Does the CEO matter? An empirical study of small Swedish firms operating in turbulent environments. Scandinavian J Manag 13(3):251–270. https://doi.org/10.1016/S0956-5221(97)00011-0

Wright M et al (2007) Internationalisation by SMEs: a critique and policy implications. Reg Stud 41(7):1013–1030. https://doi.org/10.1080/00343400601120288

Yin RK (2003) Case study research: design and methods. Sage, Thousand Oaks, CA. DOI: 10.12691/jbms-5-1-1

Zahra SA (2003) International expansion of U.S. manufacturing family businesses: the effect of ownership and involvement. J Bus Ventur 18:495–512. https://doi.org/10.1016/S0883-9026(03)00057-0

Family Ownership and Investment Decisions. An Empirical Analysis on the Role of Board Monitoring and CEO Emotional Attachment

Claudia Frisenna and Davide Rizzotti

Abstract Despite research provides wide evidence that family-controlled firms face underinvestment and low growth problems, literature provides limited insight on what factors are able to incite investment spending in family firms. Building on agency and stewardship constructs as complementary frameworks, this study investigates whether board monitoring and CEO emotional attachment might affect investment spending within family firms. Empirical results show that family-controlled firms invest less than non-family firms. However, findings also show that, within family firms, board independence and the presence of a family CEO have a positive impact on the level of investments.

Keywords Family-oriented behavior · Agency theory · Stewardship theory · Board independence · Family CEO

1 Introduction

Despite their economic relevance, researchers diverge on whether family firms constitute a valuable business structure. In particular, prior studies provide wide evidence that family-controlled firms tend to be more conservative and to face severe financial constraints, which lead to underinvestment problems, low growth, and stagnation. However, literature provides limited insight on the relationship between different board structures and investment spending in family firms. Building on agency and stewardship constructs as complementary frameworks, we suggested that both board monitoring and the presence of an emotionally involved CEO may be positively associated with the level of investments in long-term projects.

C. Frisenna (✉) · D. Rizzotti
Department of Economics and Business, University of Catania, Catania, Italy
e-mail: claudia.frisenna@unict.it

D. Rizzotti
e-mail: rizzotti@unict.it

A. Leotta (ed.), *Management Controlling and Governance of Family Businesses*, Contributions to Management Science,
https://doi.org/10.1007/978-3-030-47741-7_12

This study aims at providing empirical evidence on whether board monitoring and CEO emotional attachment might affect investment spending within family firms.

Since the research question assumes that underinvestment problems in family firms exist, we first examine the relationship between family control and investment spending. Building on prior studies, we test the benchmark hypothesis of the existence of a negative relationship between family ownership and capital expenditures (H1).We find that family-controlled firms invest less than non-family firms.

Then, focusing on family-controlled firms, we investigate whether board monitoring and CEO's emotional attachment are able to incite the level of investment expenditures. In order to capture the effects of board monitoring, we focus on board independence, as in the agency perspective, the monitoring role of the board and its effectiveness are mainly entrusted to independent directors. Consistently, with the agency assumptions, we hypothesize that *within family firms, board independence is positively associated with the level of capital expenditures* (H2).

In order to capture the effects of CEO's emotional attachment, we focus on the presence of a family CEO, as stewardship theorists suggest that the degree of emotional involvement, self-identification, and commitment is higher when the person who runs the firms is a family member than an external professional manager (Miller and Breton-Miller 2006). Consistently, with the stewardship constructs, we hypothesize that *within family firms, the presence of a family CEO is positively associated with the level of capital expenditures* (H3).

The empirical analysis is based on a sample of 121 Italian listed firms, with 946 firm-year observations over the period 2006–2014. Italy constitutes a suitable setting because of the high presence of firms with ownership concentrated in the hands of a family, which keeps corporate control through several generations (Brunello et al. 2003; Prencipe et al. 2008).

Empirical results show that family-controlled firms invest less than non-family firms. However, findings also show that, within family firms, board independence and the presence of a family CEO have a positive impact on the level of investments.

These results suggest that both an effective board monitoring and a strong CEO's emotional commitment are able to mitigate agency conflicts and to incite investment spending.

In the following sections, we describe the research design and the empirical results of our analysis.

2 Research Method

2.1 Institutional Setting

The Italian context constitutes a suitable setting to address the role of the board independence and the CEO's emotional attachment on investment decisions of family firms, for the following reasons. First, Italian financial market is characterized by a significantly prevalence of family ownership, with 73% of family listed firms (Bianchi and Enriques 1999; Prencipe et al. 2014; Volpin 2002). Second, Italian family owners tend to hold the firm's majority stake and to keep the firm's control for a long term (Brunello et al. 2003; Prencipe et al. 2008). The high financial involvement and the desire to preserve the control constitute the determinant of the risk aversion and financial constraints which in turn cause underinvestment problems and low growth. Third, the Italian governance system is characterized by a weak effectiveness of external governance devices, such as the market for corporate control and the activism of institutional investors (La Porta et al. 2000; Melis 2000; Brunello et al. 2003). Therefore, the protection of minority shareholders highly depends on the monitoring of independent directors and on the CEO's commitment toward firm's sustainability. Fourth, Italian family firms are mostly characterized by close owners-managers relationships (Rizzotti et al. 2017). In particular, Prat et al. (2010) find that, among Italian family firms, a fidelity model system is well established in which family owners usually appoints faithful managers among the set of friendly relationships, in order to protect family interests. Therefore, professional executives may have greater incentives to safeguard the trust of the family owners, in order to keep their position for a long time (Volpin 2002; Brunello et al. 2003).

Finally, Italian Code of Good Governance is particularly concerned with the protection of small shareholders' rights, mainly entrusted to independent directors. Indeed, since the first version of 1999, the Code stressed the monitoring role of independent directors. The revised versions of 2006 and 2011 have further strengthened the role of independent directors recommending an effective monitoring, especially in cases of potential conflict of interests between majority shareholders and small investors.

The 2006 Code version, in essence unchanged in the later versions, provides the following criteria to define a non-executive director as independent: (i) lack of relevant business relationships with the firm and its subsidiaries, managers, executive directors, and its controlling owners; (ii) lack of ownership of a portion of shares that could enable the director to exert a dominant influence over the firm, also considering any agreements with other shareholders which could give them the power to control the firm; and (iii) lack of kinship with corporate executive directors or other persons who are in the situations referred to in points (i) and (ii). As well as the formal compliance with these requirements, the 2006 and 2011 revised versions add the need for the board independence to be, and appear outside, evaluated in its substance and constantly for the entire mandate.

Unlike other countries, such as UK or USA, where it is required that at least half of the board of directors is composed of independent members, until 2011 the Italian Code did not specify a number of independent directors, simply recommending the participation of a number of independent members adequate to provide an objective judgment. Instead, the 2011 version requires the inclusion of at least two independent directors and a proportion of board independence equal to one third for the firms belonging to FTSE-Mib index.

Table 1 Sample selection process

Italian listed firms	206
Financial and Insurance firms	−53
Cross-listed firms	−3
Firms with missing data	−29
Final Sample	121

The initial sample consists of 206 Italian listed companies. We exclude 53 financial and insurance companies, 3 cross-listed firms, and 29 firms with missing governance data. The final sample consists of 946 firm-year observations of 121 non-financial listed companies, during the period 2006–2014.

2.2 Sample

The empirical analysis is based on a sample of Italian listed firms. The initial sample consists of 206 Italian firms listed in December 2015. We exclude 53 financial and insurance firms (NACE REV 2 Code), because the regulation and the nature of their assets differ from those of other firms. Moreover, we remove three cross-listed firms in order to avoid noises due to different governance regulation. We also drop 29 firms with missing governance data. Table 1 summarizes the sampling process.

The final sample consists of 946 firm-years observations from 121 Italian listed firms covering the period 2006–2014.

2.3 Variables

Dependent Variable. The dependent variable in the analysis is the fixed component of long-term investments, measured as the annual amount of capital expenditures scaled by total assets (*Capex*).

Independent Variables. The first variable of interest relates to the measure of family control. The definition of family firms constitutes an empirical challenge as there is not a unique measure of family influence over corporate decisions. Therefore, the definition of family firms needs to be contingent with the question that must be addressed (Prencipe et al. 2014). For the purpose of this study, which assumes that the high family's financial involvement and the unwillingness to dilute family control may lead to underinvestment problems, we adopt the involvement approach which focuses on the power of the family to affect strategic decisions. In particular, we define a firm as family-controlled firm if the family holds the majority of firm's shares. This definition is the most adopted operationalization of family businesses (Salvato and Moores 2010), as it ensures that the family has the power and the incentives to affect corporate decisions, regardless of the presence of the family members in the governance structures. Therefore, in order to test the first hypothesis, we include a dummy variable equal to 1 if the family holds the majority of firm's shares (*Family*), and 0 otherwise.

The second variable of interest is the measure of board independence, which is the ratio of the number of independent directors over the total number of board directors (*Independence*). In order to identify independent directors, we use information from the annual corporate governance reports, as Italian listed firms are required to specify both the number and the names of independent directors, on the basis of the definition provided by the Corporate Governance Code.

The third variable of interest is the presence of a family CEO. Therefore, we include a dummy variable equal to 1 if the CEO is a member of the controlling family, and 0 otherwise (*FamCEO*). To check for the CEO's family membership, we verify her/his identity through the firm's annual corporate governance report. In particular, we focus on the CEO's last name, and if it differs from that of the controlling family, we carry out further research to identify any potential kinship relations.

Control Variables. Moving from prior studies, we control for a number of factors that may affect the level of capital expenditures. The set of control variables includes institutional ownership (*Institutional*), the solvency ratio (*Solvency*), firm cash flows (*CashFlow*), firm sales growth (*SGrowth*), and industry profitability (*IndustryPerf*). We also control for fixed effects at year and firm levels.

Institutional is the percentage of shares held by institutional investors. We control for the presence of institutional owners because prior research finds that the monitoring of institutional shareholders is associated with investment decisions (e.g. Zahra 1996; David et al. 2001).

Solvency is the ratio of net income plus depreciation, deflated by total liabilities. We include the solvency ratio because prior studies show that the level of financial solidity is positively associated with investment spending[1] (Aivazian et al. 2005; Ahn et al. 2006; Firth et al. 2008).

CashFlow is the ratio of firms' generated cash flows to total assets. We control for firm cash flows because prior studies find that the availability of cash holding is positively associated with the level of investment spending (Lamont 1997; Kadapakkam et al 1998; Richardson 2006).

SGrowth is the percentage of growth in firms' sales. We include sales growth in order to control for prior firm performance, as prior studies find that firm profitability is positively related to investment spending (Kaplan and Zingales 1997; Chen and Hsu 2009).

IndustryPerf is the average ROA of firms in the same industry. We control for industry profitability as prior research finds that industry features affect investment decisions (e.g. Röller and Tombak 1993).

Finally, we control for time-invariant fixed effects, and for time fixed effects, in order to control for unobservable firm features and year effects.

[1] The main index used to proxy for financial health is the leverage index. However, when we included the leverage index in the model, problems of multicollinearity arise. Therefore, we replaced the leverage ratio with the solvency ratio, which also captures the level of financial health.

Financial accounting data are collected from Amadeus, the European database from Bureau Van Dijk, while corporate governance and CEO information are hand-collected via annual corporate governance reports.

2.4 Model

We test the first hypothesis with the regression model in Eq. (1).

$$\begin{aligned}\text{Capex}_{i,t+1} = {} & \beta_0 + \beta_1\text{Family}_{i,t} + \beta_2\text{Independence}_{i,t} \\ & + \beta_3\text{Institutional}_{i,t} + \beta_4\text{Solvency}_{i,t} + \beta_5\text{CashFlow}_{i,t} \\ & + \beta_6\text{SGrowth}_{i,t} + \beta_7\text{IndustryPerf}_{i,t} + \lambda Y_t + \eta F_i + u_{i,t}\end{aligned} \tag{1}$$

In order to test the second and the third hypotheses, we run the regression model in Eq. (1) in the sub-sample of family-controlled firms, replacing *Family* with *FamCEO*, as follows:

$$\begin{aligned}\text{Capex}_{i,t+1} = {} & \beta_0 + \beta_1\text{FamCEO}_{i,t} + \beta_2\text{Independence}_{i,t} + \beta_3\text{Institutional}_{i,t} \\ & + \beta_4\text{Solvency}_{i,t} + \beta_5\text{CashFlow}_{i,t} + \beta_6\text{SGrowth}_{i,t} \\ & + \beta_7\text{IndustryPerf}_{i,t} + \lambda Y_t + \eta F_i + u_{i,t}\end{aligned} \tag{2}$$

3 Results

3.1 Descriptive Statistics

Table 2 reports summary statistics of the key metrics. The full sample consists of 946 observations, of which 534 refer to family-controlled firms (56.45%), and 412 refer to non-family firms (43.55%). The sub-sample of family-controlled firms seems to well represent the population of Italian family firms. The range of family ownership for the sub-sample of family-controlled firms moves from 50.01 to 84%, with an average family holding of 61.31%. Among the family-controlled firms, little more than the half is managed by a family CEO (51.7%). On a univariate basis, data show that, on average, family-controlled firms invest less than non-family firms (*Capex*, 0.039 for family-controlled firms; 0.048 for non-family firms). On average, boards of sampled firms are constituted by 9 directors and no significant differences emerge between family and non-family firms. As regards board independence, data show that, on average, boards of family-controlled firms are composed by a lower percentage of independent directors (38.8%) with respect to non-family firms (41.9%). Not surprisingly, institutional ownership is lower in family firms (5.23%) than non-family

Table 2 Descriptive statistics

	Full sample (N.Obs. = 946)			Family-controlled firms (N.Obs. = 534)			Non-family firms (N.Obs. = 412)			T-test (p-value)
	1°P.le	Mean	99°P.le	1°P.le	Mean	99°P.le	1°P.le	Mean	99°P.le	
Capital expenditures	0.001	0.043	0.229	0.001	0.039	0.181	0.001	0.048	0.229	0.000
Family ownership (%)	0.000	41.624	82.300	50.014	61.309	84.009	0.000	16.110	49.296	0.000
Family CEO	–	–	–	0.000	0.517	1.000	–	–	–	
Board size	5.000	9.434	19.000	5.000	9.333	18.000	5.000	9.566	19.000	0.122
Board independence	0.111	0.401	0.889	0.143	0.388	0.700	0.111	0.419	0.889	0.002
Institutional own	0.000	8.095	83.220	0.000	5.233	20.990	0.000	11.804	87.608	0.000
Solvency ratio	0.000	0.383	0.878	0.034	0.394	0.916	0.000	0.369	0.786	0.015
Cash flow	−0.237	0.057	0.233	−0.065	0.068	0.220	−0.438	0.043	0.250	0.000
Sales growth	−0.665	0.049	1.131	−0.659	0.045	1.100	−0.705	0.054	1.131	0.297
Performance (%)	−38.000	2.117	23.440	−19.620	3.818	24.700	−42.090	−0.092	18.720	0.000
Industry performance (%)	−9.869	1.926	8.555	−9.869	2.403	8.555	−9.869	1.307	8.555	0.000

firms (11.80%). Moreover, data show that family-controlled firms are, on average, more creditworthy and have higher cash availability than non-family firms (*Solvency*, 39.4% for family firms; 36.9% for non-family firms; *CashFlow*, 0.068 for family firms; 0.043 for non-family firms). In addition, family-controlled firms report higher performance than non-family firms (*Performance*, 3.82% for family firms; −0.09% for non-family firms).

3.2 Empirical Results

Table 3 reports correlations among the main variables, which summarily confirms the predictions. Actually, data show that the level of capital expenditures is negatively correlated with family control and positively correlated with board independence. However, data show a negative correlation between the level of capital expenditures and the presence of a family CEO.

Moreover, level of capital expenditures is highly positively associated with firm cash flow, and with the industry performance. Findings also show a non-correlation between the family control and board independence, while the latter is negatively correlated with the presence of a family CEO.

The correlation analysis shows the existence of significant correlations between some predictors. In order to face concerns of multicollinearity, we run the VIF analysis. The VIF values show that the analysis is not affected by multicollinearity problem (VIF of the predictors are all lower than 5.0).

Table 4 reports the empirical results concerning the relationship between family ownership and capital expenditures. Findings show the existence of a negative relationship between the family control and the level of investment spending (*Family*, $\beta = -0.011$; p-value $= 0.079$). Therefore, evidence confirms that family-controlled firms tend to invest less than non-family firms.

Findings also show that the level of capital expenditures highly depends on the degree of firm's solvency (*Solvency*, $\beta = 0.043$; p-value $= 0.001$), and on the availability of cash holding (*CashFlow*, $\beta = 0.065$; p-value $= 0.001$).

Table 5 reports the empirical results concerning the impact of board monitoring and the impact of an emotionally attached CEO on the level of capital expenditures in family firms.

As regards the role of board monitoring, findings show that board independence is positively associated with the level of capital expenditures (*Independence*, $\beta = 0.038$; p-value $= 0.010$). This result confirms that the monitoring of independent directors incites investment spending in family-controlled firms.

As regards the role of emotional attachment, results show that, within family-controlled firms, those managed by a family CEO invest more than those managed by a professional manager (*FamCEO*, $\beta = 0.012$; p-value $= 0.064$). Therefore, evidence confirms that the presence of a family CEO has a positive impact on the level of capital expenditures.

Table 3 Correlation matrix

	Capex	Family	Independence	*FamCEO*	Institutional	Solvency	CashFlow	SGrowth	IndustryPerf
Capex	1								
Family	−0.095*	1							
Independence	0.130*	−0.013	1						
FamCEO	−0.124*	0.564*	−0.136*	1					
Institutional	0.004	−0.068*	0.021	−0.089*	1				
Solvency	−0.005	0.086*	−0.125*	0.111*	0.038	1			
CashFlow	0.279*	0.118*	−0.006	0.033	0.183*	0.371*	1		
SGrowth	0.059	0.012	−0.061	0.047	0.087*	0.124*	0.243*	1	
IndustryPerf	0.075*	0.125*	0.035	0.069*	−0.021	0.149*	0.198*	0.260*	1

The symbols *, **, ***, denote significance at 10%, 5%, 1% respectively

Table 4 Regression of capital expenditures on family control

Capex	Exp. sign	Coefficients	*p*-value	Std. err
Intercept		0.026 ***	0.003	0.009
Family	–	−0.011 *	0.079	0.006
Independence	?	0.016	0.100	0.010
Institutional	+	0.000	0.853	0.000
Solvency	+	0.043 ***	0.001	0.013
CashFlow	+	0.065 ***	0.001	0.019
SGrowth	+	0.004	0.324	0.004
IndustryPerf	+	0.000	0.838	0.001
Year-fixed effects		Yes		
Firm-fixed effects		Yes		
Obs.# 946				
R^2 12.76% (*p*-value 0.000)				

The symbols *, **, ***, denote significance at 10%, 5%, 1% respectively

Table 5 Regression of capital expenditures on family CEO and board independence

Capex	Exp. sign	Coefficients	*p*-value	Std. err
Intercept		0.003	0.794	0.011
FamCEO	+	0.012 *	0.064	0.006
Independence	+	0.038 **	0.010	0.015
Institutional	+	−0.001 *	0.058	0.000
Solvency	+	0.046 **	0.017	0.019
CashFlow	+	0.053 *	0.076	0.030
SGrowth	+	0.002	0.675	0.005
IndustryPerf	+	0.000	0.593	0.001
Year-fixed effects		Yes		
Firm-fixed effects		Yes		
Obs. # 534				
R^2 13.15% (*p*-value 0.000)				

The symbols *, **, ***, denote significance at 10%, 5%, 1% respectively

Surprisingly, we find that, other things being equal, institutional ownership in family-controlled firms is negatively related to capital expenditures, even if the magnitude is rather low (*Institutional*, $\beta = -0.001$; *p*-value = 0.058). Finally, as expected, results show a strong positive impact of the solvency ratio and the cash availability on the level of investment spending (*Solvency*, $\beta = 0.046$; *p*-value = 0.017; *CashFlow*, $\beta = 0.053$; *p*-value = 0.076.

4 Conclusions

A critical concern of family firms' behavior is the low propensity to invest and growth. While literature provides evidence that family- controlled firms face underinvestment and low growth problems, it provides limited insight on what factors are able to incite investment spending in family firms.

The purpose of this study is to shed some light on the relationship between family ownership and investment expenditures, by exploring the role of board monitoring and CEO's emotional attachment.

Findings confirmed that family-controlled firms invest less than non-family firms. However, findings revealed that, within family firms, board independence and the presence of a family CEO have a positive impact on the level of capital expenditures.

Taken together, two interesting insights for investors and the financial community emerge from this analysis. First, the commingling between personal's wealth and firm's wealth typical of family businesses can lead to sub-optimal investment level, which may damage small investors' wealth in the long run. Second, the criticalities related to conservative investment decisions are weaker in family businesses with independent boards and in those managed by a family CEO. Therefore, the governance structure of the family firms is one of the key factors that must be accurately observed in assessing firm's future growth prospects.

The study provides several contributions to the literature. First, it provides evidence supporting the importance of board monitoring in limiting family-oriented particularistic behaviors. Second, empirical results confirm the existence of heterogeneity in family firms' behavior (Chua et al. 2012; Chrisman et al. 2012), showing that it can be due, at least partially, to a different board structure. Third, this study provides evidence on the bright sides of family involvement in managerial positions.

This study has two main limitations. First, this study focuses on the level of investment spending, but it does not examine the efficiency of such investments. Actually, while findings suggest that board monitoring and CEO's emotional attachment are able to encourage investments in family-controlled firms, results do not provide evidence on whether corporate resources are invested efficiently.

References

Ahn S, Denis DJ, Denis DK (2006) Leverage and investment in diversified firms. J Financ Econ 79(2):317–337. https://doi.org/10.1016/j.jfineco.2005.03.002

Aivazian VA, Ge Y, Qiu J (2005) The impact of leverage on firm investment: Canadian evidence. J Corp Finan 11(1):277–291. https://doi.org/10.1016/S0929-1199(03)00062-2

Bianchi M, Enriques L (1999) Has the 1998 reform of Italian listed company law fostered institutional investor activism? CONSOB, Rome

Brunello G, Graziano C, Parigi BM (2003) CEO turnover in insider dominated boards: The Italian case. J Bank Finan 27:1027–1051. https://doi.org/10.1016/S0378-4266(02)00244-3

Chen HL, Hsu WT (2009) Family ownership, board independence, and R&D investment. Fam Bus Rev 22(4):347–362. https://doi.org/10.1177/0894486509341062

Chrisman JJ, Chua JH, Pearson AW, Barnett T (2012) Family involvement, family influence, and family centered non-economic goals in small firms. Entrepreneurship Theory Pract 36(2):267–293. https://doi.org/10.1111/j.1540-6520.2010.00407.x

Chua JH, Chrisman JJ, Steier LP, Rau SB (2012) Sources of heterogeneity in family firms: an introduction. Entrepreneurship Theory Pract 36(6):1103–1113. https://doi.org/10.1111/j.1540-6520.2012.00540.x

David P, Hitt MA, Gimeno J (2001) The influence of activism by institutional investors on R&D. Acad Manag J 44(1):144–157. https://doi.org/10.5465/3069342

Firth M, Lin C, Wong SM (2008) Leverage and investment under a state-owned bank lending environment: evidence from China. J Corp Finan 14(5):642–653. https://doi.org/10.1016/j.jcorpfin.2008.08.002

Kadapakkam PR, Kumar PC, Riddick LA (1998) The impact of cash flows and firm size on investment: the international evidence. J Bank Finan 22(3):293–320. https://doi.org/10.1016/S0378-4266(97)00059-9

Kaplan SN, Zingales L (1997) Do investment-cash flow sensitivities provide useful measures of financing constraints? Q J Econ 112(1):169–215. https://doi.org/10.1162/003355397555163

La Porta R, Lopez-de-Silanes F, Shleifer A, Vishny R (2000) Investor protection and corporate governance. J Finan Econ 58(1):3–27. https://doi.org/10.1016/S0304-405X(00)00065-9

Lamont O (1997) Cash flow and investment: evidence from internal capital markets. J Finan 52(1):83–109. https://doi.org/10.1111/j.1540-6261.1997.tb03809.x

Melis A (2000) Corporate governance in Italy. Corp Gov Int Rev 8(4):347–355. https://doi.org/10.1111/1467-8683.00213

Miller D, Le Breton-Miller L (2006) Family governance and firm performance: agency, stewardship, and capabilities. Fam Bus Rev 19(1):73–87. https://doi.org/10.1111/j.1741-6248.2006.00063.x

Prat A, Bandiera O, Guiso L, Sadun R (2010) Italian managers: fidelity or performance. In: Boeri T, Merlo A, Prat A (eds), The ruling class: management and politics in modern Italy. Oxford, Oxford University Press. https://doi.org/10.1111/j.1468-0335.2012.00927.x

Prencipe A, Bar-Yosef S, Dekker HC (2014) Accounting research in family firms: theoretical and empirical challenges. Eur Account Rev 23(3):361–385. https://doi.org/10.1080/09638180.2014.895621

Prencipe A, Markarian G, Pozza L (2008) Earnings management in family firms: evidence from R&D cost capitalization in Italy. Fam Bus Rev 21(1):71–88. https://doi.org/10.1111/j.1741-6248.2007.00112.x

Richardson S (2006) Over-investment of free cash flow. Rev Acc Stud 11(2–3):159–189. https://doi.org/10.1007/s11142-006-9012-1

Rizzotti D, Frisenna C, Mazzone R (2017) The impact of family owners' monitoring on CEO turnover decisions and the role of trust. J Manag Gov 21(3):599–621. https://doi.org/10.1007/s10997-016-9367-z

Röller LH, Tombak MM (1993) Competition and investment in flexible technologies. Manag Sci 39(1):107–114. https://doi.org/10.1287/mnsc.39.1.107

Salvato C, Moores K (2010) Research on accounting in family firms: past accomplishments and future challenges. Fam Bus Rev 23(3):193–215. https://doi.org/10.1177/0894486510375069

Volpin PF (2002) Governance with poor investor protection: evidence from top executive turnover in Italy. J Financ Econ 64(1):61–90. https://doi.org/10.1016/S0304-405X(02)00071-5

Zahra SA (1996) Goverance, ownership, and corporate entrepreneurship: the moderating impact of industry technological opportunities. Acad Manag J 39(6):1713–1735. https://doi.org/10.5465/257076

Discussing and Concluding Remarks

Antonio Leotta

A journey throughout the family business scenery has been undertaken. What motivated this journey was for the authors to share an experience with each other and with the readers. It was a learning experience that has probably offered a deeper understanding of the family business world. The journey was first ideal and then real.

The first part of the book was indeed theoretical. After drawing an overview of family business characteristics and features, the extant literature on the main family business topics, namely managerialization and professionalization, succession, internationalization and relations with financial markets, has been summarized and discussed. The critical approach followed in this discussion has entailed to consider all the topics as the challenges a family business has to face. The theoretical part ends with a final chapter which, drawing on the main arguments developed in the previous chapters, proposed a conceptual framework aimed to re-order all the family business challenges discussed earlier in a systemic view centred on the concept of governance package. A more extended concept of governance has been proposed, drawing on the management control studies focused on lateral relations. Indeed, the concept of governance we proposed is considered useful for governing family business challenges, since these challenges involve networks distributed in time and space. Challenges that involve networks distributed in space are: managerialization and professionalization, as the related processes run amongst family and non-family members, requiring an alliance between family and managerial principles and values; internationalization, which requires a family business to coordinate domestic and foreign markets; relations with financial markets, which need an alliance between family business CEO and financial investors. Challenges involving networks distributed in time are limited to family business succession, the outcome

A. Leotta (✉)
Department of Economics and Business, University of Catania, Catania, Italy
e-mail: antonio.leotta@unict.it

A. Leotta (ed.), *Management Controlling and Governance of Family Businesses*,
Contributions to Management Science,
https://doi.org/10.1007/978-3-030-47741-7_13

of which depends on an agreement between old and new generations about the vision of the business.

The concept of governance we proposed is also based on a relational view which underlines the interdependences amongst the challenges. Family business studies indeed highlight that, in family businesses, growth and development, managerialization and professionalization are intertwined with succession. Also, family business studies noticed how an international growth of a family firm absorbs financial resources. Therefore, governing family business challenges require governing the network shaped by interdependent challenges.

The conceptual lenses developed in the first part of the volume were used to go on a journey around real business cases. Two methodological approaches were adopted. The main approach relates to interpretive case studies, aimed at developing deeper understanding of the processes of managerialization and professionalization, succession and internationalization, highlighting interdependences amongst these processes. A quantitative approach was also followed. Statistical data were collected on Italian listed firms, aimed at providing empirical evidence on whether board monitoring and CEO emotional attachment might affect investment spending within family firms.

Now, at the final step of this trip, we can adopt the conceptual lens, developed in Chapter "Governing Family Businesses. A Research Map", in order to make sense of the empirical evidence. In doing so, we discuss the governance systems package used to deal with the challenges reported in Chapters "Learning Financial Language to Face On-going Challenges. The Case of Greenlife", "Professionalization and Managerialization: Original Levers From Molino Nicoli Spa", "Beyond the Founder. Which Conditions can Favor or Hinder the Professionalization of Family Firms?", "Internationalization in Family Businesses. The Case of Mamagra" and "Family Ownership and Investment Decisions. An Empirical Analysis on the Role of Board Monitoring and CEO Emotional Attachment".

Our analysis of how the family business challenges empirically observed were faced by an appropriate governance systems package needs to be developed: first, discussing the challenges in terms of lateral relations amongst the main actors involved, so considering the two most relevant characteristics of interdependence and complexity that can be referred to each challenge; second, examining the particular features of the governance systems package adopted to govern those challenges, namely exchange of knowledge, cooperation as well as competition, flexibility as well as standardization and shifts in the leadership role; third, highlighting the role of the four structures, namely economic, institutional, social and technical structures, which compose the governance systems package, and how they have been combined in dealing with the challenges.

In developing our conceptual framework, in Chapter "Governing Family Businesses. A Research Map", we outlined the family business challenges discussed in Chapters "Professionalization and Managerialization: Original Levers From Molino Nicoli Spa", "The Survival of Family Businesses: The Challenge of Succession" and "The Growth of Family Businesses: The Path to Internationalization" and "Investment Decisions in Listed Family Firms: Risk Aversion and Emotional Attachment", considering the relations amongst the main actors involved as distributed in space, as in the cases of managerialization and professionalization, internationalization and relations with financial markets, or distributed in time, as in the case of succession. Moreover, such relations present the characteristics of interdependence and complexity, as discussed theoretically. The case studies have confirmed both these characteristics. We first offer a discussion of the characteristics of the lateral relations and the particular features of the governance systems package for each case, since it requires a focus on the principal processes examined in each case. Then, we summarize the main governance structures observed both from all the cases and from the statistical evidence.

The case of Greenlife, examined in Chapter Learning Financial Language to Face On-going Challenges. The Case of Greenlife, is very emblematic in terms of interdependence amongst the processes of professionalization and managerialization, internationalization and succession preparation. Greenlife is in its growing phase and is consolidating its presence in the US market. A need for control and for professional and managerial competences comes out for accompanying the firm in its growth. The entrance of a new professional, non-family manager was a response to this need and was an opportunity for convincing the family members about the usefulness of managerial practices, such as financial statement analysis, product cost analysis and reporting. In dealing with internationalization, professionalization and managerialization challenges, the founder was not the only person who orchestrated the relations amongst various actors. The founder's son and daughter played a central role as well. Indeed, they were increasing their responsibility in Greenlife, preparing themselves to their future roles of leader. Such intertwined processes defined the interdependence amongst the relations between the family members. In the company a transfer of leadership from the founder to his son and daughter, which was in progress, made the decision-making process a-centred, and had an impact on what family members expected from the new professional managers, therefore influencing the relations between family and non-family members. To this articulated picture, the introduction of managerial practices, promoted by the new professional manager with the engagement of external advisors, added further complexity, since it increased the number of actors who played a role in all the processes. In such a context, the complexity of relations was very high, being different the points of view of family and non-family members, but being also different the points of view within the family members themselves. In the dynamics involving professionalization, managerialization and succession preparation, the process of internationalization played a minor role, since Greenlife was already present in the US market when the professionalization process was starting.

The governance systems package, which led all these processes, was supposed to manage the lateral relations outlined above by means of mechanisms which would have balanced the competition and cooperation emerging between the founder's children and the new professional manager. This was evident during the implementation of the financial statement analysis. In a discussion where all the actors participated, several misunderstandings emerged. The external advisors played a relevant role in that moment by clarifying the main financial concepts and the related language. In this sense, the managerialization process favoured the learning of financial language. This brought the founder's children and the new professional manager to agree on their respective roles: the founder's children were supposed to increase their managerial skills and experience, while the external manager was required to help their learning process in order to make them ready for the leadership of the business. Speaking the financial language facilitated the sharing of knowledge between the family members and the professional manager. Furthermore, the introduction of financial statement analysis, first, and of the cost analysis and reporting, second, led Greenlife organization towards an increasing role of the procedures and systems which were supposed to standardize and de-personalize the most important decision-making processes. Finally, from the above arguments, a shift in leadership role was also evident. During the professionalization, the managerialization and the succession preparation processes, the decision-making approach changed its features from being centred to the founder towards being a-centred and spread amongst the founder, the new external manager, the founder's children, with a supporting role played by the administrative staff and the external advisors.

The dynamics described in the case of Molino Nicoli are in part similar to the Greenlife case but differ in the complexity of the former business, which was higher. In the story of Molino Nicoli development, professionalization was gradually introduced by the past managing director, who was the founder of the business and the father of the family, and became, recently, the president of the firm. The current president started an injection of new professional skills and experiences by hiring external managers, most of them with long experience in other important and larger companies. In the Molino Nicoli case, the key lever of professionalization process is the same as in the succession process, namely the current president's awareness of the need for a gradual preparation of his heirs to take the leader positions of the business. With this awareness, the president was strongly willing to hire new external managers with long experience and skills. This was aimed at endowering the company with experienced and skilled professional trainers who can prepare the successor for the business. Therefore, given the quality of the new professional managers, the professionalization process informed stimulated the managerialization of the business. An agreement between the new managing director and the operation director (currently the Vice President), who were non-family and family members, respectively, was aimed at introducing a learning by doing approach involving high experienced workers. This showed that the successful exit of professionalization favoured the managerialization of the firm by promoting the alliances between family and non-family members. The managerialization process was formalized by the managing director in a formal plan and then analysed with the operation director. The introduction of the management accounting function and the designation of a family member as management accountant was the main result of the managerialization process. The management accounting function was endowed with a family member, as responsible for the function, and with an advanced information system, an ERP, which denoted the decision to invest in the function. This was the exit of a long training process which increased the experience of all the workers and of the new chief of the management accounting function. The interdependence between professionalization, managerialization and succession processes seems to follow a sequential order in this case. The way to deal with this interdependence was therefore to increase gradually the complexity of the knowledge and skills of managers and workers, first by hiring new skilled and experienced managers from outside, second by following a learning by doing approach and a path of training on the job. It was an internal couching made possible thanks to the new professional skills imported from outside.

In terms of the main features of governance package, exchange of knowledge, balances between competition and cooperation, flexibility and standardization were conducted in a way similar as in the Greenlife case, but what differed was how competition and cooperation were perceived and interpreted. In the Molino Nicoli case, the presence of external, professional managers was higher and more relevant, being characterized by various experienced and skilled managers who interpreted competition as continuous improvement of the daily procedures and business processes. The adoption of a functional organizational structure, combined with a process-oriented approach, stimulated an inter-functional cooperation. The shift in the leadership role occurred when the professionalization started, thanks to the long experience of the new managing director, which legitimated him as the leader of the managerialization process. Therefore, the professionalization process was enacted by the founder as a way to delegate professionals to the training of his future heirs. The shift in the leadership role in this succession process, which is currently still in progress, moved from the incumbent to professionals, to prepare the successors for the future.

The comparative case study discussed in Chapter "Beyond the Founder. Which Conditions can Favor or Hinder the Professionalization of Family Firms?" highlights relevant differences in governing professionalization after succession has been completed. In both the Teseo and Volta cases, succession and professionalization intertwined. In the Teseo story, professionalization started earlier and favoured succession process. In the Volta case, succession preceded the attempt to professionalize the firm. Therefore, in order to understand the origin of different exits of professionalization between the Teseo and the Volta cases, particular attention has to be paid on the relationship between the incumbent and the successor, but also on the relationships between family and non-family members. In the Teseo case, the incumbent and her daughter shared a common vision of how the family should handle the business. Since family members did not have the technical competences needed to lead the business during its development, the founder realized the need for the family to stay a step back and leave more room to skilled and experienced professional managers. The strategy of growth through acquisition was consistent with the need to acquire the managerial experience developed in the company Teseo took over. The choice to take over a second company gave Teseo the chance to increase its customer portfolio with new companies. The choice of the family to stay in the background of the business brought the owners to hire an external manager, who was later appointed CEO. The same attitude was kept by the founder's daughter, when the succession process was over. This consistent attitude followed by both the founder and her daughter made the interdependence between family and non-family members very high, increasing the relevance of the different levels of business knowledge and experience characterizing the controlling family and the management. In other words, the complexity of the family–non-family member relations was high, and the relations were governed as lateral ones. The exchange of knowledge was managed through recruitments which allowed the firm to acquire knowledge and experience from outside. The balance between cooperation and competition as well as between standardization and flexibility was resolved in favour of cooperation and standardization. High collaboration was in place between the owner and the CEO, and professionalization was managed in order to increase the level of standardization, de-personalizing the organizational processes and procedures. The leadership of the professionalization process was always kept by the non-family CEO.

Very differently, the dynamics described in the Volta case highlighted that the founder's vision of how the family should handle the business was not the successor's vision. This was also due to the phases of the business life cycle which differed before and after the succession was completed. Indeed, when the founder involved his daughter for future succession, the business was in its growing phase, namely in its entrepreneurial stage, and when the founder's vision and his insights were very helpful for the business to seize new opportunities, decision processes were centred to the entrepreneur and could be run very fast. It was when the succession was over that the rapid expansion of the business worldwide, with the increase in the market and organizational complexity, made the presence of managerial competences more urgent. The general manager was hired just in the pregnancy period of the founder's daughter, but it was just on paper. A sense of competition, rather than cooperation, seemed to characterize the attitude of the successor, who never left the management of the business. The involvement of family members in key business functions was symptomatic of the family CEO's desire to keep the control over the business, considering the business and its future development as dependent on the family. Consequently, the exchange of knowledge was limited to family members, while professional managers were considered as "strangers". No shift in leadership role actually occurred, since family members continued controlling various innovation processes, included managerialization. The exit of the general manager was a failure as the leadership approach remained the same as in the entrepreneurial stage of the business.

The case of Mamagra reported in Chapter "Internationalization in Family Businesses. The Case of Mamagra" showed an internationalization which followed a succession process and was based on a fruitful partnership between Calabrian and Italian food tradition and culture and foreign market dynamics and specificities. The serene business atmosphere, where all family members and co-workers were involved in all the business matters, and a managerialization process introduced during the firm international growth were all relevant conditions that contributed to make the international strategy successful. The decision to internationalize the business was firstly supported by the introduction of a management control reporting, even if at its informal stage, which helped family managers to make a rational choice of the foreign markets where to increase the sales volume. Indeed, the choice of foreign countries was made in some cases according to their attractiveness, such as in countries where, at the same price, the value of the domestic product was higher than the value of the corresponding competitor products; in other cases, the criterion was that the price on the foreign market was potentially higher than the price on the domestic market and lower than the price of competing foreign products. The cost reporting developed by Mamagra family management was therefore able to support the family entrepreneurs in a revenue analysis. The partnership between the family and regional tradition and the foreign market trends was established thanks to the hiring of foreign professionals, employed in the commercial area of the business. A first partnership with foreign actors was indeed realized within Mamagra organization. A second type of partnership was of commercial nature and followed the direct export strategy implemented in the earlier step of the internationalization process. In summary, Mamagra, in the earlier stages of its internationalization path, relied on direct export. Subsequently, as it became progressively familiar with the foreign country, it started collaborating with local intermediaries (indirect export) to mitigate the risk of the investment. In this gradual approach, the interdependence amongst the family firms and the foreign market actors increased, being accompanied with a growing complexity. While the governance elements were characterized by an increasing weight of a standardized and formalized procedures, even if investments remained flexible; an increasing weight of cooperation with foreign agents upon competition; a shift in the leadership role moved from family managers to family and professional, foreign managers, in the latter internationalization stages, when the exchange of knowledge was directed from the professionals, hired from foreign countries, to the family managers.

Discussing the four structures of the governance systems package is useful for a deeper understanding of the interrelationships existing amongst all the family business challenges described so far. In doing so, we can usefully combine the field evidence on professionalization and managerialization, internationalization and succession with the statistical evidences on relations between family firms and financial markets. From all the evidences outlined so far, our discussion will be directed to make sense of each type of structure comprised in the governance systems package, namely economic, institutional, social and technical structures, which has been properly defined in Chapter Governing Family Businesses. A Research Map. Moreover, our discussion will be aimed to make order amongst the four types of structures.

The technical structure refers to the constraining features of transaction, production technologies, information and financial flows, managerial systems and practices. Such a kind of structure can induce the management to perceive a knowledge gap, as in the Teseo case, where the heir realized the need to hire a professional, experienced manager, later appointed as CEO. The development of management accounting systems, based on sophisticated information systems, is observed in the managerialization process followed in the Molino Nicoli case, where an ERP was implemented, and required the development of managerial competences which was searched for outside the family firm. This is an episode when the technical structure influenced the social and the institutional ones. The technical structure also reflects different features and trends between domestic and foreign markets, especially when these differences are historically embedded and have to be considered as given, as in the Mamagra case.

The social structure pertains to the systems of values and principles, which, in the field of family business, has been properly emphasized by the Social Emotional Wealth perspective. In professionalization and managerialization challenges, the social structure highlights the divergence/convergence between family and professional principles and values; in succession, it emphasizes the dialectic between old and new generation values. While professionalization-managerialization and succession seem, from the case evidence, to be reciprocally interdependent challenges, internationalization appears to be influenced by the formers. In the case of Mamagra, the successful international path was the exit of a positive experience of succession and was also accompanied by a starting managerialization and professionalization.

When a family is pursuing a qualitative and/or quantitative development, the family CEO may require additional funding. Then, the ability of the firm to attract new investors strongly depends on how the firm communicates of being endowed with an institutional structure composed of rules and mechanisms which protect the investors' interests. In the case evidence on professionalization, managerialization and succession, the institutional structure is also the outcome of the combination of the social and technical structures. The institutional dimension ensures the stable equilibrium reached by the dialectics between the social and the technical structures. Therefore, it is the outcome of a long process of institutionalization. In professionalization, the institutional structure refers to the appointment of a professional manager as CEO, as in the Teseo case; in managerialization, it refers to the institution of a management accounting function, as in the Molino Nicoli case. In succession, the presence of an institutional structure is reflected in the existence of a formalized succession plan, as in the Molino Nicoli case again.

Finally, the economic structure refers to the presence of performance measures, relying on consolidated and shared concepts of efficiency and competitiveness. It is the main exit of managerialization, when family principles and values have espoused the managerial ones. Actually, the presence of such managerial culture could be informal, as in the Mamagra case. This means that the institutional structure is still in progress. When the institutional structure is formalized, it is often supported by the economic structure. The existence of incentive rules and mechanisms, discussed about the relations between family businesses and financial markets, requires the functioning of an economic structure which makes such rules working. At the same time, the use of management accounting reporting in the Mamagra case was not accompanied by a management accounting function, which was still absent. But such reporting practice gave the family management the economic structure necessary to make rational choices about the foreign areas where to expand their business. Similarly, the introduction and adoption of financial statement analysis and product cost reporting and analysis, which in the Greenlife case were accomplished by a consulting team, were not supported by the presence of a management accounting function. The main effect in the Greenlife case was the introduction of the accounting and financial language: its speaking allowed the diffusion and the sharing of economic and accounting concepts which enriched the family members' skills, facilitating the managerialization process.

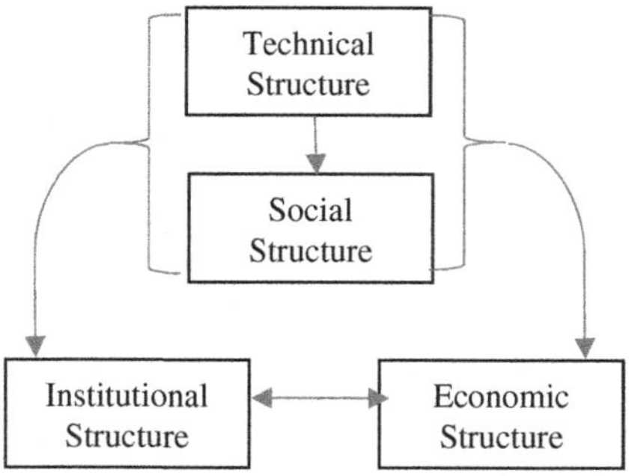

Fig. 1 Interdependences amongst governance structures

The above discussion suggests that the four types of structures follow an intentional order which makes explicit the interrelations and interdependence observed in the discussed evidence. What resulted is sketched in Fig. 1 and summarized in the following.

The technical and social structures are the antecedents of the institutional and economic structures. The technical structure, referring to the main constraints characterizing operation, information and financial processes, has a given content. However, it can give input to the set of principles and values shared within the family and non-family member relations, namely the social structure, to act towards a certain direction. Combined with the social structure, the technical structure can stimulate changes in the institutional and/or in the economic structure.

Figure 1 represents what can be seen from a zoomed look taken at Fig. 2, in Chapter "Governing Family Businesses. A Research Map", which sketched the theoretical framework applied to the interpretation of the empirics observed from the field and the statistical analyses. This shows how the empirical research has contributed to enrich the initial framework built on the extant literature and on the theoretical arguments developed in Chapter "Governing Family Businesses. A Research Map". The real journey experienced around the Italian family firms, in their operational, information and social processes, in their relational dynamics, but also in their accounting figures and practices, has given something that no logical analysis can grasp. The real journey in discussion has allowed the researchers a real experience about the family businesses' life.

In the final step of our journey, we, as researchers, are aware that the continuous life of family businesses is at work for attracting new research interest, but our hope is, to some extent, to have contributed to the interest coming from the family business practitioners, such as entrepreneurs, professional advisors, family and non-family managers, who can translate the experience from this journey into an experience of life.

The manufacturer's authorised representative in the EU is Springer Nature Customer Service Centre GmbH, Europaplatz 3, 69115 Heidelberg, Germany. If you have any concerns regarding our products, please contact ProductSafety@springernature.com

Printed and bound by CPI Group (UK) Ltd, Croydon, CR0 4YY
30/09/2026
02225505-0007